Beginning Teaching: Beginning Learning

Third Edition

Edited by
Janet Moyles

Open University Press

Open University Press
McGraw-Hill Education
McGraw-Hill House
Shoppenhangers Road
Maidenhead
Berkshire
England
SL6 2QL

email: enquiries@openup.co.uk
world wide web: www.openup.co.uk

and Two Penn Plaza, New York, NY 10121–2289, USA

First published 2007
Reprinted 2011

Copyright © The Editor and Contributors, 2007

A catalogue record of this book is available from the British Library

ISBN 13: 978 0335 221 301 (pb) 978 0335 221 318 (hb)
ISBN 10: 0335 221 300 (pb) 0335 221 319 (hb)

Library of Congress Cataloguing-in-Publication Data
CIP data applied for

Typeset by YHT Ltd, London
Printed in Great Britain by Bell & Bain Ltd., Glasgow

The **McGraw·Hill** Companies

Beginning Teaching:
Beginning Learning

Third Edition

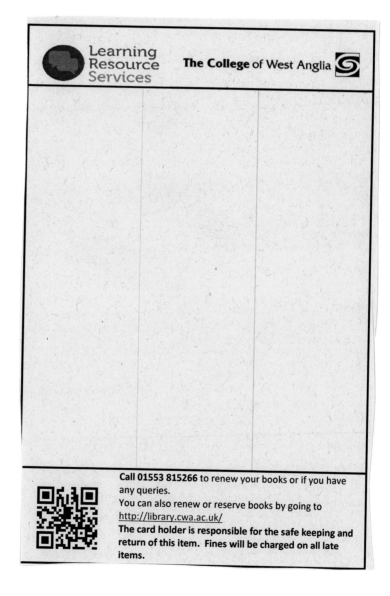

Contents

Part 3   Organizing for teaching and learning

Part 4   Supporting and enhancing learning and teaching

List of figures and tables

Figures

Tables

Notes on the editors and contributors

Siân Adams was an early years advisory teacher later moving to Leicester to study for her PhD on teachers' reflective practice within the context of playful learning. Siân was engaged in several research projects relating to effective, playful pedagogy in the early years, including *SPEEL* (*Study of Effective Pedagogy in the Early Years*) (DfES 2002) and *Recreating the Reception Year* (ATL 2004). Her latest book (with Janet Moyles) is *Images of Violence* (Featherstone Publications 2005).

Deborah Albon is Senior Lecturer in Early Childhood Studies at London Metropolitan University. She has worked as both a nursery nurse and teacher in a range of early childhood settings as well as in a primary school. Her current doctoral research is focused on young children's experiences of food and eating in early childhood settings, re-searching alongside practitioners, parents and young children.

Alan Bradwell is a Senior Lecturer in the Faculty of Education at Anglia Ruskin University. He leads the education studies and research strands of the BA ITT (Primary) degree. His research interests are how student teachers negotiate the conflicting knowledge communities of school and university in becoming 'academically literate'; and the use of critical theory to gain understandings of educational privilege and deprivation.

Wasyl Cajkler is Senior Lecturer in Education at the University of Leicester, with a background in English and foreign language teaching, who contributes to both primary and secondary PGCE programmes. In recent years, he has worked extensively with teaching assistants helping to establish professional development opportunities from short courses to degree level programmes. He has also led a three-year systematic literature review into the perceived contributions of teaching assistants to support learning in both primary and secondary schools.

Penny Coltman is a Lecturer in Early Years Education and the director of the Early Years and Primary PGCE course at the Faculty of Education, University of Cambridge. She has a research interest in early mathematical development and an enthusiasm for science. Penny is a member of the team involved in the Cambridge Independent Learning (CIndLe) Project. She also enjoys writing for BBC Worldwide and has written materials linked to series, ranging from David Attenborough to Bob the Builder.

Tricia David is now retired but continues her involvement in the field of Early Childhood Education and Care, through writing, conference presentations, grandmothering, and so on. She was greatly honoured to be awarded the title of Emeritus Professor by Canterbury Christ Church and Sheffield Universities (the latter for three years). Having reached the age her contemporaries, the Beatles, sang about, she is also happy to have time for 'doing the garden, digging the weeds'.

Dan Davies is Professor of Science and Technology Education, Head of Primary Education and Assistant Dean of Education at Bath Spa University. He taught in primary schools in London before moving into teacher education at Goldsmiths, University of London. He has published widely in the fields of primary science and design & technology education.

Aline-Wendy Dunlop is Chair of Childhood and Primary Studies in the Department of Childhood and Primary Studies at the University of Strathclyde in Glasgow. She is also Lead-Director of the National Centre for Autism Studies. Her main areas of current research interest are leadership in early education, additional support needs, social interaction and understanding in autism, the empowerment of families of very young children, educational transitions and positive behaviour in the early years.

Nick Easingwood is Senior Lecturer for ICT in Education and acts as the ICT Co-ordinator for the Faculty of Education of Anglia Ruskin University in Chelmsford, Essex, in England. He leads the Primary Post-and Professional Graduate Certificate of Education (PGCE) and contributes regularly to these and undergraduate programmes, teaching both professional studies and ICT. He has co-written several publications on ICT in primary education.

Nansi Ellis is Deputy Head of Education Policy and Research for the Association of Teachers and Lecturers, where she works with teachers and support staff, developing policy and advice on early years and primary issues, children's services and professional development. Formerly a primary teacher, she subsequently managed QCA's early years team. She is currently putting early years theory into practice, learning to play with her own baby boy.

Hilary Fabian is Head of Education and Childhood Studies at the North East Wales Institute (NEWI). She has taught young children in the UK and with the forces schools in Germany. Her work in the university sector includes teaching at the Manchester Metropolitan University, the University of Edinburgh and NEWI. Her MSc, PhD and publications reflect her interest in transitions, particularly children starting school and the way in which induction is managed.

Kathy Hall, a former primary teacher, is Professor of Education in University College Cork, Republic of Ireland. Previously she was Professor of Education at the Open University, Professor of Childhood Education and Head of Educational Research at Leeds Metropolitan University. She has carried out research on assessment, literacy, learning and inclusion, and has written extensively on these topics. She is currently leading a major, interinstitutional project for the DfES – a three-year longitudinal study of modern foreign languages in the primary school.

Linda Hargreaves is Senior Lecturer in the Cambridge University Faculty of Education teaching MEd/MPhil, educational research methods and psychology of education. A former primary and early years teacher, she was an observer on the 1970s ORACLE project and has used observation in subsequent research, most recently in the ESRC's Teaching and Learning research programme, 'Social Pedagogical Research in Groupwork' (SPRinG) project. She is currently Director of a national project on the status of teachers and the teaching profession.

Jane Hislam is Programme Director of an undergraduate degree for teaching assistants and lecturer in Primary English on the Primary PGCE course at the University of Leicester. Her research and teaching interests are in the area of language and literacy, in particular oral storytelling, children's literature and the teaching of grammar to primary age pupils. She is Director of a research project entitled 'Song and Story with Under Five Year Olds'.

Alan Howe is Senior Lecturer in Primary Education and Primary Science Co-ordinator at Bath Spa University. He taught in primary schools in London, Bristol and Bath before moving into teacher education. He has published widely in the fields of primary science and creativity in primary education. He is joint author of *Science 5–11: A Guide for Teachers, Teaching Science and Design & Technology in the Early Years*, and *Primary Design & Technology for the Future,* all published by David Fulton.

Rajinder Lall is Lecturer in Primary English on the Primary PGCE course at the University of Leicester and also works on an undergraduate degree for teaching assistants. Her research and teaching interests are in the area of diversity and equality issues in education and working with children who have English as an additional language. She has extensively used oral storytelling in English and other languages in the classroom and worked closely with many colleagues in schools. She is also a trustee for the Leicester Complementary Schools Trust.

Karen McInnes is a Senior Researcher with Barnardo's UK policy and research team. Previously she was a Senior Lecturer in early years education at Bath Spa University College and has worked with young children, both as a teacher and speech therapist. Recent research projects have involved acting as a consultant researcher to a local Sure Start programme and developing outcomes for local children's centres. She has published on various aspects of early years education.

Jeff Meiners is a Lecturer at the University of South Australia's School of Education. He has worked widely in movement, arts and dance education, teaching people of all ages, as leader of a dance education team and has facilitated dance and movement projects across Australia and in Papua New Guinea, England and Portugal. He was a 2002 and 2005 Australian Dance Award nominee for Services to Dance Education and is a member of the Australia Council's Dance Board.

Roger Merry taught for six years before joining the School of Education, University of Leicester, where he is now a Senior Lecturer. He has worked extensively on the Primary PGCE and doctorate programmes, and is currently in charge of the MA in Primary

Education, with distance learning students from all over the world. His main interest is in children's learning, with publications including academic articles and books and materials for teachers and children.

Janet Moyles is Professor Emeritus at Anglia Ruskin University and an early years consultant. She has worked as an early years teacher and head, and also run early years initial and inservice training courses for teachers on play and learning and effective/ reflective pedagogy. She has directed several research projects including *Jills of All Trades?* (ATL 1996), *Teaching Fledglings to Fly* (ATL 1997), *Too Busy to Play?* (Leicester 1997–2000), *SPEEL – Study of Pedagogical Effectiveness in Early Learning* (DfES 2002) and *Recreating the Reception Year* (ATL 2004).

Theodora Papatheodorou is Professor in Early Childhood Education and Research at Anglia Ruskin University. She has long and diverse teaching and research experience in the field of early childhood. Her work has been widely disseminated by publications and presentations at international journals and conferences, respectively. She is the author of the book *Behaviour Problems in the Early Years* (Routledge 2005).

Sacha Powell is Senior Research Fellow in the Department of Educational Research at Canterbury Christ Church University. She works on a variety of research projects, primarily in childhood and community studies. She has a particular interest in constructions of early childhood internationally, and regularly works with colleagues in the People's Republic of China. Her current research focus is on play policies and strategies and their impact on opportunities for children's and young people's play and informal recreation.

Gillian Robinson is Reader in Education, Director of Research Degrees and Lecturer in Art and Design at Anglia Polytechnic University. Her book *Sketch-books: Explore and Store* was published in 1995 and by Heinemann USA in 1996. Her continuing research interests are focused on the value of sketchbooks and journals as a cross-curricular tool for developing creativity and thinking skills. She is also a practising painter, working mostly in mixed media.

Jenny Rogers is an experienced early years teacher, psychologist and teacher-educator. She developed the current Professional Course of the Primary PGCE at the University of Leicester where she is Co-Director of the MA in Primary Education and supervises the research of masters and doctoral students. She has published widely in the area of young children's learning, including mathematical development, and leads an international research project on early learning and problem-solving.

Wendy Schiller has worked in Canada, South Africa, PNG and Australia with indigenous populations and taught at tertiary level in Canada and Australia. Wendy has edited and authored 11 books, 25 book chapters and over 35 journal articles. She is currently Professor and Director of Research at de Lissa Institute of Early Childhood and Family Studies at the University of South Australia. Wendy was recently awarded an Order of Australia Medal (OAM) for services to early childhood education.

Alison Shilela is Associate Dean in the Faculty of Education at Anglia Ruskin University. She has taught in England, France, Zambia, Senegal and Germany in the primary, secondary and post-compulsory sectors. She worked for the Cambridge Multicultural Education Service and taught Namibian refugees in Zambia. Alison's commitment to teaching for social justice is now reflected in her research focused on engagement with critical pedagogy through curriculum development in higher education from an international perspective.

Wendy Suschitzky is a part-time tutor working in initial teacher education at the University of Leicester. She has worked in early years and community education. Her main interests are mentoring, teacher education and diversity issues in young children's education.

David Whitebread is a Senior Lecturer in Psychology and Education in the Faculty of Education, University of Cambridge, and a former director of the Early Years and Primary PGCE course. His research interests are concerned with learning in young children, including the role of play, thinking skills, and the development of self-regulation and independent learning. His publications include *The Psychology of Teaching and Learning in the Primary School* (RoutledgeFalmer 2000) and *Teaching and Learning in the Early Years*, 2nd edn (RoutledgeFalmer 2003).

Sylvia Wolfe is a tutor on the Primary PGCE course in the Faculty of Education, University of Cambridge, and an affiliate member of the Educational Dialogue Research Unit at the Open University. Prior to studying for a PhD, she had extensive experience working in an advisory service and as a class and language support teacher with a particular expertize in early years practice. Her research interests are in investigating classroom communication, particularly the role of dialogue in effective teaching and learning, and raising the achievement of bilingual pupils.

Maulfry Worthington is the co-author of *Children's Mathematics*: *Making Marks, Making Meaning* and is engaged in further research on children's mathematical graphics for her doctorate (Free University, Amsterdam). She has taught in the full 3–8 year age range for 25 years. Maulfry has worked as a National Numeracy Consultant and lectured on Primary and Early Years mathematics and Early Years pedagogy in Initial Teacher Education. She is joint founder of the international *Children's Mathematics Network*.

Acknowledgements

Many thanks and much appreciation should go to the students, tutors and others associated with the range of institutions represented in this book who have contributed in various ways to the production of this third edition. They have all worked hard to produce a worthwhile and exciting new volume which we all hope will ensure this book continues to support the important task of educating our new early years and primary teachers and the staff who work with them. This is no mean feat in the current age where education is expected to be the panacea for many of society's challenges and teachers are under pressure to produce better and higher standards of learning and behaviour.

Further acknowledgements are given in individual chapters.

Abbreviations

We have tried to keep educational jargon to a minimum in the book but, inevitably, there are certain acronyms or phrases given specific meaning in education.

ALS	Additional Literacy Support
ATs	Attainment Targets and tests within NC subjects
Citizenship	Part of the NC related to children developing social and political awareness
CWDC	Children's Workforce Development Council
DES	Department for Education and Science, later to become the DfE
DfE	Department for Education, the previous name for the DES
DfEE	Department for Education and Employment, the government body in charge of education prior to 2000
DfES	Department for Education and Skills
EAL	English as an Additional Language and EFL (English as a Foreign Language)
Early years or Early childhood Education	Applied usually to the education of birth–7/8-year-olds but increasingly focused on birth–5-year-olds in the Foundation Stage
ECEC	Early Childhood Education Centre
ERA	Education Reform Act
EYFS	Early Years Foundation Stage – guidance on curriculum for children aged birth–5 years in all settings, e.g. nurseries, playgroups, reception classes
HEI	Higher Education Institution, e.g. university, college
ICT	Information Communications Technology
ITE	Initial Teacher Education (preferred by most academics to ITT)
ITT	Initial Teacher Training
KS1 and KS2	The NC gives four age-related stages of education, with Key Stages 1 and 2 relating to primary children aged from 5–7 and 7–11 respectively
LEA	Local Education Authority
NC	National Curriculum
NQT	Newly qualified teacher
OfSTED	Office for Standards in Education, the body which governs school and ITE/ITT course inspections
Parents/carers	Anyone who has the legal guardianship of a child
PE	Physical Education
Pedagogy	The study of teaching and learning

PGCE	Post-graduate Certificate in Education Professional Graduate Certificate of Education
PPA	Planning, Preparation and Assessment
Pupils	Children in the context of school/ing
QCA	Qualifications and Curriculum Authority
QTS	Qualified Teaching Status
RE	Religious Education
SATs	Standard Attainment Tasks
SEN	Special Educational Need(s)
STA	Specialist Teaching Assistant
TAs	Teacher Assistants (sometimes called Classroom Assistants or Learning Support Assistants)
TDA	Teacher Development Agency, which has charge of all ITT/ITE courses
TE	Teaching experience (or TP, teaching practice or placement)
Year groups	Those years which now constitute the years of schooling for primary childen from age 5 to 11, e.g. Year 1 = 5–6-year-olds, Year 2 = 6–7-year-olds, through to Year 6 = 10–11-year-olds. There is a designated Year R for reception children (those who are approaching 5) now within the EYFS.

Introduction

Janet Moyles

Cameo 1

(From a student teacher's journal about work with a Year 4 class) 'The best moment this half-term was when all the children together performed a dance/drama about the water-cycle from beginning to end – five weeks' work – and said they really enjoyed it! I felt a great sense of achievement because, in the first week's dance session, they didn't have a clue – and neither did I!'

Cameo 2

The student has spent nearly a week with a class of 5-year-olds on her first teaching experience. In planning the final day, the teacher has suggested that Julia might take the class for the Friday morning and 'try out' being a class teacher. Plans have been made and Julia goes through in her mind just how everything will go. The morning is spent on various activities and runs quite smoothly, if rather noisily. The teacher, who has just entered the classroom, reminds the student that the children will need some time to pack away the equipment. Julia uses what she believes to be the teacher's method of getting the children to put everything away, saying clearly 'Listen everybody . . . it's time to stop now. Put your things away and go and sit on the carpet.' Pandemonium reigns. The children appear to have gone berserk, rushing around the room, colliding with each other and dropping things on the floor. Even worse, the classroom looks like a herd of animals has passed through – and the teacher's standing there watching!

In the beginning . . .

Beginning teachers, whether students or those entering their first teaching posts, rightly have high ideals about the kind of teachers they want to be and the kind of classroom ethos they want to foster. Nearly always, as in the first cameo, they share a delight in actually being with children and participating in the fun and enjoyment of new learning. These are, however, only a very few aspects of the role of teacher, albeit arguably the best bits! There are many skills and attributes needed, as will be evidenced through the chapters of this book. Many of these will be acquired through the processes of initial teacher education courses but since there are now a great multiplicity of standards for students and newly qualified teachers, the time on courses for thinking more widely about the professional aspects of teaching, as well as curriculum content, has become somewhat limited.

The second cameo serves to emphasize that children and teaching can seemingly be extremely unpredictable and that the balance of primary classroom life is sometimes poised on a ruler edge (if not quite a knife edge). The student did everything 'right' yet the outcome was disastrous for her confidence, at least in the short-term. What this situation highlights is that it is not sufficient merely to emulate the actions and behaviours of another in order to learn to teach. How simple it would be if one could walk into a classroom armed with subject knowledge, the desire to teach and a belief that what one taught is what the children learn. The real world is far less predictable but infinitely more varied, exciting and challenging!

Whereas we all might wish that someone could wave a magic wand and save us from Julia's encounter in Cameo 2, these experiences are all part of learning to be a teacher. From the outset you need to be clear of one thing: *no one can teach you how to teach* any more than anyone can teach you how to learn. Both happen in tandem – or at least they should do – hence the title of this book *Beginning Teaching: Beginning Learning*. Learning to teach is all about what *we as teachers* bring that develops our professional personalities in harmony with our own personalities.

Every teacher is a mix of the personal and the professional and, whereas the professional may take a few knocks in the beginning stages like Julia, keeping the personal esteem intact is vital; I may be an awful teacher but that does not mean I am inevitably an awful person!

In any profession, the learning curve between a state of being a 'novice' and that of being an 'expert' (Casbergue and Allen 1997; Muijs and Reynolds 2005) is inevitably steep because there are always so many new issues to deal with simultaneously. Even when a certain level of expertise has been gained, new initiatives often challenge existing securities. Whatever apparently rigorous and difficult roles people have had in previous experiences, entrants to the teaching profession (as well as those with significant experience) may suddenly find themselves confronted with an overload of challenges. Because foundation stage and primary education concerns birth to 11-year-old children – and often fairly large numbers of them at once – these challenges are nearly always immediate and unrelenting: the children just do not go away while we get our acts together! What needs to be acknowledged is that, with support and encouragement from others, the vast majority of people succeed as effective teachers and thoroughly enjoy their vocation. Any teacher education course, of whatever duration or type, is only the *start* of a professional career; the beginning of learning about teaching – and about ourselves!

Intentions of this book

The third edition of this book, like its two predecessors, addresses all those just entering teaching either as students or as newly qualified teachers. It will also be of interest to those whose job it is to help these individuals learn about pedagogy. The original book grew out of increasing concern on the part of course tutors that there is too little time (especially on PGCE courses) to cover all the underlying issues that make the early and primary years of education and school, different and special. This still obtains – and even more so given that the foundation stage now covers working and playing with children from birth! This demands yet another level of understanding and knowledge that we have tried to address in this new edition.

By undertaking this third edition and incorporating some of this new thinking, we hope to redress the necessary balance to ensure not just a *trained* teaching workforce but an *educated* and *reflective* workforce, something now emphasized by both the Teacher Development Agency (TDA) and the Children's Workforce Development Council (CWDC).

Like its predecessors, this book does not aim to do everything or be all things to all people. We have used the expertise of individual contributors to raise issues which they think are important for new teachers (and, indeed, early years practitioners). Clearly there is more about which we could have written; this is why we give further reading at the ends of chapters so that readers have easy access to other informative sources.

First, a brief background to the current context of primary and early years education would seem useful. Second, the structure of the book is explained and information given regarding the chapters.

The context of early years and primary education

In England, as in many other countries in the world, a deep economic recession in the 1980s led to relatively high levels of unemployment. On the understandable basis of attempting to give their children more than they themselves had experienced, being 'in work' became the ultimate goal of many parents for their children and, parallel to this, came the pressures of being 'well educated' in order ostensibly to achieve such employment. Rightly or wrongly, education – or more properly *schooling* – became viewed, by politicians and the general public alike, as the panacea for many of society's problems. Huge pressures of accountability were put on teachers and it was inevitable that what was taught in the name of education also came under national scrutiny.

It was within this framework that the National Curriculum (NC) for England and Wales became a legislated requirement in 1989, standards for new teachers were imposed in 1998 and performance-related pay for qualified teachers appeared in 2000 – to name but a few! This focus on teaching, learning and curriculum is set to continue for many years. Some things have changed for the good; in the earlier book, the issue of early years education featured way down any list of educational and political priorities. However, growing knowledge from research, in particular, about children's development, the early formulation of dispositions to learning in our youngest citizens and new information on brain functioning, as well as downward pressures from Key Stage 1 (KS1) of the NC, have put early years firmly on the political and public agenda, culminating in 2001 with a Select Committee Report to the government on the early years and the many issues that it embraces (House of Commons Education and Employment Committee 2001). First in 2000 came the *Curriculum guidance for the foundation stage* (QCA/DfEE 2000), *Birth-to-Three*

Matters Framework followed in 2003 (DfES 2003), then *Every Child Matters* (2003 – now a major influence on all education and care policies); and, since then, CGFS and 0–3 have been combined into the *Early Years Foundation Stage*, DfES 2006). The Children's Workforce Development Council (CWDC 2006) has been instigated to look at training for Early Years Practitioners, intended to bring the level of early years personnel up to teacher-level qualification by various routes.

The NC curriculum for primary aged children has, since 1989, undergone a number of both reductions and extensions, resulting in the current documentation used in schools, the subject of which is the focus of all initial teacher education (ITE) courses. All ITE providers are also visited by government inspectors and judged on the basis of their ability to deliver all components of the curriculum but, especially, English and mathematics. Currently, attempts are being made to broaden the curriculum again, particularly in the light of current concerns, such as child obesity (partly due to an earlier downgrading of subjects, such as physical education in schools) and a perceived lack of 'creativity' and problem-solving abilities in today's children.

Inspection reports on ITE provision (as they are for individual schools) are available for public scrutiny through the OfSTED website (www.ofsted.gov.uk). The full NC has to be taught *by law* to all children aged 5–11 years in state primary schools, with maths and English (from 1995) being formally assessed in KS1 at age 7 years and KS2 at age 11 years. The EYFS curriculum is taught to all children from birth to 5 years of age and carries its own assessment profile based on early learning goals. The DfES's website includes very full information on all of this, including support with teaching activities (www.dfes.gov.uk).

The NC and EYFS aim to reflect the entitlement of all children to have access to a broad, balanced and relevant curriculum, which accounts for differentiation, progression and continuity, in order that every child should achieve his or her full potential. In practice, this means that the subject part of the NC has to be extended to incorporate all the broader curriculum aspects, such as citizenship and personal and social education. With EYFS the six areas of learning and 4 main principles embrace a wide range of content and processes, not least a thorough understanding of children's learning and development See Moyles (2007). Clearly, just in content terms, there will be much that new teachers will need to learn and address in order to show their capabilities and competence across such a broad curriculum sweep.

It needs to be remembered that a subject-dominated curriculum takes *knowledge*, and the handing *down* of that knowledge, as its basis. However, it is widely acknowledged that, for all children up to 11 years of age, the *processes* of their learning are far more important. As Muijs and Reynolds (2005: 24–5) point out:

> During childhood [the] process of selectively strengthening and pruning connections in the brain is at its most intense ... it is most pronounced between the ages of 2 and 11 as different development areas emerge and taper off. During these periods, the brain demands specific and extensive (stimulating) inputs to create or consolidate neural networks.

To teach early years/primary aged children effectively, one must first recognize what they already bring to the learning situation, just as education and training courses try to use the existing strengths of students as the basis of professional development.

The subject dominance, particularly of the National Literacy and National Numeracy Strategies, has impacted heavily on teacher education and new standards are continually being developed to show what students are expected to accomplish (Jacques and Hyland 2000; TDA 2006). So while a major part of course time is to be spent on subject curriculum, students are also assessed – and self-assess – on a significant number of standards, all of which must be met for *Qualified Teacher Status* (QTS) to be awarded. Standards similarly exist for the *Early Years Professional Status* award (CWDC 2006). Further standards are incorporated into the induction year processes for NQTs (see www.tda.gov.uk). In addition, there are specific periods of time (dependent on the overall length of the course) that students must spend in schools in direct contact with practising teachers and children. (Since around 1993, the relationships between institutions and the people within them have been known as 'ITT partnerships'.) Both tutors and teachers, during OfSTED inspections, award students specific grades for aspects of their teaching and, in order to be successful, partnerships must demonstrate high degrees of congruence between these gradings and those of the inspectors. As with other aspects, there are changes being made to the requirements, which mean that tutors and students, as well as partnership teachers/mentors, need continually to change and adapt practices to meet the current situation. There are also specific standards for early years teachers which must be met. For all teachers, the current standards contain the following headings:

- S1: Professional values and practice (8 standards);
- S2: Knowledge and understanding (8 standards);
- S3: Teaching: planning, expectations and targets (5 standards); monitoring and assessment (7 standards); teaching and class management (14 standards).

Within these headings are also a number of sub-headings which indicate that teaching and learning must also occur within history or geography, physical education, ICT, art and design or design and technology, performing arts and religious education. Clearly these are extensive areas to be covered and yet the list provides glimpses of much more that needs to be understood and explored by students; issues such as children's thinking, creativity, observation, behaviour, working alongside other adults. Hence the need for a book of this type, which explores some of these vitally important areas and a selection of related issues that we feel are important for beginning teaching and learning about teaching.

The structure and content of the book

This third edition has four parts: the first five chapters address the issues concerning those who will teach our youngest children but are an important read for all those who want thoroughly to understand children up to the age of 11 years. The second part (six chapters) explores a variety of curriculum-related issues; while the third part (five chapters) looks at many of the organizational aspects of teaching, including developing play and children's independence. In part four (five chapters) observation, assessment, equality and behavioural issues are discussed with a final chapter looking at the all-important role of reflection for all teachers. Each chapter is written in a straightforward style and begins with cameos of classroom life as experienced by beginner teachers and children so as to offer an immediate point of reference with everyday encounters. Each chapter also concludes with its own thought-provoking questions and suggested further reading.

In the first of the five chapters constituting Part 1, we begin at the beginning with a new chapter by Tricia David and Sacha Powell on teaching birth to 3-year-olds. The authors stress the importance of understanding where and how learning begins so that practitioners and teachers can build on children's strengths and understanding – truly starting from the child! They present some of the research on early child development and its implications for teaching very young children. They urge readers to address the phenomenal learning likely to have occurred in the very early years and not to assume that learning only begins at school age. This is followed by a chapter on working in the *Foundation Stage* in which Nansi Ellis argues that early years teachers are often the most passionate about their work and find this the most exciting and rewarding period in which to engage in children's learning. She argues that this stage is vital to all the children's futures both as school pupils and as people and welcomes the current focus on early years education and the closer working relationships formed with parents at this stage. This chapter is followed by a new chapter from Karen McInnes on multi-disciplinary working practices in which she considers the range of professionals who work in a children's centre: the role of the early years teacher and how multi-disciplinary working may be successfully achieved. Karen gives a brief overview of policy and research which has led to the formation of Children's Centres (a new concept in education and care) and takes an in-depth look at the joys and challenges of joint working and how different professionals might work together. In Chapter 5, Debbie Albon examines the TDA standards in relation to working in partnership with parents/carers and encourages reflection by beginner teachers upon its importance. She offers ideas on how the standards might be achieved in practice and stresses the need to develop good communication skills.

In Chapter 4 of Part 1, Hilary Fabian and Aline-Wendy Dunlop write about the different transitions children make in their lives and outline aspects for the beginner teacher to consider for children who are just starting school and highlight the importance of friendship and curriculum continuity during transitions, as well as exploring practical aspects, such as preparing the classroom and structuring the day.

Roger Merry and Jenny Rogers begin Part 2 by examining closely how children learn. They concentrate on aspects, such as perception, memory and learning strategies, review some general trends in children's development up to the age of 11 years and also include reference to the current research into cognitive development and brain studies, a growing feature of cognitive theory. This is followed by a new chapter by Dan Davies and Alan Howe who use the science and design/technology curricula as the basis of examining the effective teaching of thinking skills to early years/primary children. They emphasize that, in effect, thinking skills are cross-curricular and show how learning experiences which are relatively open-ended, involve trying things out, testing ideas and communicating discoveries, generally make use of and develop these skills. They offer advice on how such experiences can be structured and developed in order that children begin to learn to select and apply appropriate skills autonomously.

Jane Hislam and Rajinder Lall explore story-*telling* (as opposed to story-reading) in

Chapter 8 and consider it from the angle of different cultures and presentations. They delve into the different responses children have given to being told stories and give examples of how beginner teachers might develop these important skills to promote literacy and oracy among children. This creative theme is then carried on in Gill Robinson's Chapter (9) in which she outlines children's entitlement to an art programme which is rich and multifaceted, motivating and challenging, and which takes account of the individuality of each child. Gill, like Dan and Alan, points out that the most meaningful and rewarding work in art results from an engagement with the process where children have been involved in first-hand experience and with experimenting and investigating.

Nick Easingwood has updated his chapter on ICT (Chapter 10) as a tool in early years and primary education. In this exciting chapter he has outlined the growing use of whiteboards and networked communities within schools and gives many useful practical suggestions on what you can do to truly incorporate ICT across the curriculum. In a new Chapter 11, Wendy Schiller and Jeff Meiners (Australian colleagues) explore issues related to children's learning through physical activity, something now considered much more vital in the UK, given levels of children's obesity and sedentary lifestyles. The examples used in this chapter are from the early years of school and raise issues relevant to a range of primary schools and early childhood settings. Discussion includes the importance of children's interests, the broader context for physical activity and the teacher's skills, special talents or qualifications. Attention is given to ground rules for inclusion and co-operation, large and small group management, encouraging safety including 'safe touch', supporting diversity and children's positive approaches to lifelong participation in physical activity.

Part 3 contributions begin with Maulfry Worthington (Chapter 12) writing about planning for and developing play, the sort of play in which young children freely engage and which is highly significant, not only in a general sense for their well-being and social development but also to support their intellectual development. She emphasizes that genuine child-initiated play is spontaneous and belongs to the child and that teachers and other practitioners must adapt their ways of working to suit this vital element of childhood. In Chapter 13, Janet Moyles revisits the issue of planning for learning in both playful and more formal contexts and examines how beginner teachers can plan for children's learning within the context of their own interests and motivations while still complying with subject curriculum requirements. The theme of children's own motivations and independence continues in Chapter 14, where David Whitebread and Penny Coltman review their own and others' research into the development of independence and autonomous thinking in early years/primary settings. They stress that the aim of good teachers should be to make themselves redundant. If we are to effectively educate our young children, we must enable them to become independent, or what might more properly be termed 'self-regulating' learners. This is followed (Chapter 15) by a look at how the organization of the classroom environment, if properly planned and executed, can support both the children's and the teacher's work and play. Rather than dealing with the pragmatics of the classroom, the emphasis is on delving into teachers' beliefs and values, behavioural and home/school issues, children's independence and the processes of teaching and learning, to understand how structures and routines affect potential learning opportunities.

The final chapter in this section is a brand new contribution from Wasyl Cajkler and

Wendy Suschitzky who explain the working roles and relationships of teachers and teaching assistants (TAs). They outline very clearly how the TAs' roles have developed over the past few years and what beginner teachers can expect by way of support from these variously trained adults.

Part 4 begins with a new chapter, Assessing Children's Learning, by Kathy Hall (Chapter 17). There can never be enough information given about assessment and Kathy makes an excellent job of exploring a range of key assessment themes: assessment purposes, assessment evidence, formative assessment and feedback, national testing and prioritizing assessment for the promotion of learning. She also stresses that acknowledging the learner's take on their own learning is fundamental to good assessment practice in the primary school and that observation is such a vital feature of making quality assessment. Observation is then the focus of Chapter 18, with Linda Hargreaves and Sylvia Wolfe, who further stress the centrality of observation to the processes of assessment, evaluation, reflection on practice and action research. They emphasize that observation must remain a key part of the professional practitioner's repertoire and suggest some simple pencil and paper recording techniques, before considering the use of more technologically advanced but easily accessible tools, such as video, MP3 and computerized systems. Throughout, they offer examples from observation-based research projects to inspire beginning teachers to examine similar themes in their own practice.

With the inclusion of children with special and additional needs into mainstream schools, no book like this would be complete without a chapter on behaviour issues in early years and primary education. In Chapter 19, Theodora Papatheodorou explains the different types of behaviour which many teachers, especially those just beginning their careers, may find challenging, and outlines certain parameters and criteria that determine whether a behaviour becomes challenging in the classroom. She then explores a range of strategies for dealing with the child and the behaviour. Differences in children occur for many reasons, one of which may be related to different cultural backgrounds: Alison Shilela and Alan Bradwell, in Chapter 20, explore the relationship between understandings of race equality manifested in the learning context and the lived experience of learners and practitioners. They stress the need for collective commitment to engage with the dynamics of difference by taking into account the rapidly changing nature of the primary school workforce, the increasingly diverse ethnic profile of our primary children and the reality of underachievement for some children. This chapter will give readers much food for thought, as will Chapter 21, the final chapter in which Siân Adams underlines the vital need for all teachers and practitioners to work on their own continuing professional development through reflection on and about practice. She raises many questions to guide the beginning teacher to make considered responses to episodes that frequently occur in the classroom, emphasizing that reflective practice is a highly complex process that involves thinking critically at many different levels. It is not an add-on but a vital part of the role of early years and primary teachers and practitioners.

The very brief conclusion to the book ensures that the voices of beginning teachers are heard as they explain to readers their experiences in the early days of teaching and learning.

As will be obvious by now, the scope of the book is very broadly based but by keeping the focus on the learning partnership between the beginner teacher and the children, it is hoped that the book will be manageable and useful like its predecessors. Whatever the intensity and rigours of the primary curriculum, the children and their teachers both need to gain enjoyment and satisfaction from the educational process and a real desire to continue learning: school and learning should be fun for everyone. Beginner teachers are usually welcomed by the children because they bring new ideas and different ways of doing things. As one 8-year-old child wrote in a letter to a student – 'We are very greatful that you came to help us in your spare time and we're sorry that your liveing'!! [sic]

Here's the hope that you will always be able to see the humorous side of school.

References

Casbergue, R. and Allen, R. (1997) Evolution at novice through expert teachers' recall: implications for effective reflection on practice, *Teaching and Teacher Education*, 13(7): 741–55.

CWDC (2006) *Early Years Professional Prospectus.* Available online www.cwdcouncil.org.uk (accessed 15 September 2006).

Department for Education and Skills (2003) *Birth to Three Matters.* London: Sure Start.

Department for Education and Skills (2003) *Every Child Matters.* London: HMSO.

Department for Education and Skills (2006) *The Early Years Foundation Stage: Consultation on a Single Quality Framework for Services to Children from Birth to Five.* London: DfES.

House of Commons Education and Employment Committee (2001) *Early Years First Report*, vols I and II. London: HMSO.

Jacques, K. and Hyland, R. (2000) *Achieving QTS: Professional Studies: Primary Phase.* Cleveland. Learning Matters.

Moyles, J. (ed) (2007) Early Years Foundations: Meeting the Challenge. Maidenhead: Open University Press.

Muijs, D. and Reynolds, D. (2005) *Effective Teaching: Evidence and Practice.* London: David Fulton.

Qualifications and Curriculum Authority/Department for Education and Employment (2000) *Curriculum Guidance for the Foundation Stage.* London: DfEE.

Teacher Development Agency (2006) *Professional Standards for NQTs.* Available online http://www.tda.gov.uk (accessed 26 June 2006).

Suggested further reading

Day, C. (2004) *A Passion for Teaching.* London: RoutledgeFalmer.

McGrath, M. (2000) *The Art of Peaceful Teaching in the Primary School.* London: David Fulton.

Moyles, J. (ed) (2007) Early Years Foundations: Meeting the Challenge. Maidenhead: Open University Press.

Muijs, D. and Reynolds, D. (2005) *Effective Teaching: Evidence and Practice.* London: Sage.

Pollard, A. (2005) *Reflective Teaching: Effective and Research-based Professional Practice* (2nd edn). London: Continuum.

PART 1
EARLY BEGINNINGS

1 Beginning at the beginning

Tricia David and Sacha Powell

Cameo 1

Cy (aged 2) is pushing a little wooden trolley along the pavement. Every few yards he stops and peers down intently. On the third stop, his father apologizes (I am behind them), confirming what I had already concluded: Cy is fascinated by the grid covers, apparently they are one of his special interests whenever he goes for a walk.

Cameo 2

Manjit (11 months) sings to herself at nursery with comforting sounds she has developed to accompany her mother's lullabies and which she now uses to lull herself to sleep.

Introduction

These very young children have begun their lives with parents who are gently patient and who have learnt what pleases, interests and soothes their individual children. We may never know why a particular behaviour, event or object becomes meaningful or attractive to a baby or toddler: individuality is one of the wonders of life. However, we can observe and note these predilections because they can help us understand a child so that we can 'tune in' to ways of supporting them emotionally and furthering their learning.

In this chapter, we will present some of what is known about early child development and its implications for teaching very young children. Although it is important to regard the whole of the Foundation Stage – from birth to 5 – as one stage of education, it is also important to think about the different phases within that stage. We must build on the phenomenal learning that is likely to have occurred, rather than asking what we expect children to be able to do when they reach Key Stage 1, imposing unrealistic and meaningless goals and downward pressure, and assuming learning only begins in school!

We will focus on the years from birth to 3. Research on development, together with examples of theory and practice interspersed with cameos from the lives of children in their homes and early childhood education and care (ECEC) settings, will explore what *teaching* means and what we know about babies and very young children learning.

The 'new' Foundation Stage

Provision for children in the earliest phase of life has a chequered history in the United Kingdom (David 1990) and it has only been in the past two decades that governments have begun to recognize the need for thoughtful expansion of services. Much of the emphasis of the New Labour government, since 1997, has been on the development of 'care' to enable mothers to continue in or re-enter the workforce (Campbell-Barr 2005). However, with the inception of the Sure Start Unit within the Department for Education and Skills (DfES), attention has also been paid to children's learning. For children aged between 3 and 5, the *Early Learning Goals* (QCA/DfEE 2000) had been initiated and for those working with children from birth to 3 a *Framework to Support Children in their Earliest Years* (DfES 2003). That Framework has now been incorporated into the *Early Years Foundation Stage* covering children from birth to 5 (DfES 2006).

Two interrelated issues highlight the focus of this chapter: what do we mean by the terms 'education' and 'care'? And is it appropriate to talk about 'teaching' such young children? Unfortunately the history of the ECEC field in the UK, with some provision being labelled 'care' (so mothers could work, or for children of ill or 'feckless' parents) while other forms of provision (such as nursery schools and nursery classes attached to primary schools) have been labelled 'education', has led to a divide that pervades both thinking and the provision itself. While it is accepted that all forms of provision can and should offer both care and learning (Bennett 2003), differences in staffing ratios, staff education and qualifications, and conditions of service have slowed down the integration of services. Many personnel in the ECEC field, especially those in what was formerly called the 'care sector', are reluctant to use the terms 'education' or 'teaching' because to them such terms smack of formality and schooling. In fact, Baroness Massey, chair of the All-Party Parliamentary Group for Children, took Schools Minister, Lord Adonis, to task on behalf of early years organizations in June 2006, arguing that 'teaching' should be removed from the Childcare Bill. He responded by quoting Bernadette Duffy, head of Thomas Coram Nursery Centre, that 'teaching' is 'Not instructing in a formal way but engaging and interacting with children, introducing them to new ideas and encouraging their well-being' (Weinstein 2006: 5). The problem is that if we cannot explain what we do to help children learn and do not regard it as a form of teaching, people outside of the field believe the work is simple, negating its complexity and seriousness. Further, it can mean that some working in ECEC settings are overly *laissez-faire*, leaving children to their own devices while others think that to satisfy OfSTED inspectors they must teach formally, indicating a lack of understanding about how young children learn (David *et al.* 2000).

But are critics correct to think what we mean by 'education' or 'teaching' as applied to very young children is formal and adult-led? What is sad about believing such a view of education is that it does not hold true for any age group. In this chapter we will show how babies and children learn through talk and play sometimes alone, sometimes with others, especially those they love and who love them (Gopnik *et al.* 1999).

The origin of the word education is, after all, from the Latin verb *educare* – 'to lead out' – in other words, when we act as teachers who educate rather than merely instruct, we enable the learner to use the talents they have 'inside' and help them move onward/outward to greater and more complex levels of understanding and knowledge.

In fact, while endorsing play as the main mode of learning in the EYFS, this view of what is meant by teaching young children is stressed by the DfES: 'Teaching means systematically helping children to learn so that they are helped to make connections in their learning and actively led forward, as well as helped to reflect on what they have already learnt' (DfES 2006: 30).

Babies and young children learning

Babies come into the world seemingly programmed to be eager to learn and to interact with those they find around them (Trevarthen 1995; Karmiloff and Karmiloff-Smith 2001). Our own observations and recent research (Bloom and Tinker 2001) confirm that very young babies are intentional even before they can express those intentions in language:

> At bath time, a game had built up over several weeks in which Nic's Mum poured water from a cup onto Nic's tummy or hand, singing 'Water on your tummy' or 'Water on your hand' each time. This game began when Nic was just a couple of months old and continued because he seemed to enjoy the sensations. By the time he was five-months-old, Nic was leading the game by sticking his tummy out of the water or wafting his hand in front of the cup so that his Mum would follow his lead and sing 'Water on your tummy/hand' as appropriate. This game lasted until Nic decided it was his turn to commandeer the cup, and the game changed to one of self-soaking and cup exploration!

> One of the clips exemplifying an adult's intervention to support learning with babies can be seen on the tape in the *Birth to Three Framework* pack. Two babies are seen sitting near each other with a number of balls. They are 'testing' the balls, holding one in each hand, banging them on the floor followed by one ball against the other. One senses immediately that soon one baby will 'test' a ball on the second baby's head or back. When this does indeed occur the practitioner subtly places her hand where the baby can 'test' the errant ball, gently showing him what is permissible and what is not, while allowing the exploratory play to continue.

All these babies are exploring their worlds – the people, objects and materials in them, their properties and reactions. The main messages from research about how babies and young children learn are that:

- they are actively making sense of the world literally through their senses – through seeing, hearing, touching, smelling and tasting;
- their ability to explore and experiment increases as they become physically more able;
- they engage in proto-conversations (taking turns at making noises and meaningful gestures) and later in conversations using the languages they have heard around them with familiar adults and children;

- they observe behaviour, mimic modelling by others, can join in fantasy play and become 'mind readers' who, by age 2, know what makes others 'tick';
- they need warm, sensitive relationships in which they are accepted and loved unconditionally;
- they need opportunities to observe and to interact with other children;
- their ability to learn is impaired by severe deprivation, exposure to violent or frightening experiences, extreme lack of stimulation or too much adult direction, too little opportunity to engage from choice with people and objects and too much extraneous noise (for example from a television that is never switched off).

(See also David *et al.* 2003; Robinson 2003; Gerhardt 2004).

A major influence on current recognition for the birth to 3 age range by governments in many countries has been the contribution from neuroscience (Shore 1997), suggesting that:

- brain development occurs as a result of a complex interweaving of genetic potential and experience;
- early experiences affect the 'design' of the brain, ultimately influencing the nature and extent of adult capabilities;
- early interactions impact on the way the brain is 'wired' as well as creating the context for development and learning;
- brain development is non-linear and at 'sensitive periods' particular learning is optimized;
- children's brains are much more active than adults' and levels of activity drop during adolescence.

While some claims about brain development are questioned (for example, Thompson and Nelson 2001), the researchers Gopnik *et al.* (1999), who collated evidence from scores of research studies, suggest young children learn best through relaxed, happy play and interaction with those they love and who love them.

Aspects of early learning

Babies have an immense drive to explore. They are curious and sociable; they want to know what everything in their world does and what they can then do with whatever has attracted them – be it a person, an object, behaviour pattern or event. Babies do not have to be overtly taught to communicate, to experiment or to adopt the habits and rituals of their communities. They observe and manipulate who and what they find around them. They are capable of recognizing what is permissible, what invites praise and affection (and the converse) in their families and society, and most emulate the role that has been bestowed upon them. However, that is not to say that children themselves have no hand in determining their role in the group. In the past few decades, psychologists have begun to acknowledge that each child co-constructs their individual world and role in it through interaction with more powerful others – usually their parents and family members. Each society (and subgroups within that society) will have a dominant view of what early childhood should be (Rosenthal 2003). Thus family life and nursery experience will vary from country to country (OECD 2001; David and Powell 2005).

Just as older pupils and students have different preferences with respect to learning styles (see Chapter 6), so do young children. Most young children learn by experimenting through hands-on play experiences. Some will be avid watchers, especially of a 'model' they admire.

Practitioners need to evaluate their work, reflecting on their records of what has gone on in order to ensure they offer a range of visual, auditory and kinaesthetic experiences to babies and children as in the following cameo.

Cameo 3

From his earliest days, Jamie was eagerly mobile, starting with 'worming' his way down and across his mother's body (at 2-days-old,) seeming to prefer left over right breast. His ever-increasing control over his body delighted him as he exerted energy and great concentration, moving his body up, down, to and fro. He watched his own limbs with intense interest over the nine months it took him to achieve (his) goals of sitting, crawling and pulling himself up to stand. Only walking evaded him and by making appropriate arm movements and vocal signals he could enlist the help of a pair of hands under the armpits to help him become prematurely bipedal.

By contrast, his twin brother was an observer. He lay quite still taking in his surroundings, listening to the sounds, breathing the scents, receiving the kisses, cuddles and loving words. As he found greater control over his body it was to sit and explore in intricate detail that gave him great pleasure or, when beginning to crawl, to look back at his legs to see what they were doing behind him.

The concept of *learning dispositions* also contributes to our deep understanding of early learning. Carr (2001: 22) tells us that learning dispositions are:

> about responsive and reciprocal relationships between the individual and the environment ... a repertoire of familiar and privileged processes of contribution and communication ... learners recognise, select, edit, respond to, resist searches for and construct learning opportunities.

According to Carr (2001: 39), dispositions reflect the children's theories about learning places, providing a narrative – 'what learning is, and ought to be, all about'. They can help the children avoid, resist, or change the learning environment but it is often the adults who hold the power and 'control the agenda' (2001: 46).

Brooker's research (2002) demonstrated how children entering Year R displayed very different dispositions from each other as a result of their families and cultural backgrounds. They came to school with varying accumulations of *cultural and social capital* and had different experiences of family *habitus*. Brooker found that in order to learn at school the children needed to be compliant, prosocial, independent and involved and that all the children displayed these characteristics, but some less frequently than others and these tended to be the children who were overlooked and given little support by staff. They had not acquired a school-like 'habitus' because they came to school from a very dissimilar home culture to that of the classroom. While the children were struggling to maintain their parents' values and beliefs, they were being subjected to those of school staff. They showed, as Anning (1997) also found, tremendous strength and adaptability but for some the 'recognition and realization of rules of the discourse were just too mysterious to access' and their subsequent academic progress was increasingly at risk (Brooker 2002: 155). This research should sound alarm bells for ECEC practitioners. Without constant evaluation and reflection (see Chapter 21) concerning what we think babyhood and early childhood are 'for' and how we should provide for such young children, we put them at risk.

Assisting early learning

Having established that babies and young children are avid learners – from birth, in fact even in the womb – how are we to help them learn?

The *Birth to Three Framework* (DfES 2003: 5) states that:

- learning is a shared process and children learn most effectively when, with the support of a knowledgeable and trusted adult, they are actively involved and interested; .
- caring adults count more than resources and equipment;
- schedules and routines must flow from the child's needs;
- children learn when they are given appropriate responsibility, allowed to make errors, decisions and choices, and respected as autonomous and competent learners;
- children learn by doing rather than being told;
- young children are vulnerable. They learn to be independent by having someone they can depend upon.

Because of the holistic nature of early learning and in order to emphasize the inter-connectness of all areas of children's development, the Framework was organized as four Components – *a Strong Child; a Skilful Communicator; a Competent Learner; a Healthy Child* – rather than through the traditional areas adopted by developmental psychologists, who are increasingly aware that different areas of development influence one another.

By providing materials and props that are appropriate and likely to arouse interest in a child or a small group, an adult can spark play activities, observe and sometimes 'weave themselves into' a child's 'narratives', *scaffolding* learning. But this is *not* about the teacher (who may be the child's parent) leading, directing or monopolizing! It's about perceptive observations and dialogue, dialogue that is sometimes spoken, but is some-times simply actions. For example, it might be:

- giving a cuddle and letting go when the child is attracted by something or someone else;
- looking into a child's eyes and showing full attention and acceptance;

- watching them try something and smiling when they look for approval or reassurance;
- providing a piece of equipment that will move the chosen activity on;
- being willing to listen and be directed by the child or group of children.

When the sensitive intervention in the child's play involves shared speculations or the introduction of something new, the adult is said to have capitalized on a *teachable moment*.

Play and learning

Play has been advocated as the best vehicle for children's learning for many years but prescribed goals or outcomes can make it difficult to give children time and space to learn through play. Play is unpredictable and fluid. To be true play, an activity must be directed by the players. The advantages of capitalizing on play are that it involves:

- children's intrinsic motivation and curiosity to engage;
- self-imposed 'questions' about the play activity which are meaningful and relevant to the child (or children) involved;
- many possibilities, rather than a 'right answer' to be sought, so play is non-threatening, although it is often challenging;
- 'ownership' and control of the situation by the learners which strengthens both motivation and learning;
- the 'what if' quality of play which encourages creativity; rules can be invented and broken;
- social aspects, encouraging interpersonal skills, although it can be solitary;
- different forms of play that exercise the body and the mind ... play is 'an integrating mechanism' (Bruce 2005: 60);
- pleasure!

(David and Nurse 1999: 173–4)

Nevertheless, we should heed Sutton-Smith's (1979) argument that play can be used as a disciplining power strategy to shape children by the dominant expectations of their communities (David *et al.* 2000; Rosenthal 2003). Bennett (2003) argues that overly prescriptive, pre-primary-style curricula tend to limit children's autonomy and may prevent the development of the whole child. He suggests that the earliest years of life are for learning to live in society and for sharing a society's fundamental values. Our own work would lead us to concur with that view. Young children are deeply interested in what life, death and the world are all about and how we live together. Loris Malaguzzi, the prime spirit of Reggio Emilia nurseries, argued that for deep learning to take place, a child's environment must enable cognitive aspects of development to interface with those of affectivity and relationships (Edwards *et al.* 1998). Similarly, Shonkoff and Phillips (2000) state that the establishment of rich, strong, mutually rewarding relationships is the key task of the early years.

How do we know when to intervene in play to promote learning?

The importance of close observation and especially being a sensitive, familiar 'other' cannot be underestimated. Intimate 'portraits' of young children, recording their development (see Campbell 1999; Arnold 2003), can be particularly enlightening when the observing researcher is a family member, for young children are at their most relaxed and as a result display their knowledge and abilities more readily. Elfer and Selleck's (1999) research showed how important it is for staff in ECEC settings to be aware of the ways in which children show their pleasure or discomfort and to be attentive to these, often subtle, signals (see Linden 2006). This reinforces the need to keep close contact with parents and other family members and to ask them to contribute to the setting's information on their children (see Manning-Morton and Thorp 2001; Bruce 2005).

Teaching by capitalizing on *teachable moments* is not easy. It requires we really get to know our children and their families; that we carry around any preset goals in our heads and note when children show evidence of reaching these, rather than setting up special teacher-led activities that we think will achieve this. We must 'feel our way', be 'intuitive practitioners' (Claxton 2000) – formal in our heads but informal with the child/ children.

Simple examples of how we do this without even realizing it include our enthusiastic 'Yes, Mummy/Daddy!' when a baby babbles 'Mumumum' or 'Dadadad', or providing a spoon when feeding. Similarly, we might intervene spontaneously in fleeting engagements with toddlers, who may surprise us by taking our suggested props further than we imagined they could.

> **Cameo 4**
> Two-year-old Callie was playing at cafés with her Mum and Nana. Although Callie had only limited experience of cafés, her Mum asked for a menu – it could have been an imaginary menu or a book to represent a menu – but Nana spotted some paper and pens nearby and Callie immediately said 'I do it, I do it.' Afterwards she told Mum and Nana what was on the menu – chicken and chips, for example. You can see in Figure 1.1 she has varied the script for the different items.

Conclusion

Rinaldi's (2006: 72–3) conclusions on teachers' competency, based on her long experience in Reggio Emilia echo our own – the competency of teachers of very young children is:

> defined more in terms of understandings than of pure knowledge ... It is a sensitivity to knowledge ... in a situation where only the surface is visible ... Proceeding by trial and error does not debase the didactic paths; indeed it enriches them on a process level ... as well as on the ethical level.

Figure 1.1   Callie's menu

Questions to set you thinking

1   Look at the *Early Years Foundation Stage Document* and think of some alternative
    ideas for what might constitute effective practice in the examples given.
2   In the examples of Nic and Callie, think of alternative responses their family
    members could have made and what might have happened.

References

Anning, A. (1997) *The First Year at School*. Buckingham: Open University Press.

Arnold, C. (2003) *Observing Harry*. Maidenhead: Open University Press/McGraw-Hill.

Bennett, J. (2003) Starting Strong: the persistent division between care and education, *Journal
of Early Childhood Research*, 1(1): 21–48.

Bloom, L. and Tinker, E. (2001) *The Intentionality Model of Language Acquisition*. Monograph of
the Society for Research in Child Development, 66(267): 4.

Brooker, L. (2002) *Starting School: Young Children Learning Cultures*. Buckingham: Open University Press.

Bruce, T. (2005) *Early Childhood Education* (3rd edn). Abingdon: Hodder Education.

Campbell, R. (1999) *Literacy from Home to School: Reading with Alice*. Stoke-on-Trent: Trentham
Books.

Campbell-Barr, V. (2005) The economy of childcare, unpublished thesis submitted to Canterbury Christ Church University/UKC, Canterbury.

Carr, M. (2001) *Assessment in Early Childhood Settings: Learning Stories*. London: Paul Chapman/ Sage.

Claxton, G. (2002) *Building Learning Power*. Bristol: TLO Publishing.

David, T. (1990) *Under Five: Under-Educated?* Milton Keynes: Open University Press.

David, T. and Nurse, A. (1999) Inspections of under fives' education and constructions of early childhood, in T. David (ed.) *Teaching Young Children*. London: Paul Chapman.

David, T. and Powell, S. (2005) Play in the early years: the influence of cultural difference, in J. Moyles (ed.) *The Excellence of Play* (2nd edn). Maidenhead: Open University Press.

David, T., Goouch, K., Powell, S. and Abbott, A. (2003) *Birth to Three Matters: A Review of the Literature*. London: DfES.

David, T., Raban, B., Ure, C., Goouch, K., Jago, M., Barrière, I. and Lambirth, A. (2000) *Making Sense of Early Literacy: A Practitioner's Perspective*. Stoke-on-Trent: Trentham Books.

Department for Education and Employment/QCA (2000) *Curriculum Guidance for the Foundation Stage*. London: DfEE.

Department for Education and Skills (2003) *Birth to Three Matters*. London: Sure Start.

Department for Education and Skills (2006) *The Early Years Foundation Stage: Consultation on a Single Quality Framework for Services to Children from Birth to Five*. London: DfES.

Department for Education and Skills (DfES) (2006) *The Early Years Foundation Stage: Consultation on a Single Quality Framework for Services to Children from Birth to Five*. London: DfES.

Edwards, C., Gandini, L. and Foreman, G. (1998) *The Hundred Languages of Children*. New York: Ablex.

Elfer, P. and Selleck, D. (1999) Children under three in nurseries. Uncertainty as a creative factor in child observations. *Europeans Early Childhood Education Research Journal*. 7(1): 69–82.

Gerhardt, S. (2004) *Why Love Matters: how Affection Shapes a Baby's Brain*. Hove: Brunner-Routledge.

Gopnik, A., Melzoff, A. and Kuhl, P. (1999) *How Babies Think: The Science of Childhood*. London: Weidenfeld and Nicolson.

Karmiloff, K. and Karmiloff-Smith, A. (2001) *Pathways to Language: From Fetus to Adolescent*. Cambridge, MA: Harvard University Press.

Linden, J. (2006) Just a thought, *Nursery World*, 106(4025): 12–3.

Manning-Morton, J. and Thorp, M. (2001) *Key Times: Developing High Quality Provision for Children Under Three*. London: UNL/London Borough of Camden.

OECD (2001) *Starting Strong: Early Childhood Education and Care*. Paris: OECD.

Qualifications and Curriculum Authority/Department for Education and Employment (2000) *Curriculum Guidance for the Foundation Stage*. London: DfEE.

Rinaldi, C. (2006) *In Dialogue with Reggio Emilia*. London: Routledge.

Robinson, M. (2003) *From Birth to One*. Maidenhead: Open University Press/McGraw-Hill.

Rosenthal, M. (2003) Quality in early childhood education and care: a cultural context, *European Early Childhood Research Journal*, 11(2): 101–16.

Shonkoff, J. and Phillips, D. (eds) (2000) *From Neurons to Neighborhoods: The Science of Early Childhood Development*, Washington, DC: National Academy Press.

Shore, R. (1997) *Rethinking the Brain: New Insights into Early Development*. New York, NY: Families and Work Institute.

Sutton-Smith, B. (1979) *Play and Learning*. New York, NY: Gardner-Halstead.

Thompson, R.A. and Nelson, C.A. (2001) Developmental science and the media: early brain development, *American Psychologist*, 56(1): 5–15.

Trevarthen, C. (1995) The child's need to learn a culture, *Children and Society*, 9(1): 5–19.

Weinstein, N. (2006) Early years experts want 'teaching' taken from Bill, *Nursery World*, 106(4025): 5.

Suggested further reading

Arnold, C. (2003) *Observing Harry*. Maidenhead: Open University Press/McGraw-Hill.

Bruce, T. (2005) *Early Childhood Education* (3rd edn): Hodder Abingdon/Education.

David, T., Goouch, K., Powell, S. and Abbott, A. (2003) *Birth to Three Matters: A Review of the Literature*. London: DfES.

Gerhardt, S. (2004) *Why Love Matters: How Affection Shapes a Baby's Brain*. Hove: Brunner-Routledge.

OECD (2001) *Starting Strong: Early Childhood Education and Care*. Paris: OECD.

2 Foundation stage – expectations and vision

Nansi Ellis

Cameo 1

At the beginning of each day, parents are invited to choose an activity to share with their child. Rebecca and her mum choose to paint a picture. While Rebecca paints, the teacher talks to her and her mum about the wedding they attended the previous weekend. Later, the nursery nurse invites Rebecca, who has dressed up as a bride and assembled a 'wedding party' in the role play area, to talk to the class about the wedding. This prompts Rupal to talk about his brother's wedding and the beautiful red sari the bride wore.

Cameo 2

Ben had recently watched a film which told a story of animals threatened by the melting of polar ice-caps. He talked constantly about ice and why it melted. A parent-helper made different sized blocks of ice, some of which had toys and natural objects frozen inside. Over the next week, Ben was engrossed for long periods playing with the ice, trying different ways of melting it, breaking it into smaller pieces, using water and sand and taking it outside into the sun. The teacher spent time with him, and they discussed hot and cold things, freezing and melting, and considered other things they might freeze. Ben helped the teaching assistant to make ice cubes for the children's mid-morning drinks.

Introduction

Foundation Stage teaching is hugely exciting and rewarding. You will work closely with children, their families and communities. The children you teach will be enthusiastic, eager to find out about the world. They will want to do everything 'now'. You will encourage them to become more secure in their skills and abilities and more confident explorers and learners.

Children change daily, and we face the challenge of supporting their learning and harnessing their eagerness. We need to be creative to maintain their enthusiasm and flexible to meet their immediate needs. We want to light a fire in these children's lives for learning, to set them on a course which will motivate them to keep learning throughout their lives. But expectations, particularly those placed on schools to aim towards specific outcomes and to meet targets, can make it hard to hold on to our vision for children and their learning.

Your professional practice is being shaped by your vision and values (see Chapter 13). As a professional you will explore and challenge your beliefs about children, about education and about learning (see Chapter 13). For example, do you agree with Dahlberg that the child is 'an active and creative actor … a subject and citizen with potentials, rights and responsibilities, a child worth listening to and having a dialogue with, who has the courage to think and act by himself' (Moss and Petrie 2002: 7)? Or are children 'adults in the making', to be valued (or feared) for what they will become? Are they innocent, to be protected, or dependent with needs to be met? Are children 'our future', able to change the world for the better if we can provide them with the means now?

Is our vision for education about preparing children for the future, or providing opportunities in the now? Is it about meeting their needs or about developing their interests? Is it about supporting children as they show a 'readiness' to learn, or about challenging and motivating them at the edges of their capabilities?

And what of young children's learning? Is it about 'being filled with knowledge'; being a 'lone scientist', making sense of the world by adding to and refining world pictures with every new discovery; or being 'social learners', co-constructing knowledge in community with peers and adults who will challenge and support? Some beliefs can lead to very prescriptive teaching, for example, the erroneous belief that the earlier a child learns something (perhaps reading or writing), the more successful they will be at a later age. Others may take us down strange paths that are not supported by evidence, such as rigid interpretations of 'learning styles' or the unquestioning adoption of a 'brain gym' approach. As with everything to do with young children and learning, there are no simple answers.

Our beliefs about children, learning and education may at times clash with national expectations, initiatives and prescribed practices. But it is important to keep these questions in mind and to discuss them with others, including the professionals with whom you work and with children's parents. Otherwise, we risk being swayed by every fashion, or teaching only according to our own personal whims.

Aims and values

The new *Early Years Foundation Stage* (EYFS) starts with children. It brings together *Birth to Three Matters* (BTTM) and the *Curriculum Guidance for the Foundation Stage* (CGFS), along with the five outcomes from *Every Child Matters* (see Chapter 1). The vision for this new EYFS should be underpinned by what we believe about children and their learning, which (in my view) should include the fact that children:

- are learners from birth;
- learn holistically (not in 'subjects');
- learn through first-hand experience;
- learn best through play, when they are active participants, talking and learning with others, and when they have time to be engrossed;

- learn best when they know they are valued and they value themselves;
- prosper in warm, caring relationships;
- learn best when they feel safe, and when they are healthy.

As we consider and discuss our beliefs, we become clearer about our aims for young children, such as:

- supporting their development as independent, confident, life-long learners and thinkers;
- enabling children to learn about and to value themselves and their achievements;
- supporting children in developing caring relationships, and to participate in their communities;
- enabling children to develop emotionally, socially, physically and intellectually and to enjoy extending their skills, understanding and knowledge of the world about them.

An EYFS that is truly integrated means continuity for children, sharing of information between providers and a shared understanding of children and their learning, so that starting in nursery or reception class is not a huge leap (see Chapter 5). We will need to work hard to realize this vision.

Getting to know you

As with all new relationships, we will need to spend time finding out who the children 'are', and what makes them 'tick'. They will have had very different experiences: some may never have been away from home without their parents or familiar adults; this may be their first experience of school with its strange rules and big, noisy children. They may speak little or no English (see Chapter 20), they may be fluent readers or they may be unable to tie their own shoelaces. In an ideal world, an integrated EYFS would mean that we have much more information about these children from their previous settings, but there are other ways in which we can get to know the children.

Links with parents

Initially, and over time, we can learn a great deal from parents and carers who will be able to tell us:

- what interests and excites their child;
- what activities they enjoy doing together;
- whether the child finds anything particularly challenging – and how they deal with difficulties;
- what expectations parents have, and what messages children are receiving about school;
- the important events in the child's life.

If parents and carers feel welcome and valued, their children are more likely to feel the same. Having routines at the start of the day (Cameo 1) can set a positive tone for the session and enable parents to talk to their child at home in more specific terms ('Did you enjoy painting today?' rather than 'What did you do at school today?') It also offers opportunities for parents and teachers to talk about the children and their experiences. By making space for parents and finding different ways of explaining what their children are doing and why, we can involve parents in their children's learning and justify our own practices.

Just as our professional practice is shaped by our vision, parents too will have beliefs and expectations about what education is about and how children learn. They will want their child to be happy, to enjoy school and to make friends. They also want their child to 'do well'. While, as teachers, we may aim to foster independent learning through following children's interests, as in Cameo 2 (see also Chapter 14), to parents this seemingly random choice of activities may be at odds with their expectations of 'real learning'. This may be particularly the case in the reception class where many parents will expect to see children sitting together and listening to the teacher or engaged in familiar activities, such as reading, writing and counting. Parents' expectations of the purpose and structure of school will be reflected, to some extent, in their children's attitudes. Some children will have been told that they must 'sit still, work hard and do what the teacher tells you': some of these children will flounder when faced with opportunities to choose activities, to act independently and to play. Others may have learnt the importance of keeping clean and tidy: outdoor and messy play may be anathema to them. Yet others will already have picked up ideas about gendered or cultural behaviour and may refuse to use the computer, play with dolls or engage in role play. Our visions for our classroom practices may well clash with parents' expectations, and as professionals we will need both to understand the expectations and to explore and explain our vision, if we are to build effective links with parents.

Assessment practices

Part of the excitement and the challenge of teaching young children is that they change every day. Regular assessment through observation allows us to find and value the positive in every child (see Chapter 18).

The *Foundation Stage Profile* (a requirement for reception teachers and finalized at the end of the reception year) is one form of assessment. It is a very real example of where expectation and vision may conflict, but it is also possible to use the Profile as part of a wider process of assessment for learning. By observing children as they play, and engaging in real, sustained conversation with them, we can find out not only what they know and can do, but how they see themselves and their world. By engaging in sustained, shared thinking (Sylva *et al.* 2004), as the teacher does in Cameo 2, we can challenge them from where they are, rather than moving them towards a prescribed outcome. Assessment is only partially about recording what we see and hear: we will gain much more useful information about children's learning (as opposed to what they can do) if we ask open-ended questions, in particular about what children think, or why they're doing things in a particular way. We don't need slavishly to record everything we find, but we do need to find ways of remembering those aspects which will inform our planning, and those things we will want to share with parents and others (see Chapter 17). Some of these findings will be recorded in the FSP, but it is much harder to fall into a 'tick-box trap' of assessment if we hold on to our own aims of getting to know individual children.

Developing curriculum

How should we plan the curriculum in the FS? This may seem a strange question – we already have a curriculum document. But it is important to remember that the EYFS is not in itself the curriculum: it provides guidance as we develop our curriculum, and it gives a set of outcomes which most children should achieve. We may feel that there is an expectation that we will work through the stepping stones or focus exclusively on the ELGs, but it is vital that we continue to think about how our aims for children will be addressed through our own provision.

What's in a curriculum?

A curriculum is made up of knowledge, skills, dispositions and feelings (Katz 1998). The FS curriculum starts with real children, with Rebecca and Rupal and their wedding stories, and with Ben and his fascination with ice. Of course, we work in real schools and we are expected to plan a curriculum that takes these children towards the early learning goals or key stage assessments. This means both knowing the children and knowing where they need to go, but it also provokes a continuing challenge to hold on to our own vision.

A traditional school curriculum prioritizes knowledge as a key part of children's learning, and is often planned in terms of subjects. The primary national strategy, *Excellence and Enjoyment*, has encouraged a rethink of curriculum provision, with many schools moving towards a more topic-based approach. Obviously, knowledge is important, and young children need to develop their knowledge and understanding of the world, but there are also a range of skills and dispositions that children need in order to learn (see Chapter 6).

Children have been developing their skills from birth: they have learnt to communicate, to move, to think and to create (see Chapter 1). Young children are constantly refining their physical and creative skills, learning, thinking and communication skills, skills in relationships and in managing their own emotions. The curriculum we plan should reflect this continuing development. Dispositions can broadly be defined as:

> relatively enduring 'habits of mind', or characteristic ways of responding to experience across types of situations (including persistence at a task, curiosity, generosity, meanness, the disposition to read, to solve problems). Unlike an item of knowledge or a skill, a disposition is not an end state to be mastered once and for all. It is a trend or consistent pattern of behaviour.
>
> (Katz 1998)

We need to consider the dispositions children need in relation to our aims for them to develop as learners and thinkers, in strong relationships, and to continue to explore the world around them. Ben (Cameo 2) shows developing dispositions of curiosity, responsibility, independence, interdependence, motivation and persistence. He is taking charge of his own learning, testing things out and considering new ideas: making sense of his world through his play (Moyles 1989; Bruce 1991). This is his own self-directed play, but structured both by the resources provided and skilled interventions from the teacher. Children's skills, dispositions and knowledge can and should be developed through play (see Chapter 12). With sensitivity we can plan our curriculum, starting from what we know about the children, building on children's play and moving them forward through sensitive involvement.

This kind of curriculum can also readily help children to move towards the early learning goals. Importantly, many of those goals reflect skills and dispositions, for example, self-confidence, self-esteem and making relationships; imagination; expressing and communicating ideas; and moving with confidence and imagination (see also Chapter 11). We need to try to focus on those, rather than on 'bits' of knowledge.

What of teaching children to read and write? Changes to the literacy strategy, brought about after a recent review (Rose 2006), mean that FS teachers will be under pressure to teach a programme of synthetic phonics to children by the time they are 5-years-old. Phonics teaching obviously helps children to decipher the words on the page and potentially to spell words when they begin to write, but it is not the only, nor arguably the most important aspect of learning to read. And just because it can be taught in a 'fun' and multi-sensory way does not make it part of children's play. If we wish to encourage children to become independent learners and thinkers, teaching them to decode is not enough (Moyles 2006). We need to provide opportunities for them to enjoy books and stories, to want to read and write and to talk about and understand words and contexts rather than concentrating solely on mechanical skills. Reading and writing can be taught in a meaningful way, consistent with our vision of children's wider education, if as FS teachers we develop a good understanding of how children learn to communicate and we continually question new strategies and methods offered.

Curriculum planning

In planning the curriculum we need to focus on what we want children to *learn*, rather than what we want them to *do*. This also helps to shape the dispositions and attitudes to learning that will support children's development as learners. Research by Adams *et al.* (2004) showed that planning which focuses largely on what children would do in an adult-provided activity, rather than on what they might learn, and which prioritizes coverage of the six areas of learning and the stepping stones, too often leads to children undertaking repetitive and simple tasks, instead of extending and challenging their thinking, or enabling them to refine their views of the world.

In planning the curriculum, we should return to our original aims:

- What do we want children to learn (rather than, what activities shall we provide for them?) and how will we know when they have learnt something?
- How will our curriculum enable children to develop as learners, communicators and thinkers?
- What are the interests, skills and needs of the children we currently teach?

- How will our curriculum encourage children to develop and extend their understanding of the world in which they live?
- What resources can we provide (indoors and outside) for children to explore their learning in contexts that are meaningful to them?

Working with others

Teachers do not often work in isolation. Rebecca's teacher (Cameo 1) has spoken to her assistant about her morning conversation and the assistant feels confident about taking Rebecca's interest forward later in the day. Cameo 2 is underpinned by conversations between the different adults about planning the curriculum which lead to a range of opportunities for Ben to take his learning forward. Over the past few years changes have taken place that increasingly influence who we work with and how (see Chapter 16). In particular, the 10 per cent PPA time, introduced in schools by the Workload Agreement, is bringing about changes that mean that, perhaps more than at any other time, we need to learn to work with, and to manage, other adults in order to make sure that we can continue to meet our aims for children's learning.

Continuity and 'joined-up services' have become increasingly important to policy-makers and practitioners alike (see Chapter 4). *Every Child Matters* (DfES 2003) grew from a need to make sure that children and families didn't 'fall through gaps' in provision because different professionals failed to share information. As FS teachers, we are expected to work more and more closely with professionals in health and social care, sharing information and supporting children's well-being.

Although the FS already straddles school and 'pre-school' provision, intending to provide continuity and ensure that children experience the same high quality of care and education whatever the setting they attend, children are already 3-years-old when they begin the FS. Continuity for children in their experiences pre- and post-3 is vital, and we need both an understanding of BTTM, and the time to work and learn with those who work with children from birth to 3. Currently, FS teachers are trained to work with children over 3, but many argue that we need a profession that can work with *all* young children from birth.

Conclusion

What is likely to make you an effective FS teacher? An effective teacher is a strong pedagogue, one who knows about children, their learning and development, and who has an understanding of children's worlds and of the world in which they will grow up; one who is willing to question the expectations placed on them and our children, and to uphold and continually develop their vision. As professionals, we have a duty to continue to learn about how children learn, by keeping up-to-date with research and by observing the children we teach, as well as questioning our beliefs and those of others about children, their learning and their play. Working with others, professionals in different fields as well as those within education, can challenge us further to question, to think, to improve and to enjoy our teaching. We may also be challenged to change our practice, but we will want to evaluate the changes we make to see if they do indeed make a positive difference to children and their learning. What are the dispositions we need to develop in order to become effective FS teachers? We must question the beliefs which underpin every new strategy, explore the evidence and decide what fits with our own professional aims for the children.

Questions to set you thinking

1   What is your professional vision of FS education? What principles and beliefs underpin this vision, and how are these reflected in your teaching, planning and record keeping? How far is your vision supported by the expectations of your school or of government strategies? For example, are you expected to prepare children for school routines and a KS1 curriculum, or do you see your role as challenging this expectation and developing routines and curriculum that are relevant to the children?

2   How will you ensure your vision is based on up-to-date research and thinking about FS practice? Does your Local Authority, your union or your local university offer any support? How will this form part of your continuing professional development both in your induction year and beyond?

3   How can you plan towards outcomes while remaining focused on individual children, their needs, their talents and their ways of learning? Does your planning format and assessment record enable you to do that?

4   How will you evaluate your own practice? Can you do this both in the light of your vision for the FS and of the expectations placed upon you? What skills and dispositions do you need to be a strong and effective teacher? How will you develop (or hold on to) your questioning skills, curiosity or persistence?

References

Adams, S., Alexander, E., Drummond, M.J. and Moyles, J. (2004) *Inside the Foundation Stage: Recreating the Reception Year*. London: Association of Teachers and Lecturers.

Bruce, T. (1991) *Time to Play in Early Childhood Education*. London: Hodder and Stoughton.

Department for Education and Skills (2003) *Every Child Matters*. London: HMSO.

Katz, L.G. (1998) A developmental approach to the curriculum in the early years, in S. Smidt (ed.), *The Early Years: A Reader*. London: Routledge.

Moss, P. and Petrie, P. (2002) *From Children's Services to Children's Spaces*. London: RoutledgeFalmer.

Moyles, J. (1989) *Just Playing: The Role and Status of Play in Early Education*. Milton Keynes: Open University Press.

Moyles, J. (2006) Literacy Learning, Young Children and Play: Why a diet of phonics doesn't work, in S. Featherstone and R. Bayley (eds) *L is for Sheep*. Lutterworth: Featherstone Publications.

Rose, J. (2006) *Independent Review of the Teaching of Early Reading. Final Report*. London: DfES.

Sylva, K., Melhuish, E., Sammons, P., Siraj-Blatchford, I. and Taggart, B. (2004) *The Effective*

Provision of Pre-School Education (EPPE) Project. Technical Paper 12. The Final Report. London: DfES/Institute of Education, University of London.

Suggested further reading

Adams, S., Alexander, E., Drummond, M.J. and Moyles, J. (2004) *Inside the Foundation Stage: Recreating the Reception Year.* London: ATL.

Bennett, N., Wood, L. and Rogers, S. (1997) *Teaching through play: Teachers' Thinking and Classroom Practice.* Buckingham: Open University Press.

Brooker, L. (2002) *Starting School: Young Children Learning Cultures.* Buckingham: Open University Press.

Carr, M. (2001) *Assessment in Early Childhood Settings: Learning Stories.* London: Paul Chapman/ Sage.

3 Do we understand each other? Multi-disciplinary working in Children's Centres

Karen McInnes

Cameo 1

This Children's Centre has developed from a Sure Start local programme and is attached to a primary school. The manager of the Centre was previously a member of the senior management team of the Sure Start local programme. All the staff in the centre have been working together for a long time as part of the Sure Start team and comprise: a family support team, an early years team, a speech and language therapist, a health visitor, a midwife and a child-minder network co-ordinator. An early years teacher works part-time in the Children's Centre and part-time in the Foundation Stage in a local school.

Cameo 2

This Children's Centre was originally a local authority nursery school situated alongside a social services day nursery. The two early years services were amalgamated. They were designated an Early Excellence Centre and then a Children's Centre. The head of the Centre was a nursery school head teacher and has two deputies: one with an education background and one with a social services background. The other staff members are: a training and development manager, an inclusion manager, a speech and language therapist, a child psychotherapist, a social worker and a fathers' development worker. There are three teachers working with the 3- and 4-year-olds and one working with the 2-year-olds.

Introduction

Over the last nine years in England under 'New Labour', there has been a vision not only to increase spending on early years provision, but also to change the make up of early years services and the ways in which they were being delivered to children and families. Since 1997, there have been significant changes in early years services and provision through a variety of government reforms and initiatives (Sylva and Pugh 2005) which beginner teachers need to understand. This chapter sets out to further this understanding through laying out some of the major policies and initiatives over the past few years and how they will impinge on teachers' knowledge and working lives before discussing the role of early years teachers.

Background policies and initiatives

In 1998, the *National Childcare Strategy* heralded the development of Early Excellence Centres. These Centres were designed to provide care and education for children from a few months old to 5 years of age. Most Early Excellence Centres were developed from existing early years provision or from local networks of services. The Centres were designed to provide high quality nursery care and education, parent education and training and other services required by families, often in socially disadvantaged areas (Wyse 2004).

Additionally in 1998, Sure Start was launched with the aim of tackling social exclusion at community level. This led to the development of Sure Start local programmes, comprehensive programmes focused on children aged from birth to 4 years and their families. They were envisaged as 'one stop shops' in the 20 per cent most disadvantaged areas and were generously funded to provide a range of services and activities. Their core services included:

- outreach and home visiting;
- support for families and parents;
- support for good quality play, learning and childcare experiences;
- primary and community healthcare.

All involved qualified teachers who chose to work with young children in collaboration with other early years staff.

The programmes were innovative in many ways. They were outcome-based, they covered all aspects of children's development as well as purportedly strengthening families and communities. They supported inter-agency commissioning and provision of services and included parental participation and capacity building. Initially, 250 programmes were funded, followed by additional funding being given for further development as a result of the *Inter-departmental Childcare Review* (DfES 2002). Many programmes were developed from existing Family Centres and local authority Early Excellence Centres and had varying accountable bodies ranging from the statutory and voluntary sectors to small community initiatives and the private sector.

There is an on-going national evaluation of the Sure Start programme and the most recent report, focusing on early impacts on children and families, highlights several beneficial effects from the local programmes but also some adverse effects (Melhuish *et al.* 2005). One such example is that teenage mothers living in Sure Start areas with 3-year-olds appear to experience greater behaviour problems than those of non-teenage mothers. The same report notes, however, that the SS programme appears to 'enhance growth-promoting family processes somewhat' (2005: 52). Other positive impacts from another aspect of the evaluation (Anning *et al.* 2005: 1) show that:

- children are getting more support in their early learning experiences for speech and language and emotional development and extra opportunities for physical and literacy development;

- through the provision of childcare, parents are increasing their opportunities to work, to volunteer and to undertake training.

The *Neighbourhood Nurseries Initiative* (NNI) followed Sure Start and provided financial incentives to increase the number of childcare places particularly to enable parents to return to work. They were often located within Sure Start local programmes.

Alongside this, the Foundation Stage was developed and the *Curriculum Guidance for the Foundation Stage* (QCA/DfEE 2000) was introduced. This has had a very direct impact on all teachers and other practitioners working with young children, because is literally guides the curriculum they provide in schools and settings, catering for children up to the end of the reception year (see Chapter 2).

In 2003, Lord Laming's Report was produced, following the death of Victoria Climbié (the young black child who died through abuse and neglect at the hands of relatives). The report highlighted the lack of co-ordination between different children's services, and deficiencies in accountability or responsibility among them, as well as a lack of overall leadership. This heightened the depth of change in the early years agenda and services concerned with children and families and resulted in the *Every Child Matters* Green Paper in September (DfES 2003). This paper contained four main areas:

- a stronger focus on parenting and families;
- earlier intervention and effective provision;
- workforce reforms;
- accountability and integration at local, regional and national level.

It also specified five broad outcomes necessary for children's and young people's well-being. These were: be healthy, be safe, enjoy and achieve, make a positive contribution and achieve economic well-being (see also Chapters 1 and 2). These have formed the basis of many other subsequent documents which will be discussed later.

Also in 2003, the *Birth to Three Matters Framework* was introduced, which is a framework for practitioners working with children from birth to 3 years, and mapped on to the *Curriculum Guidance for the Foundation Stage*. Both frameworks are underpinned by clear principles and both acknowledge the centrality of play for young children's learning (see Chapter 12). These two frameworks are now integrated to form a new single *Early Years Foundation Stage*.

Finally, the Children's Centre programme was developed at this time. This built on Early Excellence Centres, neighbourhood nurseries and Sure Start local programmes. Like Sure Start, there was a promise of a centre in the 20 per cent most disadvantaged communities. Now, however, according to the ten-year strategy also introduced: 'every family is to have easy access to integrated services through Children's Centres in their local community, offering information, health, family support, childcare and other services for parents and children. 2,500 Children's Centres will be in place by 2008 and 3,500 by 2010' (HM Treasury *et al.* 2004: 1).

Despite the enormous progress made in early years services and delivery over the past few years, there remain challenges ahead:

- ensuring long-term, adequate funding to provide Children's Centres and appropriately qualified staff;

- affordability of childcare for parents, especially in some parts of the country;
- ensuring there are sufficient highly qualified staff to work in the Centres;
- enabling integrated working between services.

Children's Centres – what are they and what do they do?

Children's Centres are crucial to the government's *Every Child Matters: Change for Children* programme. They will be the main vehicle for providing good quality integrated services to children under 5 years of age and their families and will form a central part of local authority provision. The vision for Children's Centres states that they 'will play a central role in improving outcomes for all young children and in reducing the inequalities in outcomes between the most disadvantaged children and the rest' (DfES/Sure Start 2005: 1).

According to the Sure Start website (www.surestart.gov.uk), in the most disadvantaged areas the core offer from Children's Centres is intended to be:

- good quality early learning combined with full day care provision for children;
- teacher input to lead the development of learning within the Centres;
- child and family health services;
- parental outreach;
- family support services;
- a base for a childminder network;
- support for children with special needs and their parents;
- support for parents/carers who wish to consider training or employment.

In more advantaged areas, there will be some flexibility so that services can meet local needs but the minimum range of services should be:

- appropriate support and outreach to parents/carers and children who are in need of them;
- information and advice to parents/carers;
- support for childminders;
- drop-in sessions and other activities for children and carers;
- links to Job Centre Plus services.

The two Children's Centres in the cameos at the beginning, which are both in highly disadvantaged areas, meet the core criteria. However, they do this in different ways and a variety of staff provide the expected functions. In their separate ways they both provide an exemplar of how Children's Centres may develop to provide the core offer but meet the needs of the local community.

Although there will be different staff in each children's centre, some staff will be generic. The main staff involved will be:

- a centre manager who may come from one of a number of backgrounds: health, social services or education;
- early years staff;

- family support staff;
- health professionals, such as health visitors, midwives and speech and language therapists;
- childminders and a childminder network co-ordinator;
- a qualified teacher;
- job centre Plus staff.

Early years staff

These early years professionals work alongside qualified early years teachers delivering early years care and learning. They are usually qualified to NVQ level 2 or 3. They will have a good understanding of child development and specifically of children's emotional and social development. Many staff at this level are undertaking further training, such as the early years foundation degree, which provides a bridge to those who wish to attain *Early Years Professional Status* (EYPS). The aim is to have an EYP in every Children's Centre offering early years provision by 2010. The EYP will be a senior member of the staff team and will be key to raising the quality of early years practices in these settings (CWDC 2006).

Health visitors

These are qualified nurses who have undertaken further training to become health visitors. All children and families are allocated a health visitor and their role is to promote health – including mental, physical and social well-being. They give help and advice to the whole family. In Sure Start local programmes, health visitors are often one of the main routes to raising awareness of Sure Start within an area and referring families to the programme.

Midwives

Midwives prepare ante-natal and post-natal care to parents and their babies and they may work in the community or in hospital settings. Ante-natal care is concerned with preparation for parenthood, conducting health checks and delivering the baby. Post-natal care may involve help with feeding, health of the mother and baby, counselling and supporting mothers with post-natal depression.

Family support service

Workers within this service often have a social care background. They provide advice and support to families on a range of issues: childcare, health and development of children, home safety and finance. They usually provide an outreach service to more vulnerable families. They aim to empower families and help them to find solutions to their problems.

Speech and language therapists

These health professionals assess and treat speech, language and communication prob-lems in people of all ages to enable them to communicate to the best of their ability. They work with children who have difficulty producing and using speech or understanding and using language. They may work individually with children or with groups of chil-dren. They may train other professionals including teachers to help them recognize speech and language problems and to provide a language-rich environment.

Childminders and childminder network co-ordinators

Childminders provide childcare in their own homes. There are strict regulations gov-erning how many children of certain ages they are allowed to look after and they are subject to OfSTED inspections. The network co-ordinator supports childminders by providing resources, training and support groups. They will often be attempting to in-crease the number of childminders in an area to help parents return to the workplace. The network should be National Childminding Association (NCMA) accredited. To achieve this they will have gone through a rigorous evaluation procedure.

Job Centre Plus staff

These are professionals who give help and advice to people who are in work or looking for work on jobs, training and in-work benefits. For those who cannot work, they provide financial advice, such as help with benefits.

The role of the early years teacher

The Effective Provision of Pre-School Education (EPPE) project (1997–2003) (and now on-going into Key Stage 2) shows the positive impact that early years provision can have (Sylva *et al.* 2003). One key finding from the project is that in settings where there is a good proportion of trained *teachers*, the quality of provision is higher and children make more progress. In particular, an early years teacher's specific knowledge is a deep understanding of cognitive development which enables young children to learn effec-tively in developmentally appropriate ways. Traditionally within Sure Start local pro-grammes, there has been insufficient emphasis on this aspect of children's development (Anning *et al.* 2005). In addition, there has often been a mismatch of learning activities to children's capabilities, resulting in the provision of activities which were either too hard or too easy. Either way children were not being motivated to engage and learn (Anning *et al.* 2005). In view of this, and in order to ensure this does not occur in children's centres, the minimum requirement is a 0.5 early years teacher in every children's centre with a remit to go beyond the provision of educational activities (Vevers 2005).

The Sure Start Children's Centres: *Practice Guidance* (DfES/Sure Start 2006) requires all teachers to do the following:

- be early years trained and experienced in working in the Foundation Stage;
- take the lead in planning;

- work with other early years staff in observing, supporting and extending children's learning;
- have knowledge of the Birth to Three Matters Framework;
- take a lead in professional development;
- have an understanding of inter-agency working and the roles and responsibilities of other professionals;
- work with parents.

In the cameos at the beginning, the teacher in Cameo 1 was a member of the senior management team of the Centre. She took the lead in planning especially with the *Birth to Three Matters Framework*. She also spent time modelling good practice. She introduced and developed good practice with observation and documentation of children's learning. As her role developed, she spent considerable time mentoring other early years workers and assisting in their professional development. As she was the only early years teacher in the Centre, she had to look outside the setting to engage in her own professional development.

In Cameo 2, there were more early years teachers and the head of Centre was previously a nursery head teacher so support and professional development for all staff was easily available. All teachers took a lead in planning and an aspect of the curriculum within the age phase they were working: 3- and 4-year-olds or 2-year-olds. They also modelled good practice and ensured continuity in planning and record keeping for all children across the Centre. As the head of Centre stated, 'They take responsibility for high quality, early years provision.'

Working together

> Effective professionals working in the field of early years need to be skilled in, and to understand the nature of collaborative practice – the ability to work with others from different professions and perspectives, often in difficult circumstances.
>
> (Leeson and Griffiths, in Willan *et al.* 2005: 132)

The Labour Government elected in 1997 has been a strong advocate of joined-up working and practice. There is concern that services operating individually and independently can have a negative impact on outcomes for children and their families. The *Every Child Matters: Change for Children* programme makes partnership working central to achieving the five outcomes.

As already stated, there will be a range of professionals working in Children's Centres and they will have undergone a variety of training – with different training comes different perspectives, knowledge, skills and language. This diversity can be a strength which can be drawn upon to enable the most effective interventions for children and families. However, it can also be problematic. Different perspectives, knowledge and skills may mean that practitioners can be focused on the family, the mother, the child or a mixture of all three. They may also be working to slightly different agendas which may not necessarily be seen as compatible, for example, promoting secure emotional and social development versus enabling the mother to return to work. Using different language and vocabulary may be a barrier to communication and understanding.

Working together effectively relies on teachers and other professionals being open to change and having a willingness to go beyond their traditional remit. They need to be enthusiastic and motivated about this way of working. Practitioners and teachers need to have a clear understanding of their own and each other's roles and responsibilities and also need to understand and celebrate the diversity in their roles (Frost 2005). They need constantly to communicate with one another in order to arrive at a common language and to understand one another clearly (Read and Rees, in Devereux and Miller 2003). Communication may take place in formal group and individual meetings. However, dialogue needs to be constant and it is often the informal, chance conversations where real understanding occurs. For this, practitioners need to have time to meet, to listen and to communicate (Williams and McInnes 2005).

Sharing is vital to this way of working and occurs in different ways. There needs to be sharing of information so that everyone has a clear understanding, sharing of knowledge and skills so that working can be collaborative and practitioners need to engage in shared training so that joint perspectives can begin to emerge (Frost 2005). Sharing a vision for the development of the Centre and how services will meet the outcomes for children and families is necessary and can only be facilitated by effective leadership (Moyles 2006). That and management support are both crucial to success (Percy-Smith 2005). Other more personal characteristics which have come through conversations to develop the cameos are: respect for one another, trust, flexibility and a willingness to negotiate.

One particular way of working that should facilitate collaborative working is the community of practice approach (Wenger 1998, in Anning *et al.* 2004; Frost 2005). A definition is 'developing shared understandings and practices within a professional community'. This necessitates a commitment to professional development and working together and involves:

- mutual engagement;
- joint enterprise;
- sharing approaches, such as tools, language, styles and actions. (Frost 2005)

It is a complex and time-consuming approach but 'through processes such as shared reflection and collaborative enquiry a community of practice approach can involve all to improve services' (Anning *et al.* 2004: 77).

Conclusion

There are, and will be, different types of Children's Centres focused on the needs of the local community but all concerned with improving outcomes for young children and their families. There is, and will continue to be, a range of professionals with different backgrounds and perspectives working in them. To be an early years teacher in this environment needs a reframing of the traditional way of working. An early years teacher must have a commitment to the following:

- multi-agency working;
- early years care and education and improving quality;

- all children under 5 and their families;
- working with parents;
- their own professional development and to those they work with.

They need to have knowledge of:

- how children from birth to 5 years learn and develop;
- the *Early Years Foundation Stage*;
- the *Every Child Matters Framework* and *Change for Children* programme;
- multi-agency working.

Questions to set you thinking

1   What additional training should early years students engage in to equip them to work in Children's Centres?
2   What different perspectives might professionals working in Children's Centres hold and how might this impact on their practice?
3   How might early years teachers in Children's Centres enable parents to participate in and facilitate their children's learning?

Acknowledgements

Thanks are due to Heather Churchill, Lynne James and Andrea Sully for their time and knowledgeable conversations.

References

Anning, A., Chesworth, E. and Spurling, L. (2005) *The Quality of Early Learning: Play and Children's Services in Sure Start Local programmes*. Nottingham: DfES Publications.

Anning, A., Cullen, J. and Fleer, M. (eds) (2004) *Early Childhood Education: Society and Culture*. London: Sage Publications.

CWDC (2006) *Early Years Professional Prospectus*. Available online www.cwdcouncil.org.uk (accessed 15 September 2006).

Department for Education and Skills (2002) *Qualifying to Teach: Professional Standards for Qualified Teacher Status and Requirements for Initial Teacher Training*, London: TDA.

Department for Education and Skills (2003) *Every Child Matters*. London: HMSO.

Department for Education and Skills/Sure Start (2005) *Sure Start Children's Centres: Practice Guidance*. www.surestart.gov.uk (accessed 15 September 2006).

Devereux, J. and Miller, L. (2003) *Working with Children in the Early Years*. London: David Fulton.

Frost, N. (2005) *Professionalism, Partnership and Joined-up Thinking*. Totnes: Research in Practice.

H M Treasury/Department for Educations and Skills/Department for Work and Pensions/ Department for Trade and Industry (2004) *Choice for Parents, The Best Start for Children. A Ten-Year Strategy for Childcare*. London: HMSO.

Interdepartmental Childcare Review (2002) *Delivering for children and families*. London: Department for Education and Skills/Department for Work and Pensions/Her Majesty's Treasury, Women and Equality Unit.

Melhuish, E., Belsky, J. and Leyland, A. (2005) *Early Impacts of Sure Start Local Programmes on Children and Families*. London: Sure Start.

Moyles, J. (2006) *Effective Leadership and Management in the Early Years*. Maidenhead: Open University Press.

Percy-Smith, J. (2005) *What Works in Strategic Partnerships for Children*. Barkingside: Barnardo's.

Qualifications and Curriculum Authority/Department for Education and Employment (2000) *Curriculum Guidance for the Foundation Stage*. London: DfEE.

Sure Start/DfES (2006) *Children's Centre Practice Guidance*. London: Sure Start/DfES.

Sylva, K. and Pugh, G. (2005) Transforming the early years in England, *Oxford Review of Education*, 31(1): 11–27.

Sylva, K., Sammons, P., Melhuish, E., Siraj-Blatchford, I. and Taggart, B. (2003) *The Effective Provision of Pre-School Education (EPPE) Project*. London: The Institute of Education, University of London.

Vevers, S. (2005) All About Children's Centres, *Nursery World*, 3 November.

Willan, J., Parker-Rees, R. and Savage, J. (2005) *Early Childhood Studies*. Exeter: Learning Matters.

Williams, J. and McInnes, K. (2005) *Planning and Using Time in the Foundation Stage*. London: David Fulton.

Wyse, D. (ed.) (2004) *Childhood Studies: An Introduction*. Oxford: Blackwell.

Suggested further reading

Devereux, J. and Miller, L. (2003) *Working with Children in the Early Years*. London: David Fulton, especially Chapter 3.

Sure Start (2005) *Sure Start Children's Centres: Practice Guidance*. www.surestart.gov.uk

Sylva, K. and Pugh, G. (2005) Transforming the early years in England, *Oxford Review of Education*, 31(1): 11–27.

Willan, J., Parker-Rees, R. and Savage, J. (2005) *Early Childhood Studies*. Exeter: Learning Matters, especially Chapter 12.

4 The first days at school

Hilary Fabian and Aline-Wendy Dunlop

Cameo 1

Lisa and Amy had been together at playgroup since they were 3 and are now looking forward to starting school together. They have made a number of visits to school and have played with bricks and sand while their mums talked with the other parents and listened to the Head telling them about reading, PE kit and medicines. On the first day at school Lisa and Amy put on their uniforms, walked to school together and their mums take a photograph of them standing at the school gate. They happily enter school but it is at this point that the problems start – the girls have been allocated to different classes, different teachers and, as a result, different friends.

Cameo 2

Jamie's best friend and hero is his dad and his favourite game is 'let's play with numbers' – adding, subtracting, multiplying are a normal part of each day as they talk about, write and play board games using numbers. Jamie is looking forward to starting school when he is 5-years-old because his dad has told him that he will be able to do maths every day. However, Jamie doesn't have any friends, and lacks the social skills needed to make friends. Furthermore when he arrives at school he is given the same number work as the rest of the class.

Introduction

It might be your first day in your new teaching job but what if it's also the children's first day at school? Most children look forward to starting school, but becoming a pupil means mastering the intricacies of the classroom, such as behaving in a certain way, understanding the classroom rules, learning the meaning of particular words and phrases used by the classroom adults and knowing the ways in which teaching and learning take place. If children find it difficult to settle into school, this might lead to disillusionment and difficulties with learning but, get it right, and a positive start:

- can help children develop an understanding of change;
- can lead to a virtuous cycle of transitions;

- is significant for children's continuing cognitive development;
- will entail parents and settings work together from the beginning of formal schooling;
- is cost-effective in the long term.

Children will therefore need support to help them mark not only the transition to school, but also to learn about learning in school by building on their pre-school experiences.

Developing a classroom culture

Many children now start school with a sense of confidence. Some children, however, face substantial differences between home and school, or pre-school and school. The degree of match is known to be a contributing factor in children's school success (Pianta *et al.* 1999). Differences include not only the physical environment, such as the building, resources, toilets, and outdoor areas, but also the cultural environment – the way we do things here. Much of the literature on children starting school discusses children being ready or adjusting to school. What is more important is that the school and your classroom are ready for the children (Broström 2002).

More often than not, children are expected to adopt the culture of the school, but Bruner (1996: 43) suggests that the culture of the classroom should merge to be a joint creation and that it is 'a complex pursuit of fitting a culture to the needs of its members and of fitting its members and their ways of knowing to the needs of the culture'. It therefore becomes a 'way of life which we continually remake for ourselves, as individuals, families, communities and societies' (Brooker 2002: 168).

Children whose home culture is very different, may encounter greater transition difficulties than average. Moving between different and sometimes poorly connected cultural worlds of home and school can disadvantage children while some of their expertise might not be acknowledged (Galton and Morrison 2000; Brooker 2002). Identity can be confusing for many children at transition as they take on the status of school pupils but might be referred to as 'the little ones'. However, this new identity can 'take on a heightened significance for minority ethnic pupils, as they mediate different expectations about ... aspirations between family, school, peers, and community elders' (Graham and Hill 2005: 53).

Many children will have experienced a number of transitions prior to starting school (DES 1990 Para.104). Some children may have attended a nursery class in the same building as the school; others a nursery or pre-school close by or on the same site. Some may well have attended more than one type of pre-school provision. Nevertheless, it should not be assumed that starting school is any easier for children who have experienced a range of settings than for those for whom this is their first transition (Dowling 1995).

Preparing the learning environment

A significant influence on children's learning is their physical surroundings, so beginner teachers will want to create an environment in which children feel confident and secure, one which is organized to promote self-reliance and decision-making skills and reflect how you think children learn (see also Chapter 6). For example, if you think children should be independent, then they should be given continuing opportunities to make real choices by, for example, finding resources for themselves without having to refer to adults (Dowling 2000 and Chapter 14).

Jamie (Cameo 2) would certainly be expecting to see numbers on the wall and number games on the shelves. If you knew about his interests before he arrived, he could even have a special number-based sticker on his peg or drawer. He would also need to be drawn into sharing time with other children productively. Here his particular skills could lend themselves to giving him some maths responsibilities, for example, putting out a certain number of items, helping with a maths game or showing another child what to do.

Arrival on the first day

When the children arrive for the first day, they will probably have made visits to the school in the previous term but if this is your first day, you might not have had a chance to meet them beforehand. You could help them remember where to go by putting up directions to the classroom and photographs of any teaching assistants. Make sure that you have a name label so parents will know who you are and give each child a name label to help you identify them.

Children benefit from a feeling of familiarity, from a calm and unhurried atmosphere, and also from a sense of novelty as they do expect school to be different. This means giving children time when they arrive to find their coat peg and say goodbye to their parent(s), and a chance to go with a friend to choose something interesting to do. Think about where the children will go and what they will do while you greet the other children and parents. Will you have activities ready? This is probably what they had during their visits and might be expecting to have something similar on their first day. Are all the children starting together? Some schools have a staggered entry time on the first day, or even over the first week or more. Indeed, some schools are now seeing the benefit of starting the new children *before* the start of term so they can have a quiet beginning to their school career.

At some point you will want to bring the children together to chat with you and introduce yourself and them to each other through 'getting to know you' activities.

Helping children and parents to say goodbye

On the first morning most children will leave their parents easily and enjoy finding their coat peg, hanging up their coat and going into the classroom. However, for some, the busyness of the classroom, the numbers of children or the thought of saying goodbye to their parents, will be overwhelming. They might be unsure about being left, shy about large groups or strange people, or anxious that their parent might not return (Fabian 2002). The anxiety of separating shows itself in different ways – by sitting passively on their own; wanting an extra hug or kiss; going straight in and not looking back; or bursting into tears as they realize that mum is about to leave. Any attempt from these children's parents to leave the classroom can be greeted with loud howls and an attempt to pull them back, so be prepared to offer advice on how long parents stay and what they can do. Stay calm and reassure children that their parent(s) will return. Distracting and involving the child in an activity either on his/her own or with others can turn attention away from the tension generated by the separation. Children might already know some of the others in the class and be guided towards them. Is there any reason why the parents cannot stay? Those children coming from Sure Start Centres are probably used to having parents with them, but be clear about the school policy on this before the first day. If the separation was tearful, encourage parents to phone later to check that their child has settled. Tell them what their child has been doing and what they are doing at that moment rather than giving bland reassurances.

Parents have high expectations and want their children to be happy and to do well at school, but if the parent responds with anxiety, that behaviour can be transmitted to the child, making a difference to the child's emotional state and reactions. Anxiety can become contagious and influence other children in the class, so make sure that your teaching assistant is prepared if several children are upset at once. If parents are encouraged to leave quickly and let you take responsibility they not only indicate that they trust you, but also help their child to develop that trust (Dalli 1999: 61).

At the pre-school stage, parents have been used to sharing their children's education with early educators. This is not easy to achieve as the sole teacher but seeing parents as part of the education enterprise is essential to children's early school success. Arrival and departure times are when parents can talk about their child's progress and needs – a photo of Lisa and Amy on the playground with a group of others would reassure their parents that they are still able to meet up but that they can also develop other friendships. Clubs and after school activities allow parents to see an active approach to learning and to get to know their 'school' child. Furthermore, seeing parents and teachers working together promotes a sense of well-being for children (Margetts 2002).

Developing belonging and friendships

Bringing together a group of children from diverse backgrounds with varied educational experiences who might not know each other can be difficult, so building positive ways of being together in class and developing a sense of belonging is important. A sense of belonging to the school community, contributes to how well children and families adjust (Dockett and Perry 2005). Developing a climate in which parents can share concerns and celebrate children's successes can help to build such a community.

The environment and routines also need to be planned to foster this sense of belonging, and be structured to give children ownership and the opportunity to contribute to the class culture. Relationships between children can be supported by providing opportunities for social interactions through grouping children for learning. Lisa and Amy (Cameo 1) had a shock when they were separated. Social aspects can be confusing for children when they are expected to work with unknown children in groups chosen by the teacher. The first teacher has a role to play in scaffolding social relationships for children. While many children start school as socially competent individuals, there are children who will benefit and be empowered through teaching them social competence and problem-solving skills which give them some sense of control over their lives and enable them to maximize their potential learning power (Fabian and Dunlop 2002).

'Buddying' can support the integration of children into the school community, promoting a caring ethos, a sense of belonging and therefore emotional well-being. One school began by inviting older pupils to complete application forms and be interviewed for the role of 'buddy'. They visited the pre-school to play and talk with children and after the visit talked about when they were in pre-school. Groups of buddies were matched with groups of pre-school children and later in the year escorted these children on visits to school. The buddies were then able to support the new intake at playtime when they started school.

Learning the rules and values of the new setting is critical to developing understanding and feelings of belonging, and essential if the frustration and emotional burden of misapprehension and exclusion are to be avoided (Edgington 2004). In mixed aged classes it is sometimes helpful to pair a new child with an older child, as they have a guide to show them round and help them with the class rules.

Anxious times

What signs do you need to look out for to identify which children are having a difficult transition to school? Jamie's tantrums are a clear sign of frustration – other indicators include:

- changes of behaviour at home;
- unwillingness to leave their parents and come into the classroom;
- frequent illness;
- wetting;
- bullying or being bullied.

It is helpful to keep a record of indicators of settling in or of insecurities and discuss this with their parents.

There are particular times in the day that might cause anxiety, such as playtime, lunchtime or assembly. The contrast between the lack of structure at playtimes with the rest of the school day can be helped by the buddy system or a Friendship Bench where older children, identified by special hats or badges, offer support to children who are on their own. Children could have lunch in the school dining hall during one of their pre-entry visits to sample a school meal and be introduced to the kitchen staff. Some schools invite parents along, too, as the food that their children eat is of concern to parents. Assembly, often in a large hall with the rest of the pupils, can be overwhelming in a large school. One example of helping children to sample this before they start, includes a short assembly with pre-school staff focused on the children's paintings and songs that they had learned in pre-school. They were then introduced to their teacher and others who would help them when they started school.

Curriculum continuity

Building on previous curriculum experiences and becoming familiar with transition records and assessments will allow you to provide continuity and progression in learning for the children. As soon as you are able, if not before the children start in school, it will be important to find out as much as you can about the children's previous learning. Part of the process will be to speak with pre-school staff, to be familiar with the curriculum they offer and to create talking and practical opportunities for the children to use existing skills and to demonstrate what they know in the new classroom. The choice of familiar stories, known activities at which children can excel, and additional challenges with already familiar materials, will allow the children to feel at home, while stimulating new interests.

New curriculum documents throughout the UK are designed to foster continuity and progression in the early stages of education – the Foundation Stage materials, the Welsh Foundation Phase 3–7 and the new Scottish Curriculum for Excellence 3–18, all share the intention to maximize the pre-school years. However, evidence shows that teaching approaches, daily programmes and learning environments, continue to be very different (Dunlop and Fabian 2006) for pre-school and school-aged children.

For children like Jamie, it is essential to recognize that particular skill and enthusiasm for one area of interest needs to be used as an entry to the parts of classroom experience that are newer or more challenging. Often records, to which parents have contributed, are passed on from pre-school. Here a balance has to be struck – read the records right away and note any important issues, contact the pre-school staff to discuss these, talk with the parents and, once you have worked with the children, make sure you go back and reread these records again just a few weeks into term. They will add further insights on every child once you know them a little yourself. However thorough the records are, do not miss the chance to spend a little personal time with every child in your class over the first few weeks. If you have portfolios from the pre-school, this is the perfect time to look at them with each child. Through even small amounts of one-to-one time you will get to know every child and will forge relationships that support both of you all school year. In this way you will genuinely begin to build on their previous experiences, and will have a good idea of their various competences.

Aim to develop contact with the various pre-schools over the year. For best practice you want to know what children have experienced in the previous year, the things that excited and motivated them, their repertoire of songs and stories, their favourite role plays and the depth of their involvement in imaginative play. These are the experiences that lay the foundation for the more formalized aspects of learning that you will introduce. Often the degree of self-regulation and independent decision-making that nursery children enjoy is underestimated when they arrive in school. Many school entrants are pre-school veterans. Going to school with children they already know often brings them wisdom about whom to play with, work with and to have as friends (Ladd 1990). With this knowledge you will be able to focus on appropriate approaches with those that are less socially skilled.

Parents want their child to be happy and safe, to succeed and to be liked and known well by the teacher. Teachers need to work in co-operation with parents to share how learning takes place at home and school and to articulate the learning achieved by their child in the classroom, at home and at pre-school. Armed with this information you will be able to plan together to co-construct each child's transitions with parents in a positive way. Effective transitions are a function of communication of all participants and of shared working – what Griebel and Niesel (2002) call 'co-construction'. At the very least this will call for:

- liaison discussions between nursery and primary staff about important overlaps and differences in the curriculum and modes of learning;
- curriculum evening for parents of new children during the first weeks of term to explain curriculum experiences and progression.

For example, at one school the teacher goes to the pre-school to meet children and after 20–30 minutes takes the children (with the teaching assistant who has worked with the children in the pre-school for one session each week and a member of the pre-school staff) on a tour of the school. The children have an activity and a story with the nursery member of staff while the teacher has a meeting with parents to answer questions. Sharing education by involving parents in their child's progress is worthwhile and valued and helps to promote their children's achievement.

Consider ways to build in progression perhaps by putting the same basic provision in place as in pre-school but including enough new materials to allow children, such as Jamie, to work at an increased level of complexity (Bayley and Featherstone 2003).

Structuring the day

For children to flourish in school, more attention needs to be paid to the classroom environment (Dunlop 2004), to playful learning and choice (see Chapter 12), to style of interaction and to building on forms of independence already achieved (see Chapter 14). School routines are usually determined by the school timetable with fixed times, such as assembly, lunch, play and hall times. A flexible and sensitive approach to appropriate routines can alleviate potential difficulties for new children. For example, the first class might have a different break time from the rest of the school, make visits to the assembly hall to see what it looks like, and start lunch earlier than the rest of the school to allow longer to choose and eat their food. Once they know their way, allow them to make decisions about when they need a drink of water, or to go to the toilet – most of them have been doing this perfectly competently in all situations for the previous couple of years. To regulate this, all you will need is a couple of cards hanging near the classroom door so that the children only go one or two at a time.

It is useful to share the day's programme visually – in this way everyone will be able to anticipate what is happening next. Later the programmes may be differentiated by group or task. Any children with additional needs that you are including in your class will also benefit from this approach. Ensure that children are not sitting for too long at a stretch and take account of the fact that young children are active learners. You will be able to encourage children's continued independence and responsibility if you communicate clearly with them and encourage them to contribute to the plans for the day. This will keep the atmosphere really positive, and save you giving constant individual reminders.

Increasingly the school quality assurance process/inspection system is evaluating the play environment in the early years of schooling. To be effective, you will need to embrace hands-on, active, practical learning as part of your teaching approach. Soon you will find that the difference this makes to children's engagement in their learning will allow you to plan the day to give you not only whole class teaching time as needed, but also time to work effectively with groups and individuals.

Evaluating your transition programme

After the children have settled, you will want to evaluate whether your systems are supporting children in their transition to school. You might not have been involved with planning the start of school for this intake, but you can learn from this experience and consider how you might approach it next time, by designing a diary of events leading up to the time children start with you. You might start by considering what is in place already and draw up a timeline in which you include a meeting between you and the preschool setting as well as dates of visits for children and their parents. Think about the activities that will be included in the programme of children's visits to school prior to entry next year and the messages that you want to convey to children about school.

By considering how children experience transitions and reflecting on this from parental and professional perspectives you can begin to assess how to improve the design of the transition process. You cannot address all areas at once, so it is best to focus on one or two areas at a time. For example, consider the messages that the school website gives about school and how it might help children and how their parents gain an understanding of the way in which learning takes place in your class.

Conclusion

This chapter has explored the importance of helping children and their parents make a successful start to school. Some of the key aspects are:

- co-construction with parents;
- communication that helps parents to know about the transition;
- curriculum knowledge of phases before and after the current phase;
- respecting individual needs in order to give children control of their lives.

Questions to set you thinking

1   How can children be helped to cope with change?
2   How can children be given some control and ownership of their transition?
3   How can parents be involved with information sharing to support their child's learning at school?

4   How does the preparation in the setting/classroom reflect what happens once the child arrives?

References

Bayley, R. and Featherstone, S. (2003) *Smooth Transitions: Building on the Foundation Stage.* Husbands Bosworth: Featherstone Education.

Brooker, L. (2002) *Starting School: Young Children Learning Cultures.* Buckingham: Open University Press.

Broström, S. (2002) Communication and continuity in the transition from kindergarten to school, in H. Fabian and A-W. Dunlop (eds) *Transitions in the Early Years: Debating Continuity and Progression for Young Children.* London: RoutledgeFalmer.

Bruner, J.S. (1996) *The Culture of Education.* Cambridge, MA: Harvard University Press.

Dalli, C. (1999) Learning to be in childcare: mothers' stories of their child's 'Settling-in', *European Early Childhood Education Research Journal*, 7(2): 53–66.

Department of Education and Science. (1990) *Starting with Quality: The Report of the Committee of Inquiry into the Quality of the Educational Experience Offered to Three- and Four-Year-olds, chaired by Angela Rumbold.* London: HMSO.

Dockett, S. and Perry, B. (2005) Starting school in Australia is 'a bit safer, a lot easier and more relaxing': issues for families and children from culturally and linguistically diverse backgrounds, *Early Years*, 25(3): 271–81.

Dowling, M. (1995) *Starting School at Four: A Joint Endeavour.* London: Paul Chapman.

Dowling, M. (2000) *Young Children's Personal, Social and Emotional Development.* London: Paul Chapman.

Dunlop, A-W. (2004) Do differences in early education environments make a difference to children's curricular experience on transition to school? Poster symposium: *Transitions in Early Education: Are There Curricular Implications?* 14th Annual Conference of the European Early Childhood Education Research Association. 1–4 September.

Dunlop, A-W. and Fabian, H. (eds) (2006) *Informing Transitions in the Early Years.* Maidenhead: Open University Press/McGraw-Hill Education.

Edgington, M. (2004) *The Foundation Stage Teacher in Action: Teaching 3-, 4-, and 5-Year-Olds* (3rd edn). London: Paul Chapman.

Fabian, H. (2002) *Children Starting School.* London: David Fulton.

Fabian, H. and Dunlop, A-W. (2002) InterconneXions, in *Early Years Matters.* Glasgow: Learning and Teaching Scotland.

Galton, M. and Morrison, I. (2000) Concluding comments: transfer and transition: the next steps, *International Journal of Educational Research*, 33: 443–9.

Graham, C. and Hill, M. (2005) Negotiating the transition to secondary school, *Topic: Practical Applications of Research in Education*, 33: 53–7.

Griebel, W. and Niesel, R. (2002) Co-constructing transition into kindergarten and school by children, parents and teachers, in H. Fabian and A-W. Dunlop (eds) *Transitions in the Early Years: Debating Continuity and Progression for Children in Early Education.* London: RoutledgeFalmer.

Ladd, G.W. (1990). Having friends, keeping friends, making friends, and being liked by peers in the classroom: predictors of children's early school adjustment, *Child Development*, 61: 1081–100.

Margetts, K. (2002) *Starting School Matters: Supporting Children's Transition to School*. Available online   http://hna.ffa.vic.gov.au/earlychildhhodmatters/docs/conference_papers/session 43a_margetts.pdf (accessed 23 March 2006).

Pianta, R.C., Cox, M.J., Taylor, L. and Early, D. (1999) Kindergarten teachers' practices related to the transition to school: results of a national survey. *The Elementary School Journal*, 100(1): 71–86.

Suggested further reading

Dunlop, A.W. and Fabian, H. (eds) (2006) *Informing Transitions in the Early Years*. Buckingham: Open University Press/McGraw-Hill Education.

Fabian, H. (2002) *Children Starting School*. London: David Fulton.

Fabian, H. and Dunlop, A.W. (eds) (2002) *Transitions in the Early Years*. London: RoutledgeFalmer.

5 The importance of partnerships with parents and carers

Deborah Albon

Cameo 1

Fatima is working in a mixed Year 5/6 class in West London, as part of her second teaching practice on a PGCE. She observes, 'I know that it is important to work with parents, but I rarely see them in my current teaching practice. The children in the age group I am working with come to school on their own and we only see the parents if there is a problem. When this happens – the class teacher deals with it, so I do not feel I am getting much experience in this area. It's also difficult because there is very little parental involvement in the school and some of the staff seem to have a very negative attitude towards the parents. If I'm honest, I am a bit nervous when parents do come in as I am worried that they won't see me as a "proper teacher".'

Cameo 2

Tanya is working in a reception class in a Foundation Stage Unit in a primary school in West London. It is her final teaching practice on a PGCE. Tanya observes, 'The school has lots of parental involvement. There is a parents' room, which is well used, and there are parent helpers that come in regularly. I sometimes feel a bit "on show" when they are in and get worried that they are judging how good I am. I also feel a bit unsure how to manage the children if their parents are in as one child in particular really plays up when his mum comes in to help.'

Introduction

These two cameos highlight just a couple of the very real difficulties you may encounter on teaching practice in achieving the Qualified Teaching Status (QTS) standards, but also highlight areas of practice that experienced teachers come across and in which they need to develop knowledge, understanding and skills.

My aim in this chapter is to encourage reflection by beginner teachers, like you, upon the importance of working with parents/carers and offer possible ideas on how you might achieve the standards related to this area in practice. In particular, the need to develop good communication skills is stressed as these are key in developing partnerships with parents and carers. You should continue to reflect upon this area of your work throughout your careers. The achievement of the standards is but the start of your professional journey.

What do we mean by 'standards'?

David (1999) notes that there is growing recognition that teachers should have knowledge and experience of working with parents/carers as part of their training. While the QTS Standards have been criticized as focusing on 'what a teacher can do, rather than what the teacher is and can become', implying a view of the teacher as a technician (Arthur *et al.* 2005: 1), the professional values standards, one of which is the focus of this chapter, tend not to be explicit in relation to how the standards are to be achieved.

Arthur *et al.* (2005: 5) define professional values as 'the complex sets of beliefs that are considered appropriate for teachers to hold, and the actions by which those beliefs may be communicated to pupils'. In this sense, standards are not value-free and may relate to values that are often left unarticulated. In relation to working with parents/carers, different schools and even individual teachers within them may have very different perceptions of what it means to work effectively with parents/carers.

The current standards regarding 'Professional values and practice' in S1.4 state that teachers with QTS: 'can communicate sensitively and effectively with parents and carers, recognising their roles in pupils' learning, and their rights, responsibilities and interests in this' (DfES 2002: 7).

In the QTS *Standards for Classroom Teachers* (TDA 2006 or www.tda.gov.uk), the first section of standards relates to 'Professional characteristics/qualities and responsibilities'. Q1.3 states that teachers with QTS should be able to do the following:

- understand and respect the contribution that parents and carers can make to the level of learners' attainment and well-being;
- communicate effectively with all children, young people, parents and carers.

While achieving the QTS standards is important, you should try to have an open mind on teaching practice and to think about how your learning can go beyond set requirements. As Perry (1997) notes, try not to think 'I've got to do this . . .' on teaching practice. Rather, try to consider what the school can offer you. Many settings will offer opportunities to go beyond the standards and it is important to make the most of these.

What do we mean by partnership with parents/carers and why is it important?

Wyse (2002) argues that it is essential to develop good relationships with all of the school community, one group of which is parents/carers. Parent support for schools has been recognized as a key determinant in the success of a child's education for many years, with the Plowden Report (DES 1967) highlighting the importance of schools and parents working together (Hurley 2005). While the word 'partnership' does not appear in the Standards, it is often applied to practice relating to working with parents/carers. If we unpick the word 'partnership', we may well come up with words and phrases such as 'two-way', 'sharing' or 'equal'. When applied to teaching, we can see that what is sometimes called a partnership, may in reality be another level of parental involvement with a school.

Pollard (2005) maintains that there are three patterns of involvement with parents/carers. These include seeing the parent as a consumer, a position that sees parents/carers as the recipients of services, with the teacher and the parents'/carers' roles as separate. The second pattern of involvement he discusses is viewing the parent/carer as a resource, a position that sees parents/carers as useful in terms of helping out in the classroom or on the Parent Teacher Association (PTA). Finally, Pollard discusses another position – one that views parents/carers as partners. This perspective on parents/carers is one that views them as partners with teachers in their children's development, with parents/carers and teachers in regular contact.

The latter level of involvement – partnership – implies a more equal relationship between home and school, with each valuing the contribution the other can bring. Hurley (2005: 93) thinks of this as ensuring schools 'address *all* parents in their roles as "co-communicators", "co-learners" and "co-decision-makers"'. For Braun (1992: 179), partnership has the following meaning:

> Where staff do not make assumptions about the neighbourhood or about in-dividual parents, but base relationships with families on an explicit recognition that they share a concern – the welfare of the child – and that each person brings different skills and experiences to that task.

Let us now explore why working with parents and carers is important in primary teaching.

Parents/carers are children's first educators. It is wrong to think that children's education begins on entry to school. All children have been learning from birth (see Chapter 1). Parents/carers have a unique knowledge of, and relationship with their child(ren) which it is important to acknowledge and build upon. Parents and carers can therefore help to provide insights into children's current interests, behaviour and learning that are invaluable to schools.

Another reason why it is important to work with parents is because studies have shown that when there is a partnership between schools and home, there is a positive impact on children's learning and behaviour. A review of a range of studies looking at parental involvement in schools (Desforges and Abouchaar 2003) has highlighted the following:

- parental involvement in a child's schooling, for children aged between 7 to 16 years is a more powerful force than family background, size of family or level of parental education;
- parental involvement has a significant effect on pupil achievement throughout the school years;
- educational failure is increased by a lack of parental interest in children's schooling;
- most parents believe that the responsibility for their child's education should be shared between parents and school – indeed, most would like to be more involved in their children's education.

Working in partnership with parents/carers can be beneficial to parents and carers as well as to teachers and children. Robson (1996) maintains that parental involvement can result in an increase in parents'/carers' knowledge, skills and confidence. This is a two-way process, as teachers' knowledge, skills and confidence are also increased through parental involvement.

Finally, in addition to the above points, parents/carers have legal entitlements to being involved in their child's education, such as being informed of their children's progress and attainment (Robson 1996). Schools are accountable to parents/carers and OfSTED looks at this area of a school's practice as part of the inspection process.

Barriers to working with parents and other professionals

The cameos presented at the beginning of the chapter demonstrate some very real barriers to working with parents/carers which may present themselves on teaching practice and, indeed, throughout people's teaching careers. We can see:

- negative perceptions of parents/carers as being uninterested in their children's education;
- a lack of confidence in how to communicate with parents/carers;
- difficulties in accessing parents/carers of older children owing to less personal contact than when children were in earlier years of schooling;
- a lack of confidence in managing children's behaviour when their parent/carer is present;
- concerns over 'being on show' and being judged by parents/carers.

These are by no means the only barriers to developing successful partnerships with parents and carers. Docking (1990) categorizes problems teachers experience into five areas:

1 ideological;
2 psychological;
3 political;
4 professional;
5 practical.

Ideological barriers relate to views of the teacher as being the 'expert' on education. Psychological barriers relate to teachers' concerns over having their work scrutinized by others – here parents/carers – and the possible challenges this might open up. Political barriers are associated with a possible lack of resources, which could support the development of partnership working. Professional barriers relate to teachers' possible lack of training and expertise in working with parents/carers. Finally, practical barriers link to time for instance. Inevitably, developing any area of practice takes time to think about and implement (Docking 1990).

However, it is not just teachers who have barriers to working in partnership, parents/carers too may find working in partnership with schools difficult owing to personal and interpersonal as well as structural barriers that present themselves when they come into contact with a school environment (Whalley and Pen Green Centre Team 2001). Parents/carers may feel undervalued, isolated, inadequate, wishing to avoid authority owing to some past bad experience, and may even be fearful on entering a school environment. Structural barriers for parents/carers may include having open evenings with no consideration given to accessibility for lone parents, who may have difficulties with childcare. Similarly, a parent/carer, who does not speak English as their first language, may not feel welcome in a school where there is little or no acknowledgement and support for them, such as signs in a range of community languages or staff that speak them. Examples such as these lead Reay (2005) to believe that a true partnership is impossible as inequalities relating to gender, race and class conspire to perpetuate an education system where white, middle-class parents and their children continue to reap educational advantages.

Try whenever you can to challenge any assumptions you might have about parents/carers. One such assumption believes that parents are a homogenous group, i.e. that they all share common beliefs on parenting and educating children. You will be used to thinking about children as having individual needs and preferences. It is therefore important to keep this uppermost in your mind in your work with parents/carers too. Therefore, in practice, one strategy for involving parents/carers might work with some and not others – a range of strategies are likely to be needed.

Achieving the standards on teaching practice – communication is the key

Fatima's difficulty on teaching practice in working with parents is common. As Perry (1997) notes, parents will often want to see the teacher with 'real' issues. However, if the teacher is confident in the trainee teacher, she may involve them in discussions. Fatima notes 'At first, my supervisory teacher was reluctant to let me get involved in discussions with parents, but as she gained confidence in me she let me join in discussions with her and a parent.' Trainee and newly qualified teachers should aim to do the following:

- *Share your thinking about any difficulties you are having:* Tanya found this very useful, 'It was really hard to admit to the class teacher that I found it nerve-racking reading a story to a group of children when one of their parents was present – especially if the child's behaviour was different when their parent was there. After talking this through with the staff I felt more part of the team and realized that everyone has difficulties with some parts of their practice at some point.'
- *Be prepared to seek further information and guidance:* Throughout your teaching careers, you should be reading and attending training to develop your knowledge, understanding and skills. Remember, achieving the standards for QTS should be seen as a beginning. Perry (1997) advises that trainee teachers talk to parents who are not related to their practice. Ask them what they want from teachers, ask them about the experiences they have had of schools and teachers both positive and negative and ask them for any suggestions they might have

regarding how to develop relationships. Some of you may also be able to draw on personal experience in this area.

What is evident from the cameos and discussion so far is that communication is a key factor in developing partnerships with parents. It is no surprise that the draft standard Q1.3 highlights the importance of effective communication. Arthur *et al.* (2005) argue that new teachers need to learn communication skills with parents. They see these as comprising:

- listening;
- knowing when to stop talking;
- not interrupting parents when they are speaking;
- not blaming parents for any difficulties;
- not labelling parents;
- giving advice sensitively;
- showing interest in the child;
- being patient and polite.

(Arthur et al. 2005: 76)

One of the difficulties in developing relationships with parents as a trainee teacher is lack of time – relationships often take time to develop. Perry (1997) offers some useful advice in this area:

- *Look at the ways in which your supervisory teacher and other classroom staff interact with parents*. Obviously it is important to observe teachers and support staff interacting with children in both teaching sessions and less formal sessions, such as playground duties, but it is also important to observe their relationships with parents. Tanya states, 'I watched the reception class teacher and the nursery nurses in their dealings with parents. One of the nursery nurses in particular was brilliant – she always seemed to put people at their ease and showed a personal interest in every parent's child. I learnt loads from watching her.'
- *Introduce yourself* – this is easier with younger children as you are likely to see parents at home time and may be able to strike up a social conversation with them. Tanya recalls, 'I was really nervous doing this to start with, but I just went out into the reception playground with the reception teacher at home time, smiled, and found that a couple of parents asked me who I was and said their child had talked about working with me. One of them actually said it was nice to have students coming in with new ideas – I had been worried that the parents wouldn't see me as a "proper" teacher, but they were fine about it.'
- *Be available at the beginning and end of day to talk to parents* – a good 'opener' is talking about something their child has enjoyed doing at school. Tanya found this easier than Fatima, owing to working with a younger age group, saying, 'I chatted to parents at the end of sessions and tried to make a point of saying something about what their child had been interested in during the day. On one occasion, I was talking about a fantastic painting of a rainbow a child had done and their dad said they had seen a rainbow at the weekend. He said that the child

had been drawing rainbows all weekend and seemed pleased that I had noticed his child's interest. I tried to find books on rainbows and sang a rainbow song at story time the next day. I made notes about this in the child's records and used this as evidence of working with parents too.'

- *Join in sessions in the school aimed at family participation,* such as curriculum workshops held in the evening maybe. In addition, trainee teachers may get an opportunity to join in INSET sessions with the school staff in the area of working with parents. Tanya was lucky enough to be able to do this. 'During my training in the reception class, I was able to do a day's training on working with families who have English as an additional language – particularly families new to this country. I was able to use this as evidence for the standards.'

- *Develop a relationship with any parent helpers* – initially this might be through informal conversation, but later in the practice this may involve organizing work with them, such as working with a group on an activity you have planned. Tanya notes, 'I would always have a chat with parent helpers – tidy up time was a good opportunity, cleaning up a messy task together! I tried to find out the types of activities they liked to be involved in. One parent said she really liked doing creative activities, so I asked her to work with a couple of children, who I had observed as enjoying collage work but wanted to extend their skills further. I talked informally with the parent at the end of the session to see how the activity had gone.'

- *Invite contributions from parents* – Fatima was surprised to find that when doing an art topic on the artist Van Gogh, when she sent home a newsletter about this explaining to parents what she was doing and why, a child came in the next day with a book on the subject. 'I was surprised and really pleased – even the class teacher was surprised! I think it made me challenge my perceptions of the parents as a group because I had not expected any of the parents to have a personal interest in this artist – I'll try not to make negative assumptions about parents again.'

- *Create a newsletter* – this might be in the form of letting parents know what has been happening in the classroom over a week or fortnight. Fatima found this especially useful as she did not have regular contact with the Year 5/6 parents in her school. 'I tried to avoid using jargon in the newsletter so it was accessible. I sent one home every fortnight during my practice and kept copies as evidence for my teaching practice file.'

- *If you are able, attend any parents' meetings* – Fatima and Tanya were unable to do this, but did find it useful to talk to their supervisory teachers when these had taken place.

- *Always thank parents for any help or support they give* – this may seem obvious, but parents are more likely to want to help you again if they feel their efforts have been valued. Tanya wrote a thank you card to the three regular parent helpers in the reception class she was training in – 'I wanted to say thank you for their support. I definitely want to try and develop good relationships with parents when I get my own class as I've really seen the benefit on this practice.'

Further to Perry (1997), I would add:

- *Always respect parents/carers knowledge of their own child(ren).* While you may hold a lot of knowledge about the curriculum, for instance, parents/carers are experts on their own children.
- *When it comes to their own child(ren), parents/carers have a unique, ongoing, emotional relationship. Their primary concern, therefore, is for <u>their</u> child – not the entire class or school* (Larner and Phillips 1994). This may seem obvious but it is vital to keep this in mind in any interactions with parents/carers.
- *Remember that at different stages in children's school career, parents/carers may have different concerns and conceptions of what your role might be* (Larner and Phillips 1994). An example of this might be that in the nursery, a parent/carer may be concerned with how their child is getting on going to the toilet independently and whether you will help them with this. Later in their child's school career, a parent/carer may be more concerned with a child's subject learning. *Any* concerns and interests a parent/carer has should be viewed as important and worthy of your attention as a teacher.

These are just some of the potential ideas when working with parents/carers. There are many more ways in which you can begin to develop partnerships. As Arthur et al. (2005: 95) point out, 'communicating, quite clearly, is the vehicle which carries all relationships, or, rather, the fleet of vehicles'.

Conclusion

Increasingly, working with parents and carers is being seen as a key element in being a teaching professional. It is therefore important to think beyond merely achieving the standards. Becoming a teacher involves developing and maintaining relationships – not just with children, but with parents and carers too.

Questions to set you thinking

1   What is your understanding of 'partnership' when applied to working with parents/carers?
2   In the setting where you are working or training, what level of involvement with parents do you see? What could you do to improve this?
3   Are all parents involved in the work of the school you are working or training in? Think here of parents who have English as an additional language, fathers, working parents, teenage parents and lesbian or gay parents. This is by no means an exhaustive list, but may help you to identify whether there are any groups you are not reaching at present. Try to think of the barriers these groups face and the strategies you might employ to increase their involvement.
4   Which parents/carers do you feel most comfortable working with? Why is this? (You will need to be very honest with yourself here.) What can you do to address this?

5 What knowledge, understanding and skills do you need to develop in order to improve your work with parents and carers? Be honest with yourself when reflecting on what your strengths are as well as the areas you need to develop.

References

Arthur, J., Davison, J. and Lewis, M. (2005) *Professional Values and Practice: Achieving the Standards for QTS*. London: Routledge.

Braun, D. (1992) Working with parents, in G. Pugh (ed.) *Contemporary Issues in the Early Years*. London: Paul Chapman/NCB.

David, T. (1999) Working with parents, in G. Nicholls (ed.) *Learning to Teach: A Handbook for Primary and Secondary School Teachers*. London: Kogan Page.

Department of Education and Science (1967) *Children and Their Primary Schools* (The Plowden Report). London: HMSO.

Department for Education and Skills (2002) *Qualifying to Teach: Professional Standards for Qualified Teacher Status and Requirements for Initial Teacher Training*. London: TDA.

Desforges, C. and Abouchaar, A. (2003) *The impact of parental involvement, parental support and family education on pupil achievement and adjustment: a review of the literature*, Research Report No. 433. London: DfES.

Docking, J. (1990) *Primary Schools and Parents*. London: Hodder and Stoughton.

Hurley, L. (2005) Communication with parents and carers, in M. Cole (ed.) *Professional Values and Practice: Meeting the Standards*. London: David Fulton.

Larner, M. and Phillips, D. (1994) Defining and valuing quality as a parent, in P. Moss and A. Pence (eds) *Valuing Quality in Early Childhood Services: New Approaches to Defining Quality*. London: Paul Chapman.

Perry, R. (1997) *Teaching Practice: A Guide for Early Childhood Students*. London: RoutledgeFalmer.

Pollard, A. (2005) *Reflective Teaching* (2nd edn). London: Continuum.

Reay, D. (2005) Mothers' involvement in their children's schooling: social reproduction in action, in G. Crozier and D. Reay, (eds) *Activating Participation: Parents and Teachers Working Towards Partnership*. Stoke-on-Trent: Trentham Books.

Robson, S. (1996) Home and school: a potentially powerful partnership, in S. Robson and S. Smedley (eds) *Education in Early Childhood: First Things First*. London: David Fulton.

Teacher Development Agency (2006) *Professional Standards for NQTs*. Available online http://www.tda.gov.uk (accessed 26 June 2006).

Teacher Development Agency (2006) *Qualifying to Teach*. London: TDA.

Whalley, M. and Pen Green Centre Team (2001) *Involving Parents in their Children's Learning*. London: Paul Chapman.

Wyse, D. (2002) *Becoming a Primary School Teacher*. London: RoutledgeFalmer.

Suggested further reading

Arthur, J., Davison, J. and Lewis, M. (2005) *Professional Values and Practice: Achieving the Standards for QTS*. London: Routledge.

Crozier, G. and Reay, D. (eds) (2005) *Activating Participation: Parents and Teachers Working Towards Partnership*. Stoke-on-Trent: Trentham Books.

Docking, J. (1990) *Primary Schools and Parents*. London: Hodder and Stoughton.

Whalley, M. and Pen Green Centre Team (2001) *Involving Parents in their Children's Learning*. London: Paul Chapman.

PART 2
BEGINNING TO UNDERSTAND CHILDREN'S THINKING AND LEARNING

6   Inside the learning mind: primary children and their learning processes

Roger Merry and Jenny Rogers

Cameo 1

Julie is 6. She is working through a sheet of basic addition problems using Unifix cubes. Given '3 plus 2' she confidently takes three cubes from the box, counting each one aloud. She next counts out a further two in the same way. She then counts all the blocks again, reaches five, and writes '5' upside down on her worksheet. The next problem is '5 plus 2', but instead of beginning with the five cubes already in front of her, she returns them to the box and starts again from scratch. Nor does she notice that her figure '5' is different from the one printed a few centimetres away.

Cameo 2

It's half-way through the literacy hour, with the whole class sitting on the carpet. The teacher has gone carefully through what the groups working independently will be doing, and has asked if anybody has any questions. No one has, and the children return to their seats. She is about to start work with her chosen group when Martin comes over. 'What do I have to do?' he asks plaintively.

Introduction

Such small incidents are so much a part of hectic, everyday classroom life that busy teachers normally have no time to stop and think about them. Yet they raise many questions, which could be of interest to psychologists as well as to teachers themselves. For instance, why doesn't Julie use the five cubes already in front of her, or correct her own figure when she sees a five written correctly? What do her actions suggest about her concept of number, her perception of the problem and her strategy for solving it? Why does Martin need to ask what to do when it has been explained so carefully and the children have been asked if they understand? What does his behaviour suggest about his attention, memory, understanding or motivation? In brief, what's going on inside these children's heads and how might teachers try to help them? These two basic questions (discussed more fully by Merry 1998), lie at the heart of this chapter.

Attention, perception and memory

Cognitive psychologists propose a view in which learners are not merely taking in things in a passive way but are in fact highly active, often making use of fragmentary and incomplete information by supplementing it with past experience and predictions. Because the learner is seen as actively constructing knowledge, this view is known as 'constructivism'. For example, research on attention has shown that, although we can scan the complex events going on around us, we can really only concentrate on one thing at a time in any depth. If you are driving along a familiar route, for instance, you may occasionally have had that sudden and frightening thought 'how did I get here?' Experienced drivers sometimes unintentionally let their attention drift after a while, scanning the road ahead only very lightly while they concentrate on something else in their minds. However, a red light or pedestrian stepping off the kerb is picked up immediately and their attention returns to their driving.

Even when we do manage to attend to something, our attempts to perceive or make sense of it rely on equally fragmentary information. As you read this text, for example, it may seem to you that your eyes move quite smoothly from one word to the next along the lines, taking everything in. But in fact, your eyes focus on one small area for a fraction of a second, then jump rapidly to another spot, all the time, whatever you are looking at. The information received by your brain is therefore very piecemeal and you rely on your past experience and knowledge to fill in the gaps. Perception is not a passive taking-in of our surroundings, but a highly active process in which the information supplied by our brains is at least as important as the information received by our senses.

Similarly, remembering something does not simply involve retrieving it from storage. As with attention and perception, what we have available to us from memory is usually only partial and fragmentary so that we again have to supplement it by using our knowledge of the world – memory, too, is partly a constructive process. For instance, you could not possibly remember every single word of this chapter so far, but if you were asked if it had contained the word 'custard' you would be able to answer with a confident 'no' because your experience tells you that such a word would not occur in this context. However, if you were asked if the word 'car' had appeared, you would be less sure and might answer 'yes' because you recalled a paragraph about driving earlier on and guessed that the word had appeared. (To save you checking, it didn't!)

The brain and learning

Psychologists and teachers are not the only ones interested in learning, however. Technical developments have enabled neuroscientists not only to understand the brain better but also to examine brain activity while people are actually carrying out various tasks, and we seem close to some major breakthroughs in understanding how these findings relate to what psychologists have been able to tell us about learning. A detailed discussion is obviously beyond the scope of this chapter, but Sousa (2006) gives a useful summary of how the brain works and discusses some implications for teachers. A major review linking schooling and brain research was provided by Bransford *et al.* (1999), and an increasing number of 'brain-friendly' approaches to teaching, such as Accelerated Learning (Smith *et al.* 2003) are based at least in part on our knowledge of how the brain works.

Two ideas from neuroscience which have become popular and familiar to teachers recently are the distinction between 'left brain' and 'right brain' learning, and the notion of modality preferences, but we need to be careful about both of them. Earlier theories about the different roles of the left and right hemispheres are still helpful, but we now know that several areas of the brain, often including both hemispheres, are routinely involved in seemingly simple activities like Julie's counting in the first cameo. Similarly, an apparently 'left brain' skill like reading aloud involves far more areas of the brain than was originally thought. Moreover, while it is true that people do tend to have some general modality preferences, such as the well-known visual/auditory/kinaesthetic, it is misleading to think of three distinct 'types' of learner, and all three modalities will often be involved in any one task. Certainly, coming out and writing something on the board, for example, is definitely not just a 'kinaesthetic' activity.

Links between neuroscience and psychology represent one of the most exciting areas of current research, and our increasing knowledge of the brain suggests that the findings of neuroscientists are very compatible with constructivist ideas about learning.

Getting ready to learn

If learning is not just a passive taking-in of information, a major implication is that we must try to prepare children for learning effectively, not just rushing straight in and presenting lots of material immediately. Children need to see how the new material is relevant to what they already know and to what they want to know. For example, in numeracy, abstract words like 'plus' and 'minus' have little relevance in everyday life, and the symbols even less. Yet most adults do not regularly have to deal with such abstract ideas in the real world, so how do 5- or 6-year-olds manage? It is well known that early incomprehension in maths can readily lead to confusion and distress for children if it is not addressed (Rogers 2006).

Time spent preparing to learn is thus time well spent, in spite of the pressure to begin 'delivering' the lesson content as soon as possible, and such preparation is important in terms of both content and attitudes. For instance, it is likely that children will have at least some prior knowledge related to the content of the lesson, but some may actually have misconceptions about it. One child, for example, is supposed to have written:

> The body consists of three parts – the brainium, the borax and the abominable cavity. The brainium contains the brain, the borax contains the heart and lungs, and the abominable cavity contains the bowels, of which there are five – a, e, i, o and u.

Clearly, it would be useful for this child's teacher to be aware of such misconceptions before starting to teach them about the human body!

Similarly, in terms of attitudes, learners need to be relaxed but alert, and confident enough not to worry if they make mistakes or don't know the answer immediately. Several learning programmes have been developed which take such ideas seriously, such as Alistair Smith's 'Accelerated Learning' mentioned above (Smith *et al.* 2003), and they again underline the idea that good teaching involves far more than the presentation of information.

Active learning

Once the children are ready to learn and we begin to present some new information to them, we must ensure that they are actively involved, not just passive recipients, and writers like Fisher (2005) offer lots of lively ideas to encourage active learning. An apparently similar idea of 'interactive teaching' was also promoted by the National Literacy Strategy, but we need to be careful here. Research by Moyles *et al.* (2003) suggests that truly interactive teaching means more than children being physically involved in waving cards in the air, for instance. They must also be cognitively involved, for instance in comparing, trying out ideas or making decisions. However, such processes do require time for children to reflect independently in ways that may conflict with the Literacy Hour's requirement for strong teacher direction and a 'sense of urgency', for example, and the need for deeper involvement is being increasingly recognized.

Bearing these introductory points in mind, we will now examine some of the cognitive processes which are at the heart of learning, and consider their implications for teachers.

Paying attention

Most teachers are highly aware of the importance of attention, not least because some children seem to have real problems with it. In the cameos, it is very tempting to blame Martin's problem on his inattentive behaviour, or to see Julie's reversed figure '5' as the result of a lack of attention to detail but, as we shall see, there could be other explanations. Some of the points below will suggest ways of trying to get through to these children but we should also be careful about interpreting poor attention as a problem entirely 'within the child'. We need to be aware of the difficulties we can inadvertently create for children – in a piece of writing, for example, expecting a child to concentrate on being creative, neat and grammatically correct all at the same time is actually making cognitive demands that many professional writers, let alone 6-year-olds, would find a challenge.

Attention and failure

Understandably, as teachers, we sometimes tend to see learning failure as a result of not paying attention, but it could equally be the other way round. Children who find it hard to cope with failure (as most of us do) may deliberately 'switch off' when confronted with a task at which they expect to fail, on the grounds that if you do not try, you cannot fail. In the second cameo, Martin may well have deliberately only half-listened to the teacher's instructions, hoping that he will get the extra one-to-one help he likes simply by asking what he has to do. 'Learned helplessness' is a phrase sometimes used to describe such behaviour and it can appear to the child that deliberately not paying attention is a good strategy for avoiding failure and getting extra help. In such cases, trying to encourage children to feel more positive about themselves as learners will be at least as important as using lively, attention-grabbing materials, and the aim of this chapter is certainly not to suggest that cognitive processes and strategies should be emphasized at the expense of attitudes and feelings. Personal factors, such as high self-esteem (Lawrence 2006) and resilience (Greeff 2005), are widely recognized as crucial in successful learning.

Attention span

It is difficult to get an accurate idea of the length of time that people can go on attending to the same stimulus without letting their attention wander. It is quite likely that, fascinating as this chapter is, your attention may well already have drifted away at least once, perhaps without you really being aware of it. For most children, the span of attention may be even shorter, probably only a few minutes at a time. Sadly, this does not mean that we can shorten the school day to ten minutes, but experienced teachers are well aware of this potential limited span of attention and take measures to get around it. Variety and change are the keys here. If good teachers are reading a story, for example, they will automatically build in some variety: a range of voices or gestures to avoid monotonous delivery; stopping to ask a question or pausing to show an illustration. They may well bring in discussion so that, although the activity is still 'reading a story', the children will be presented with different sorts of input and will be actively involved in different ways throughout.

Attention grabbers

What sorts of things 'grab' your attention? If you made a list, it would probably contain specific items such as 'a fire alarm' or 'my name' and more general ones, such as 'bright lights' or 'something unexpected'. In fact, 'attention-grabbers' can be roughly divided into two categories. Some things grab our attention automatically – sudden loud noises, movements or pain, for example. Others are things that we have learned about and which involve our experiences, expectations or interests, like hearing our own name or seeing something bizarre or new to us, just as you probably noticed this row of xxxxxxxxxxxxxxxxxxxxxxxxxxxxxxxxxxxxxxxxxxxxxxxxxx well before you actually got to them in your reading. If you watch an hour or two of children's television, you could probably learn something from other experts in grabbing children's attention, even if it is rather disheartening to see what you are, in a sense, competing with as a teacher. This is not to suggest that you dress up as Bart Simpson (though that would certainly capture the children's attention!) but that you note how children's cartoons, for instance, make use of bright colours, rapid movement, bizarre events and very short scenes in order to grab and maintain children's attention. Similarly, if you want to quieten a whole group of noisy children, it is usually better to call out a few names of the noisiest individuals rather than just say 'shh' to the whole class in a vague and optimistic way. Teachers also develop lots of techniques like 'hands-on-heads' to grab a whole group's attention, perhaps turning it into a game so that the children actually want to be among those who are attending to you.

Teacher's attention

One of the greatest compliments one of us was ever paid as a classroom teacher was by a child who said, 'You must have eyes in the back of your head, Mr. Merry!' Experienced teachers have actually developed different attentional skills in order to manage a group of children and such skills can sometimes be difficult for beginners to learn. A new teacher, going round helping individuals or groups, may get commendably involved with them only to realize ten minutes later that the other children have demolished the furniture. An experienced teacher, on the other hand, will constantly glance around the rest of the room, particularly at individuals or activities that their experience tells them could become disruptive, nipping likely problems in the bud, and letting the children know that they are being watched. Such monitoring of the rest of the room would, of course, be highly inappropriate if not downright rude in a staffroom conversation, but in the classroom it is a vital attentional skill which often marks out experienced and effective teachers.

Seeing is believing

If perception involves a great deal of 'imposing meaning', using our past experience to supplement fragmentary information, it follows that when children's experiences do not match those of the teacher, they will literally perceive things differently. The classic 'visual illusions' like the two heads/candlestick show how two people can look at the same thing and actually see something totally different, and one of the biggest problems for teachers may be to see things from the child's point of view, or to understand why they don't understand. Such different perceptions help to explain Julie's behaviour at the beginning of the chapter. If her concept of the symbol '5' was something like 'the one with two straight lines and the curly bit', she simply would not notice that hers was upside down because her 'internal model' would describe her version just as well as the correct one. Watching how children actually write letters and numbers can sometimes give a clue to understanding their perceptions – if a child forms both a 'b' and 'd' by drawing a 'ball and stick', for example, they are likely to get the two symbols confused. In such cases, teachers obviously need to draw the child's attention to the different orientation and encourage them to form the symbols in a different way, avoiding them becoming mirror images of each other.

Understanding and remembering

It will have become clear that 'attention' and 'perception' are inextricably linked, and similar links are apparent if we go on to consider learning and remembering. If we can perceive something in a meaningful way, it will be much easier for us to remember it. Take, for example, this series of letters:

> ecnetnes a etirw ot yaw ynnuf a si siht.

Once you have recognized what it is – in other words, once you have 'perceived' it – you would be able to remember it and write it down quite easily. However, you would not simply be remembering what you had seen, but would use your understanding to re-create what was there. You wouldn't actually recall the letter sequence 'ecnetnes' but would reconstruct it from your knowledge that it was the word 'sentence' backwards, and would probably write it from right to left. If the same letters had been presented in a random sequence, such as:

> ehiyw iwtfo nrte iau e asnye nnsta stc

the task of remembering it would have been virtually impossible because you would not have been able to make sense of it in the first place. A major implication for teachers is, therefore, that things which seem straightforward and obvious to us may be perceived as meaningless, problematic or complex by our children, and thus almost impossible to remember.

Learning strategies

Although it is very difficult to find out exactly what strategies children might be using, this has been a popular topic for psychologists to study. However, teachers expected to 'deliver' the curriculum tend understandably to concentrate on content – on what is to be learned rather than exactly how children should learn it. Even when we do try, we may still not give enough help. A popular and effective spelling technique, 'look, cover, write, check', for example, does seem to provide children with an overall strategy for learning spellings, but many young children still are not sure what exactly to do when we ask them to 'look at' something in order to learn it. Very simple strategies, which adults take for granted, can be surprisingly effective. For example:

- shut your eyes and try to picture the word in your head;
- repeat the letters several times over;
- actually practise writing it out a few times;
- see if the word reminds you of any others which you can spell;
- compare your version with the correct one and, if yours is wrong, concentrate on the bit you got wrong;
- if you haven't got access to the correct spelling, write your version down and see if it looks right;
- if the word is familiar but spelled in an unusual way (for example, with a silent letter) try deliberately mispronouncing it in accordance with the way it is spelled.

In general, research suggests that very young children or those with quite severe learning difficulties can improve their learning dramatically by being taught appropriate strategies, though they often do not spontaneously continue to use them for themselves.

Learning in communities

This short chapter has tended to focus on individual 'constructivist' learning processes, but the fact that much of children's learning takes place in social contexts, such as classrooms, is obviously just as important. Indeed, many psychologists now prefer the notion of 'social constructivism' which acknowledges the roles of other people and of social contexts in learning, and some say that all cognition is 'distributed' throughout a group of people, rather than taking place inside individuals' heads (Salomon and Perkins 1998).

One approach, closely related to such ideas, is called 'communities of enquiry' or 'communities of learning'. It is based in part on pioneering work by Matthew Lipman on introducing philosophy to children (Lipman *et al.* 1980) and more directly on the work of Lave and Wenger (1991) on 'communities of practice'. Learners are not only mentally active individually in the ways discussed earlier in this chapter, but also communicate with each other and work together to produce shared understandings. For an introduction and some evidence of the effectiveness of this approach, see Baumfield (2004) or Anderson (2005). We should also note that being inducted into a community of practice is of course not only important for children, but also for new teachers themselves, and if you are a beginner teacher, you will probably be very aware of the need not only to succeed in the classroom, but also to fit in the staffroom. Be sure to pay for your coffee!

Conclusion

An understanding of processes, such as attention, perception and memory, would appear to be very useful to teachers, but these processes are so much a part of us that we are rarely even aware of them, let alone willing to consider changing them: we are unlikely to decide to try a bit of 'perceiving' because we have a few minutes to spare! If so, then even the brief discussion in this chapter may help to raise that awareness a little and to give some insights not only into our own minds, but also into the minds of the thousands of children like Julie and Martin whose problems confront teachers every day.

Questions to set you thinking

1　In a topic you are teaching or will be teaching in the future, are you aware of any prior misconceptions the children might have? How could you find out?

2　Many teachers would probably feel sympathetic to the sorts of ideas about learning expressed in this chapter, but might point to various practical problems preventing them from teaching in a more 'constructivist' way. Are there any such problems in the context of your teaching? Can you do anything about any of them?

3　How do you learn? Can you find elements above in yourself?

References

Anderson, B. (2005) Can a community of enquiry approach with fiction texts support the development of young pupils' understanding? *Education 3–13*, October, 9–14.

Baumfield, V. (2004) Thinking for yourself and thinking together: the community of enquiry as a pedagogy for self-regulated learning, in E.J. Hirsch (ed.) *Thinking about Thinking: What Educators Need to Know*. Singapore: McGraw-Hill.

Bransford, J.D., Brown, A.L. and Cocking, R.C. (eds) (1999) *How People Learn: Brain, Mind, Experience and School*. Washington, DC: National Academy Press.

Fisher, R. (2005) *Teaching Children to Think* (2nd edn). Cheltenham: Nelson Thornes.

Greeff, A. (2005) *Resilience: Personal Skills for Effective Learning*. Camarthen: Crown House.

Lave, J. and Wenger, F. (1991) *Situated Learning: Legitimate Peripheral Participation*. Cambridge: Cambridge University Press.

Lawrence, D. (2006) *Enhancing Self-Esteem in the Classroom* (3rd edn). London: Paul Chapman.

Lipman, M., Sharp, A.M. and Oscanyan, F.S. (1980) *Philosophy in the Classroom*. Philadelphia, PA: Temple University Press.

Merry, R. (1998) *Successful Children, Successful Teaching*. Buckingham: Open University Press.

Moyles, J., Hargreaves, L., Merry, R., Paterson, A. and Esarte-Sarries, V. (2003) *Interactive Teaching in the Primary School: Digging Deeper into Meanings*. Maidenhead: Open University Press/McGraw-Hill.

Rogers J. (2006) Emotional responses to misunderstanding: early warning signs in mathematical communication, in M. Hunter-Carsch, Y. Tiknaz, P. Cooper and R. Sage (eds) *Handbook for Understanding and Supporting Young People with Social, Emotional and Behavioural Difficulties: Communication, Emotion and Behaviour*. London: Continuum.

Salomon, G. and Perkins, D.N. (1998) Individual and social aspects of learning, *Review of Research in Education*, 23: 1–24.

Smith, A., Lovatt, M. and Wise, D. (2003) *Accelerated Learning: A User's Guide*. Stafford: Network Educational Press.

Sousa, D. (2006) *How the Brain Learns* (3rd edn). Thousand Oaks, CA: Corwen.

Suggested further reading

Bransford, J.D., Brown, A.L. and Cocking, R.C. (eds) (1999) *How People Learn: Brain, Mind, Experience and School*. Washington, DC: National Academy Press.

Fisher, R. (2005) *Teaching Children to Think* (2nd edn). London: Nelson Thornes.

Sousa, D. (2006) *How the Brain Learns* (3rd edn). Thousand Oaks, CA: Corwen Press.

7   Exploration, investigation and enquiry

Dan Davies and Alan Howe

Cameo 1

Sarah is a science co-ordinator in a junior school. She is introducing a common investigation (vehicles rolling down ramps) to her Year 6 class (10–11 years), who will plan and carry it out independently in groups. Although these children have plenty of experience of scientific enquiry work – exploring and sorting activities in the early years, heavily 'scaffolded' investigations during Key Stage 1, with gradually more choice and freedom to plan during their junior years – she still needs to remind them of the key decisions they will have to make, tries to broaden their ideas of what is possible, and emphasizes her key learning aim for this age group of recognizing the need for repeated measurements to improve accuracy.

Cameo 2

Leanne is a newly qualified teacher with a class of 30 Year 1 children. They are beginning to learn to apply enquiry skills in simple and familiar situations and are involved and challenged by open-ended problems. Leanne explains, 'The children are very inquisitive – you have to work with that, to capture them and to raise questions. For example, we looked at a life cycle diagram and thought: what comes first, the moth or the eggs? We moved on to evolution – just from one diagram!' Leanne planned a design and technology unit of work on puppets which begun with the children handling and evaluating a collection of puppets. The children then went on to design and make their own animal glove puppets.

Introduction

This chapter will discuss how teachers can help children develop the skills they need to find out about the natural and physical world for themselves. These skills are particularly relevant to the subjects of science and design and technology (D&T), although there is a strong case for calling them 'cross-curricular skills'. As we shall see, however, there is some debate about whether young children can *transfer* skills from one situation to another.

The skills in question are 'thinking skills' (such as hypothesizing and evaluating) and 'doing skills' (such as measuring and communicating findings). Some skills seem to be a combination of both thinking and doing and defy neat categorization. One characteristic that thinking skills share is that they are 'procedural' rather than 'conceptual'; they are about carrying through a course of action, which led Harlen (1996), in the context of children's scientific learning, to refer to them as 'process skills'. Learning experiences which are relatively open-ended, involve trying things out, testing ideas and communicating what has been discovered, generally make use of and develop these skills (see Chapter 6). We shall look at how such experiences can be structured and developed in order that children begin to learn to select and apply appropriate skills autonomously.

We must start, however, by trying to define what we mean by exploration, investigation and enquiry. This can be a bewildering landscape of learning for the new teacher, and is not helped by the different usages found in official documents. *Exploration* has been defined by Howe *et al.* (2005: 11) as a 'semi-structured handling or playing with objects' which involves observation with all the senses. It may involve question-raising, although the questions may be answered through action and never articulated. Exploration may involve some of the same skills as *investigation* (for example, observing or questioning) but it is generally more open-ended, playful and less systematic than the latter (see Chapter 12). It is therefore characteristic of younger age groups, though it would be a mistake to assume that older children don't need time to explore phenomena before setting out to investigate them. Exploration can be thought of as a process within a scientific enquiry, but for young children, as an enquiry in itself.

Investigation is associated in the minds of many primary teachers with the idea of a 'fair test' in science; changing one factor and observing or measuring the effect, while keeping other factors the same. Though more goal-directed than exploration, it nevertheless allows for pupil autonomy and should be more open than the traditional school science *experiment*, in which the method – and in most cases the outcome – is predetermined by the teacher. Indeed, in the context of mathematics education, an investigation is often regarded as a problem-solving activity in which many solutions are possible (often starting with the phrase: How many ways can you find to ...?). In science, investigative work:

- encourages children to raise questions, predictions and statements which may then be tested;
- allows children to work independently to make decisions;
- allows children to plan for themselves how to go about the task;
- allows children to obtain evidence and information to test their ideas.

The ASE-Kings College London *Science Investigations in Schools* (AKSIS) project (Goldsworthy *et al.* 2000a) found that many primary teachers were placing undue emphasis on children's abilities to plan, undertake and record a 'fair test', neglecting other forms of science practical work. They proposed the broader term of *enquiry*, subsequently adopted by the *National Curriculum* (NC) in England (DfEE/QCA 1998) as the first section of the Programme of Study for Science (commonly referred to as 'Sc1'), comprising the following types of activity:

- fair testing;
- pattern seeking; observing and recording to find patterns in data, or carrying out a survey;
- classifying and identifying: arranging a range of objects into manageable sets and allocating names;
- exploring: making careful observations using all senses;
- making things or developing systems: problem-solving activities to design, test or adapt artefacts;
- investigating models: trying out explanations to see if they make sense (also called 'illustrative' activities).

From the above list it appears that we could regard both exploration and investigation as subsets within the broader heading of enquiry (see Figure 7.1).

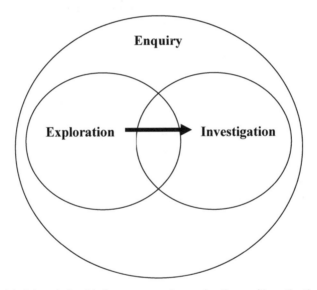

Figure 7.1 Model of the relationship between enquiry, exploration and investigation

Progression in skills of enquiry

We begin exploring progression by revisiting the class of Sarah (Cameo 1). The discussion proceeds as follows:

Teacher: What else could we put down a ramp? You could also roll cotton reels ... You could pull stuff up or push stuff down ... What could we measure?

Pupil 1: How long it takes to get down.

Teacher: So we could measure how long it takes to go down. What else could we measure?

Pupil 2: Speed.

Pupil 3: How much the force is?

Teacher:	So we could measure the force needed to pull it up. What else?
Pupil 4:	How fast it goes.
Teacher:	You could try different places on the board. How would we measure speed?
Pupil 4:	How far it goes.
Teacher:	You could measure the stopping distance . . . If the table's smoother there's less friction and we would expect it to go . . .
Pupils:	Further, faster.
Teacher:	What's the other problem with using a table?
Pupil 5:	It might fall off.
Teacher:	I'm going to ask you to come up with a test you'd like to do. You've got free choice of what you're going to change.

Here Sarah is reinforcing and rephrasing pupils' contributions to support them in taking the decisions they will need when working independently. She is treading a fine line between offering independence and scaffolding their planning of a scientific enquiry (see Chapter 14). A few minutes later, a group is working outside the classroom, comprising three boys and two girls. One of the girls (Jasmine) assumes a leadership role, leading discussion while completing the group planning sheet Sarah has provided to structure the discussion. The other girl takes a supporting role and the three boys come in and out of the discussion as their attention engages and wanders.

Jasmine:	We have to do a test, don't we? We can see how fast it goes, we can use different types of car. We can see how far it goes.
Clark:	We could test which car goes fastest.
Jasmine:	Yeah, good idea, we could test which type of car goes fastest.
Clark:	Yeah, is it the heaviest or the lightest?
Jasmine:	We're going to change the type of car.
Lydia:	What are we going to measure?
Ben:	The car.
Jasmine:	(*reading what she has just written*) We will measure or observe how fast the car goes.
Michael:	How are we going to do that?
Clark:	We could do how far it goes if we drop it and how far it slides along.
Lydia:	Yeah, so how far it goes.
Jasmine:	OK and (*reading*) we will keep these things the same . . . We will keep the height of the ramp.
Others:	Yeah.
Jasmine:	The height of the ramp the same and, anything else?
Lydia:	Oh, yeah, the same strength you push it with.
Jasmine:	Do you mean the same person?
Lydia:	Yeah, the same person pushing the car.
Clark:	The same surface.
Ben:	Don't you think you should let it go because if you push you can't get it exactly . . .
Jasmine:	Yeah, so it's a hard thing to control.
Lydia:	Stopwatch.

Jasmine: Oh, yeah, stopwatch, same person on the stopwatch.

Ben: Same two people on the stopwatch 'cos then you're just doing the average. Otherwise you might stop it a second too fast.

Jasmine: (*writing*) ... So our question is when we change the type of car, what will happen to the distance it travels? Our prediction, what do we think?

Clark: No we don't need the stopwatch because if it's just the ...

Lydia: We need a metre stick.

Jasmine: We can use a metre stick to see how far it's going, the distance.

Lydia: We could use Blutack or something to stick in it.

Michael: No because we're doing distance not weight.

Lydia: The heavier the car, more speed less friction.

Clark: So, like, all the cars we have, we're going to see how far the different cars travel.

Jasmine: The heavier it is, the farther it goes because it's got more weight to pull it down the ramp.

Michael: No, I think the lighter car will go quickly.

Jasmine: The heavier the car, the faster it goes because gravity ...

Clark: Just write that ... just say it's got more weight so it might go faster.

Lydia: 'Cos it's got more weight to pull it to the ground.

Clark: Pull it down the ramp.

Ben: It might slow down a bit quicker because the carpet ...

Clark: When it gets to the ground it might pull it instead of pushing it along.

Ben: When it's going fast down the ramp, then it's got quite a lot of speed to just push it when it gets to the ground.

Lydia: It relies on its speed.

Michael: When it gets to the bottom of the ramp there's a step and it might flip.

At this point the teacher appears and questions the group on their progress in planning the investigation:

Teacher: What would you like to change?

Jasmine: We're changing the type of car.

Teacher: And you'd like to measure ...?

Jasmine: How far it goes.

The children in this example are engaging in a high-level discussion about factors they can realistically change and the likely effects of such changes. It certainly helps to have an organized and competent 'leader' of the group, since the teacher's brief interaction does not capture the richness of the debate nor identify any of the underlying scientific misconceptions. As the children collect their equipment they will discover some of the difficulties with their plan. The plenary will be crucial in getting children to think through the implications of their planning decisions for the quality of data and what can usefully be said about it.

These children at the upper end of the primary age range may be assumed to be operating at a level towards the end of any progressive hierarchy, yet their dialogue is illuminating in that it shows the areas in which they can continue to develop, for example, in selecting appropriate quantities to measure or recognizing that a 'push' may be less 'fair' than allowing the cars to roll down the ramp. They do, however, display some awareness of reliability in measurement – Ben's suggestion of two independent observers measuring the time is higher-order thinking, and demonstrates at least one characteristic of Harlen *et al.'s* map of progression in skills:

- from simple to more elaborate;
- from being used effectively in familiar situations to being used in unfamiliar ones;
- from being used unconsciously to being used consciously and deliberately.

(Harlen *et al.* 2003: 95)

Children in this class were certainly conscious in their use of enquiry skills, as the planning process had been made very explicit by Sarah. The context was perhaps familiar, so the next stage would be to introduce something less familiar.

Feasey (2006: 147) suggests another checklist for progression:

- from using non-standard measures to standard ones;
- from 'things to change, things to measure, things to keep the same' to using the word 'factors' or 'variables';
- from taking single readings to taking repeat readings where appropriate;
- from merely reporting results to using data to draw conclusions.

The group in Sarah's class appeared to be using standard measures and to be moving towards the idea of repeat readings, though not yet to be identifying 'variables' by this name or – in the test they were planning – to be in a position to use data to draw conclusions.

Assessment for learning – recognizing children's procedural thinking

If we are to help children to make progress in developing their individual enquiry skills, we need to find out their starting points (see Chapters 17 and 18). For the primary teachers involved in the *Improving Science Together* (IST) project (McMahon and Davies 2003) there was a concern that much assessment was based on written evidence, that this was burdensome for many children and that the writing took up a considerable amount of the time available for practical work.

The AKSIS project had suggested the following requirements for teachers seeking to assess children's enquiry skills:

1 The teacher must have a model of progression for the particular scientific enquiry being undertaken and for the particular aims being addressed within that enquiry.
2 There should be ways of sharing, with the pupils, the educational aims and the criteria for judging achievement against these aims.
3 There should be ways of assessing achievement of these aims leading to

diagnosis of pupils' educational needs. This may be done by the pupils or by the teacher.

4   There should be explicit ways of helping each pupil to know what to do to reach the educational aims. (Goldsworthy *et al.* 2000b: 4)

Beginning teachers can sharpen their sense of progression by looking at the levels within NC Science Attainment Target 1 (AT1), which are exemplified in relation to particular concept areas by the *Assessing Progress in Science* materials (QCA 2003). Also, teachers need to anticipate which skills are likely to be addressed in their lessons across a unit of work or whole year (see Chapter 13). Some skills, such as observation or prediction, may be frequently occurring (Harlen 2006) so could be assessed at almost any point, while others – planning or pattern-seeking perhaps – may occur less frequently and need careful planning. We will not be able to assess the enquiry skills of the whole class at one time, so need to plan opportunities to assess different groups of children across a period of time.

To address point 2 above, a common approach is to use the acronym 'WILF' ('what I am looking for'), as in the phrase 'I am looking for children who notice something about the plant (which nobody else had observed).' This may be spoken, written or preferably discussed with the children. This helps to make success criteria clear to children who may confuse the aim of the investigation with the educational aim of the lesson, focus on surface or content features rather than procedural skills, and find it difficult to recognize the gradual learning of scientific processes (Goldsworthy *et al.* 2000a). A number of ways to assess these aims (point 3 above) are open to us:

- observing children at work can tell us whether they are using equipment carefully, correctly and accurately;
- engaging children in whole class or group discussion can help elicit particular difficulties they are experiencing in planning, executing or interpreting their enquiry;
- analysing children's written or drawn accounts of enquiry.

Harlen (2006: 28–9) suggests some common pitfalls children might encounter when transferring enquiry skills between one context and another:

Children sometimes make 'predictions' that they already know to be true and so are not a test of an idea. In setting up a test they may not control variables that should be kept constant. When observing the outcome they may focus on certain observations that confirm their ideas, leaving out of account those that might challenge them.

We also need to note that certain aspects of Sc1 are more likely to cause children difficulties than others. The AKSIS project identified specific difficulties with the following:

- transferring information from tables to graphs;
- choosing whether to use a bar or a line graph;
- understanding scale;
- describing relationships in data;

- explaining results;
- understanding why measurements need to be repeated.

To diagnose some of these difficulties, it may be appropriate to undertake a task that separates the data analysis aspects of a scientific enquiry from other parts of the process. Naylor *et al.* provide the following example:

> set up tables and charts so that learners have to extrapolate or interpolate from the data. You can get them to produce a table or chart based on information that you provide or from secondary sources, encouraging them to think of the information as clues to a puzzle.
>
> (Naylor *et al.* 2004: 51)

Such activities also closely mirror some of the assessment strategies currently used in national Standard Attainment Tests (SATs) for children aged 11. While limited in their validity to assess process skills, these tests have increasingly focused upon data interpretation and other aspects of Sc1.

To communicate clearly to children what they need to do to improve their Sc1 skills (point 4) diagnosed through the above strategies, it is helpful to find an economic way of recording the evidence from assessment. Table 7.1 is an example of a type of recording technique.

Table 7.1 Teacher's recording format: assessment for learning of enquiry skills

Group of children	Development needs to be addressed in future teaching
Most of class	Use of headings in tables to show units of measurement used
	How to phrase a generalization
	Develop phrases and vocabulary for describing patterns in graphs
Higher attainers	Improve accuracy of plotting points
Kate, Paul, Lucy, Tom, Steve B	Provide opportunity for more independence in drawing and interpreting graphs
Lower attainers	Provide a ready-made table as a model
Jim, Hannah, Mike, Suzy	Develop use of comparative vocabulary to describe similarities and differences (heavier/stretchier)

The 'next steps' identified for the categories of learners in Table 7.1 now need to be planned and shared with the groups concerned, perhaps through a note on their written work or by intervening in their own self-assessment discussions. A concern raised by this approach to diagnosing particular weaknesses in Sc1 skills might be that by placing emphasis on the parts rather than the whole it risks 'atomizing' the process for children and teachers alike. However, the responses of the teachers in the IST project suggest that teachers actually feel more confident about giving children greater opportunities for independent work when they believe the children have the skills needed to tackle it.

Planning for the development of enquiry skills

As a beginning teacher, it is unlikely that you will have the opportunity (or need) to plan for progression of enquiry skills across the school, but it may be valuable to discuss this with the science subject leader (often referred to as the science co-ordinator) to find out whether s/he has specified particular aspects of Sc1 to be developed in unit plans. For individual teachers, the overall school plan for science should suggest a focus on particular Sc1 skills in unit, weekly or lesson plans. If this is not in place, you will need to assess children's enquiry skills formatively in order to decide on appropriate learning objectives for future lessons. If you are planning for children to undertake a whole investigation, you will need to consider which parts of the investigation might need to be more strongly 'scaffolded' and where you might expect children to make more independent decisions. This would depend on where the intention was to focus teaching on a particular element (e.g. identifying patterns in results and making generalizations) and where the children are expected to apply skills developed in previous experiences, e.g. devising and using a table of results.

Whatever your resulting learning objectives, Goldsworthy *et al.* (2000b) stress the importance of making sure that children understand the purpose of the lesson and revisiting this during the lesson. This may be through use of statements, such as WILF (see above) or through asking children to explain in their own words what they are expected to be able to do by the end of the lesson. Claxton (2002) questions the extent to which the current emphasis on clearly focused learning objectives actually leads to 'better' learning. However, he also suggests that moving between focused and more diffuse forms of thinking is important in developing children's creativity, so it is important to allow children 'playing time' (within the bounds of health and safety!)

Lessons involving such open-ended enquiries in the context of design and technology ('How can we make ...?') often start with questions, so in the first lesson of Cameo 2, Leanne built her plan around 'key questions' selected to encourage the children to think for themselves:

Teacher: What do you know about puppets? Think about that with your talk partners ...
Child 1:   Water puppets?
Child 2:   Machines ...

Leanne had anticipated that the children would need time to focus on what was being asked. She produced a puppet and performed a short 'show'. She then gave the children more time to think and talk in pairs.

Child 3:   You've put your hand in it ... a hand puppet!

Ideas then came thick and fast from around the class: 'A finger puppet ... one where you pull a string ... a dressed-up puppet ... one called a Jingly Jacks!'

Leanne then introduced further key questions and also displayed on each table different types of puppets with questions, e.g.

- what is it made from?

- how does it move?
- hhat pieces have been joined?
- how well has it been made?

The children worked in carefully selected groups – Leanne had recognized that language was a vital part of this lesson so had grouped children specifically to enhance speaking and listening skills. She explained, 'Mazin speaks Arabic at home – I grouped him with Kayleigh who is very patient and supportive – but not Molly who can be quite dominant'.

Before the children set off to explore the collections, Leanne focused on associated skills that the children would need to develop in order to progress in this kind of group enquiry. She acted out a short play where two children argued over resources and tore the puppet, then another, which involved SPEAKING VERY LOUDLY TO EACH OTHER. These scenarios allowed her to make some teaching points about the need to speak, listen and co-operate in appropriate ways.

Lots of play, chatter, pretending, feeling, looking, pulling and squeezing ensued. Although the adults working with the groups endeavoured to focus on the key questions and these were returned to in the plenary, the children also had their own agenda;

> 'My crocodile (puppet) can eat.'
> 'My puppet talks like this . . .'
> 'Bear is made of fluff.'
> 'One arm doesn't move [on the marionette] . . . the string is broken.'

Leanne was not concerned about the children recording their ideas, although she gave them the opportunity to do so. In fact, by providing Post-It notes and pencils, most children elected to write (some 'emergently') during the session.

As Sarah had done with Year 6, Leanne was skilfully treading that fine line between guiding and allowing children to find their own direction in the enquiry. By the end of the session Leanne was able to identify that all children had now had practical experiences with a range of puppets, that many were able to articulate ideas about how puppets were made and that some were able to offer evaluative comments about their favourites. With these objectives met, the class was able to move on to make puppets in a creative and knowledgeable way.

Children as creative enquirers

By engaging in higher-level procedural thinking in an abstract way, through discussion of ideas and 'conjecture thinking' (Craft 2000) – asking 'What if?' questions – we can help children to take their skills of exploration, investigation and enquiry and use them creatively.

One of the 'creative thinking skills' identified in the NC is 'problem-solving'. Problem-solving is a thinking skill that has received much attention over the years, and the strategies to solve practical problems have long been promoted in design and technology (see Roden 1999). Design problems tend to be taxing, that is they are not clearly defined like mathematical problems and involve many factors, such as materials, technology and human lifestyles. We don't necessarily need to set children artificial 'problems' (for example, 'build a tower to support a marble') but we do need to support children in developing strategies that will help them think through problems in the midst of designing and making. For a food technologist, designing a sandwich that will stick together, taste pleasant and not make the bread too soggy, presents a whole range of challenging problems – it's no picnic!

Science too can provide opportunities for problem-solving activities. For example, in the topic of electricity we can challenge children to engage their prior knowledge of circuits to find the 'fault' in a circuit. The 'fault' can be set up beforehand, and might include:

- ends of wire not bared;
- 'blown' bulb;
- 'flat' battery/cell;
- two cells opposing one another.

Creativity is more than having fun or coming up with wacky ideas. It is purposeful (NACCCE 1999) and therefore seen as worthwhile and satisfying. The purpose may change during the process, but a sense of purpose must remain. A goal is most likely to be achieved through a process of raising questions, imagining possibilities, playing with materials, resources or ideas and coming up with an original solution (at least original to the child). Of course, what has just been described is a creative process and also a description of good scientific enquiry. What would 'non-creative' enquiry look like? It would be without purpose ('what is the point in this?'), without room for imagination ('follow this worksheet'), without time for play ('stop messing with those things') and without recognition of individual difference ('the answer is either right or wrong'). In other words, boring!

Conclusion

We have seen that to promote development in exploration, investigation and enquiry, we need as teachers to tread a fine line between providing enough structure so as to support the child in progressively learning a range of skills, yet have enough flexibility to engage and challenge children's personal creativity.

Questions to set you thinking

1   What are the pros and cons of teaching children the individual skills of enquiry before asking them to put the skills together in an investigative activity?
2   How might you go about assessing children's enquiry skills in the classroom? Which aspects of enquiry do you think it would be most difficult to assess?
3   How can you offer children greater opportunity for creativity in their enquiry activities? Do some curriculum areas offer more opportunities for creative enquiry than others?

References

Claxton, G. (2002) *Building Learning Power*. Bristol: TLO Publishing.

Craft, A. (2000) *Creativity Across the Primary Curriculum: Framing and Developing Practice*. London: Routledge.

Department for Education and Employment (DfEE)/Qualifications and Curriculum Authority (QCA) (1998) *The National Curriculum Handbook for Primary Teachers in England*. London: QCA Publications.

Department for Education and Employment/Qualifications and Curriculum Authority (1998) *Information Technology: A Scheme of Work for Key Stages 1 and 2*. London: HMSO.

Feasey, R. (2006) Scientific investigations in the context of enquiry, in W. Harlen (ed.) *ASE Guide to Primary Science Education*. Hatfield: Association for Science Education.

Goldsworthy, A., Watson, R. and Wood-Robinson, V. (2000a) *Investigations: Developing Understanding*. Hatfield: Association for Science Education.

Goldsworthy, A., Watson, R. and Wood-Robinson, V. (2000b) *Investigations: Targeted Learning*. Hatfield: Association for Science Education.

Harlen, W. (1996) *The Teaching of Science in Primary Schools* (3rd edn). London: David Fulton.

Harlen, W. (2006) *Teaching, Learning and Assessing Science 5–12* (4th edn). London: Sage.

Harlen, W., Macro, C. Reed, K. and Schilling, M. (2003) *Making Progress in Primary Science* (2nd edn). London: RoutledgeFalmer.

Howe, A., Davies, D., McMahon, K., Towler, L. and Scott, T. (2005) *Science 5–11: A Guide for Teachers*. London: David Fulton.

McMahon, K. and Davies, D. (2003) Assessment for enquiry: supporting teaching and learning in primary science, *Science Education International*, 14(4): 29–39.

National Advisory Committee on Creative and Cultural Education (NACCCE) (1999) *All Our Futures: Creativity, Culture and Education*. Suffolk: DfEE.

Naylor, S. and Keogh, B. with Goldsworthy, A. (2004) *Active Assessment: Thinking, Learning and Assessment in Science*. London: David Fulton.

Qualifications and Curriculum Authority (2003) *Assessing Progress in Science, Key Stages 1 and 2*. London: QCA.

Roden, C. (1999) How children's problem-solving strategies develop at Key Stage 1, *Journal of Design and Technology Education*, 4(1): 21–7.

Suggested further reading

Feasey, R. (2006) Scientific investigations in the context of enquiry, in W. Harlen (ed.) *ASE Guide to Primary Science Education*. Hatfield: Association for Science Education.

Harlen, W., Macro, C., Reed, K. and Schilling, M. (2003) *Making Progress in Primary Science* (2nd edn). London: RoutledgeFalmer.

Howe, A., Davies, D., McMahon, K., Towler, L. and Scott, T. (2005) *Science 5–11: A Guide for Teachers*. London: David Fulton.

8 Leaping oceans and crossing boundaries: how oral story can develop creative and imaginative thinking in young children and their teachers

Jane Hislam and Rajinder Lall

Cameo 1

Craig sat, mouth wide open and eyes wider still. When the teacher finished telling the class the story there was a small silence and then Craig drew in his breath and asked: 'How did you *do* that?'

Teacher:	Do what?'
Craig:	Say it without a book. Where did it come from?
Teacher:	Where do you think it came from?
Craig:	From out your head?

Cameo 2

Tutor:	Why have you not chosen so far to make that move from reading into telling?
Student:	Because I need the structure of a story, I think I won't remember it.
Tutor:	So that's what holds you back?
Student:	Yeah, the fear of forgetting it . . .

Introduction

This chapter is about telling stories orally. It encourages beginner teachers to *tell* stories, in addition to the normal practice of reading aloud. Only in doing so will you discover for yourself what makes this a distinctive and rewarding experience for pupils and teachers alike. Many teachers, including beginner teachers, may find this a daunting prospect so we have reported the voices of beginner teachers and their pupils as they explain why it is worth taking the risk.

Throughout the chapter, readers are invited to investigate the potential of story-telling, and consider some of the specific advantages for children, both as listeners and tellers. We highlight the importance of communicating through other languages as well as English with all pupils. We suggest some simple ideas for increasing a wide and meaningful story repertoire.

Although oral storytelling can certainly lead to the improvement of *written* skills, this chapter primarily explores how storytelling can enable children to draw out their imaginative, experiential and oral language resources in ways that need no justification beyond themselves.

The value of storytelling in the classroom

> Tell a good story and a child's imagination will leap across oceans and boundaries ... the adult is critical in encouraging the child to make the journey of imagination.
>
> (Naidoo 2006)

Beverley Naidoo, children's writer and teller of tales, is clear about the responsibility that rests with teachers in helping children to make sense of their own lives and those of others. Fox (1988), reporting on research she conducted into young children's narratives in the home, expressed her fear that teachers pay far too little attention in school to the power of children's narratives. Although it might be argued that narrative has been given a boost by the National Literacy Strategy, there is evidence that teachers have felt even more constrained and less able to pay attention to children's voices (and this includes oral storytelling) in the years since the NLS was introduced (Mroz *et al.* 2000; Merry 2004). Whatever successes might be claimed for the Strategy, the recent period of 'objective-led', 'text' and 'test-based' teaching has discouraged teachers from telling stories without a printed text, and from allowing pupils to tell stories without a written product. Teachers have attributed this to concerns about fitting it all in, keeping a rapid pace going in a lesson and not feeling able to deviate from the chosen teacher-led objectives (English *et al.* 2002). Despite these worries (mainly driven by concerns over OfSTED inspections), many excellent teachers and head teachers have resisted these external pressures and continued to put children's stories first.

Increasingly, there is evidence that the oral rehearsal of stories contributes successfully to children's competence in language and writing (Corden 2000). Wells' work (1986) is still relevant in demonstrating the importance for children in hearing stories told and read in their early years. Sometimes, however, the extent and nature of children's experiences in the classroom setting can be overlooked, especially in cases where children are not competent readers and writers. A teacher reported her amazement when, in response to a visiting storyteller's question 'Who can tell us a story?' one 11-year-old boy had all his classmates rapt as he told several stories from memory. The professional storyteller, who had witnessed such a situation on many occasions, was not surprised and asked the boy where he had learnt these stories. 'I go fishing early every Sunday morning with my uncle,' replied the boy, 'and while we wait for a bite he tells me stories.'

This child had a wealth of stories at his disposal but the teacher had until this time considered him to be disinterested in narratives of any kind, and certainly lacking ability as a story writer. Many teachers and educators report that oral storytelling can enable children to achieve in unexpected ways (Fisher 2005), since it appeals primarily to the creative imagination, and breaks free from the stranglehold of the formulaic and pre-scriptive agenda that sadly characterizes much literacy teaching. The stories that are defined by the National Literacy Strategy as 'fictional narrative recounts' tend to be geared to meeting specific learning objectives, such as the use of words like 'then', 'next' and 'finally'. This is rarely genuine storytelling. More likely, the child who attempts to tell the teacher a personal story spontaneously, perhaps at the end of the lesson, will be using the language needed to tell a meaningful story, but at that point the teacher may no longer be able to listen (English *et al.* 2003).

Storytelling in initial teacher training

In the context of initial teacher training, where pressures on the curriculum have also been externally driven, storytelling has also been 'squeezed' (Haggarty 2003). None-theless, many courses have continued to emphasize its key role and to encourage students to learn to tell by telling (Grugeon and Gardner 2000).

One PGCE student reported that 'In the whole group literacy lesson when one child is speaking, the answer is often of the one word variety and cannot always be heard by others in the class'. Her observations led her to develop a storytelling unit of work in her final teaching experience where gradually children's participation in storytelling, first in pairs and small groups, gave dramatic results even over a short period and enabled her mentor to hear children speak with confidence 'who had barely uttered a word before-hand'. This same student, a monolingual English speaker, began to incorporate single words and short refrains in Gujerati into her stories. She went on to say:

> All of the children were very keen to join in. Bharat and Amin, who are usually very reticent in group sessions, used the refrains and participated as fully as others. Even Iqra joined in confidently as part of the group, her words carried along by the others, and for the first time, she didn't look for reassurance from me.

Children's experience of storytelling

> 'Something has to happen in a story, and when you listen, you can imagine it.'
> 'Yes, you sort of want something to happen and you don't know if it's going to happen and then it happens and it makes you happy, or it might make you sad.'
> (Michelle and Charity, both aged 7)

Children often have firm views about the kinds of stories they like and dislike, but they nearly always talk about those they have read or heard in books. When they first hear a story told orally in school, they can be mystified. Craig's teacher (Cameo 1) described him as 'Not easily motivated'. When she was reading from a text, Craig would often work his way outwards from the group of children towards the edge of the carpet where he proceeded to see how many pencils he could snap or how quickly he could destroy Christopher's 'best ever' model. But, on this occasion, Craig sat absolutely still and 'spell-bound'. The story he had heard the teacher tell was 'Sapsorrow' (a version of

Cinderella). Craig was hooked from the moment the teacher, with no book in sight, began: *There was once a king whose wife had died. He had three daughters. Two were bad. One was good.*

What is more, Craig was able to hold the story so clearly in his mind that several days later he was able to retell the story. With an uncharacteristic degree of concentration, he elaborated on the story using elements of his own. He also talked about the story with confidence to his teacher and then to his 'talk partner'.

Why this story had such an impact on Craig, it is impossible to know. The story experience is highly personal and individual, despite its social and communal nature. Perhaps traditional folk and fairy stories have lasted so long precisely because they so powerfully engage our imaginations.

For tellers too, the experience is distinctively different from that of reading from the printed page. PGCE and BA students, with whom we have worked, have commented that they feel 'a much more direct connection with the pupils'; that 'eye contact and body language' create a sense of immediacy and tension which brings the story alive; and that they have experienced the power of holding the audience 'in the palm of their hands'.

Students' experience of storytelling

At the beginning of teacher training courses, most students have already read aloud to groups or classes. Far less frequently, students report, in these early stages of the course, that they have prepared a story to *tell*. The majority of students, in response to the question: 'What holds you back from telling a story?' say that they would be unlikely to do so without the support of the book. They say:

- I would forget the story;
- I don't know any good stories;
- I haven't learnt how to do it (the art of storytelling, e.g use of voice/sustaining interest);
- children might not concentrate or may misbehave;
- I don't like the lack of structure.

The most common response that students give to the question is that they are afraid they will forget the story. Practical activities and first-hand experience soon allow them to see that it's about internalizing the story and taking ownership of it. This is why it's good to start with personal stories before moving onto the traditional tales that lend themselves to telling, rather than attempting to learn a story from a primarily written source (see Suggested reading).

To tell a story well requires practice, craft and commitment. If the story was worth learning in the first place, then the effort of working on the story is likely to pay off. The more you do, the more confident you will feel and the more involved you will get. As Rosen (1988: 54) suggests: 'There is a value in anything that calls forth all the linguistic and imaginative potential in people, and I can't think of anything that does this as well as listening to, or telling a story.'

The told story is a much more direct form of communication than many others. Its purpose is intrinsic and is understood even by very young children. Because of this, and because it has elements of improvisation, the told story can be modified to meet the needs of the all pupils. It can be lengthened or shortened; the language can be changed; difficult words can be altered or explained within the context of story; language items can be repeated and intonation used for emphasis. It is also an ideal opportunity to include elements of other languages, and do this without artifice, embarrassment or self-consciousness. Simple greetings, warnings, sayings, rhymes and counting can be incorporated into a story and this context provides an ideal opportunity to use languages other than English in the classroom.

Benefits of storytelling for bilingual/multilingual pupils

Language competence

> Ali Omar, a Somalian boy recently arrived in the UK, listened quietly to the story of the Three Wonderful Gifts. Later, when asked to tell it to a boy from another class, he was very reluctant to speak, but as his partner nodded approval for him to continue, his story began to flow despite his difficulties with English. He had remembered the entire story ...

Children with English as an Additional Language (EAL) in our schools come from a range of cultural and linguistic backgrounds and are at different stages in acquiring English. They will have different levels of ability in their first language, from odd words and phrases to full competence. Baker (1997: 144) raises an important question about language and conceptual understanding in both languages. He introduces three threshold levels from beginner bilingual to competent bilingual:

1 low levels of competence in both languages;
2 age-appropriate competence in one of the languages; and
3 age-appropriate competence in both languages.

The latter suggests that there are positive cognitive advantages for a child who is able to use two languages without difficulty. For example, when talking to a child with a good understanding of Punjabi and English, the child is likely to have a wider conceptual image of a 'cup of tea' (English or Indian tea) and 'king' (Indian or European image, where dress and physical features are likely to differ). Of course, this is dependent on the age, experience and circumstances of each child.

Hall (1996) highlights the importance of oral traditions which can be found in many diverse cultures. Languages, such as Somali, had no written form until 1972 and all religious, academic and cultural learning was handed down orally. Teachers need to take responsibility for finding out about children's understanding and competence in their first language/s as this will have an impact on learning English. It is also worth taking some time to find out about the different languages represented in your classroom. [The Internet provides an excellent resource for doing this, for example: http://www.ethnologue.com/show_family.asp?subid=92042. This will give you useful information about children's home languages and backgrounds.]

Some EAL children will have learnt their first language informally at home in the early years of their lives and as they get older may attend complementary schools, after-school language clubs and places of worship where they will formally continue to gain competence in their first language (Gregory 1996). Some children whose parents are bilingual will be competent English speakers but may be reticent in their 'first language'. All children will be different.

Language awareness and acceptance

For all children, finding out about languages is valuable and rewarding. Often teachers rely on raising awareness about European languages as these are more familiar and acceptable to them, but can be daunted by the thought of introducing an Indian sub-continent language in schools, especially where children's first language is English. Monolingual teachers, in particular, may not have access to, or know much about other languages and may worry about mispronouncing words. Perceived, or genuine, parental reluctance for their children to speak in home languages in school may become further barriers for the teacher and inadvertently contribute to a racist model which puts language into a hierarchy of importance, with European languages being at the top and languages from places such as Africa and the Indian sub-continent coming lower down.

If you are bilingual/multilingual, you are obviously particularly well placed to use your first language in telling stories, thus creating further interest and enjoyment for the children. Parents and other adults may need encouragement to tell the stories they learnt in their home country/language (see Chapter 5). They may place value only on written texts (Medlicott 1997).

Access for EAL children and good practice

The more able bilingual child, who shows good competence in both languages is an excellent resource for any teacher and could support the class teacher with telling stories using their first language. It is important to remember that good practice for bilingual children is good practice for all children. For example, the chance to join in, the repetition of simple words and phrases, good use of gestures, actions and props make for a valuable learning experience for all, but especially for children who have little or no English. It provides the opportunity to listen, think and make connections with their conceptual understanding of the world (see Chapter 6).

Where do stories come from?

Craig was impressed that the story just seemed to come from nowhere. In reality, of course, the story was not a spontaneous invention but was 'known' to the teller. Craig's teacher talked explicitly to the children about how her version of the Cinderella story was just one of countless others similar in theme that have been told and written down over thousands of years. She explained that she had 'seen' the story, rather than read it

(Minghella 1988). She brought in books, including a Chinese version (see Internet, e.g. http://www.surlalunefairytales.com). She told more 'rags to riches' stories with similar themes and objects – rings, shoes, coats of feathers – so that the children began to appreciate the range and diversity of stories from around the world. She asked the children if they had heard or seen any other versions of the story. The idea of stories linking together in this way fascinates children (Zipes 1995).

You can begin to build a repertoire of your own stories that suit the different age groups and contexts you work in. These should always be stories that appeal to you personally. Betty Rosen (1988) gives excellent advice explaining that in preparing to tell a story you should:

- find a story you like massively; a story your imagination will relish, cherish and nourish;
- get all the facts and details together, even those you will later reject: there's a lot of lesson preparation involved, although, with luck, your pupils will never guess!
- decide what you are going to include, note it down in sequence and, in the process, consider particularly carefully how you are going to begin;
- visualize the start precisely; by this I mean allow the opening situation to occupy – take over – your imagination. This will go a long way towards ensuring that you will speak with your own voice, a story that has become your own.

The best place to start is with a storyline that is already familiar to you, for example:

- stories from your own experience;
- stories told to you, perhaps as a child;
- stories you already know well, e.g. traditional tale.

A story we often tell to students is the Three Wonderful Gifts. This is a story neither of us have read but heard from storyteller, Grace Hallworth, so many years ago now that the version we tell is very much our own. It is a story we both like enormously! It is a story with a very simple structure in which a father sends his three children to seek their fortune. All three are given a wonderful gift which they are told they must only use in great need. They return in one year and one day to discover that their father is mortally ill. The three wonderful gifts are then used to bring him back to life. This story has plenty of scope for repetition and allows children to be creative within a framework. It ends with a 'dilemma' that allows for pupil discussion. We tell this story collaboratively, using English and Punjabi.

In order to prepare to tell the story, we decide which are the main threads of the story and find a visual way to bring to mind the *whole* story. For this, story maps can be very useful (see Figure 8.1). There are other ways of 'memorizing' the story but be wary of writing it out word-for-word. This may inhibit the flexible nature of the process: you may be tempted to read it out! Rosen (1988) recommends you work hard on the opening to the story by visualizing everything, even the details you will not actually say. We find this pays off!

We usually begin something like:

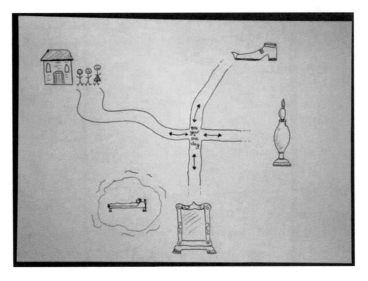

Figure 8.1 Teacher's story map

> *There was once an old man. He had three sons.* (You can change this to any combination of sons/daughters!) *One day he gathered his children around him and said: 'The time has come for you to go out into the world'. So they packed their bags and in them they put: rice/chowl, water/pane and lentils/dal* (children can give their contributions in other languages) *and off they went down the road. They walked and they walked … for a very long time until they came to a cross-roads …*

The student retold this story in a large inner city school while her student partner told another story to a parallel class. After hearing the stories, each class created their own story maps (see Figures 8.2 and 8.3) in order to exchange stories across the classes. Ali Omar had contributed little in English to his lessons up until now, having only recently arrived in the UK, but by telling his story to an attentive fellow pupil, he was able to articulate his thoughts which otherwise may have remained unnoticed. For Ali, this empowering moment was only one of many as boundaries were crossed and oceans leapt.

Conclusion … remember

- storytelling works – children are more engaged;
- it is social and participative and provides an opportunity for all to be successful;
- plenty of repetition but not forced or artificial;
- it allows for more frequent and natural use of mother tongue;
- it can bridge gaps in understanding and experience.

So …

- just have a go!
- look for a story you really like and prepare it;

Figure 8.2 Example of group story map (1)

Figure 8.3 Example of group story map (2)

- think about the kind of story it is and how it needs to be told;
- it takes a bit of nerve to tell a story rather than open the book and read, but just by doing it, you start to gain confidence, and the children's responses are what makes you want to carry on;
- find out from pupils, parents, colleagues and others the stories they know and enjoy ... not necessarily what's in books – new arrivals might bring stories with them – *value these*!
- find out what languages are spoken in your class, and who understands whom;
- learn some words and phrases from children's first languages, even if you are an English-only speaker;
- try to be an attentive listener and give children the time to communicate;
- provide opportunities for pupils to hear plenty of stories;
- give children time to recreate and retell stories in lots of different contexts;
- find ways for children to work collaboratively – storytelling is a communal activity but reaches each individual on a personal level;
- give feedback to individuals and groups about their storytelling and think about rewarding and praising children's oral work;
- provide audiences who value children's talk;
- make tapes and videos of children's storytelling activities;
- look for opportunities to transfer gains from storytelling into other curriculum areas.

Questions to set you thinking

1   What is your experience of telling, or being told, oral stories?
2   What kinds of oral stories do you enjoy?
3   What kind of stories do children in your class have to tell?
4   How might the orally told story engage children more deeply?

Acknowledgements

Beverley Naidoo for inspiration for the title. Thanks to Philippa Hurford and the children of Parkfield Primary School, Birmingham, and to all our past and present BA and PGCE students at University of Leicester, in particular Angela Burne, Dan Cammidge, Suzanne Goodger, Jennie Green and Felicity Nagington.

References

Baker, C. (1997) *Foundations of Bilingual Education and Bilingualism*. Avon: Multilingual Matters.
Corden, R. (2000) *Literacy and Learning Through Talk: Strategies for the Primary Classroom*. Buckingham: Open University Press.
English, E., Hargreaves, L. and Hislam, J. (2002) Pedagogical dilemmas in the National Literacy Strategy: primary teachers' perceptions, reflections and classroom behaviour, *Cambridge Journal of Education*, 32(1): 9–26.

English, E., Hargreaves, L. and Hislam, J. (2003) Can we talk about that later? The tensions and conflicts of teaching interactively in the literacy hour, in J. Moyles, L. Hargreaves, R. Merry, F. Paterson and V. Estarte-Sarries (eds) *Interactive Teaching in the Primary School: Digging Deeper into Meanings*. Maidenhead: Open University Press.

Fisher, R. (2005) *Teaching Children to Think* (2nd edn). Cheltenham: Nelson Thornes.

Fox, C. (1988) Learning from children learning from home, *Language Matters*, 2: 1–4.

Gregory, E. (1996) *Making Sense of a New World: Learning to Read in a Second Language*. London: Paul Chapman.

Grugeon, E. and Gardner, P. (2000) *The Art of Storytelling for Teachers and Pupils: Using Stories to Develop Literacy in Primary Classrooms*. London: David Fulton.

Haggarty, B. (2003) Memories and Breathe: professional storytelling in England and Wales: an informal report by email.

Hall, D. (1996) *Assessing the Needs of Bilingual Pupils: Living in Two Languages*. London: David Fulton.

Medlicott, M. (1997) Can we use our own voice? *Storylines*, 4(2): 6–8.

Merry, R. (2004) Are we allowed to ...? Teacher autonomy and interactive teaching in the literacy hour, *Education 3–13*, 32(3): 19–23.

Minghella, A. (1988) *Jim Henson's Storyteller*. London: Boxtree.

Mroz, M., Smith, F. and Hardman, F. (2000) The discourse of the Literacy Hour, *Cambridge Journal of Education*, 30(3): 379–90.

Naidoo, B. (2006) Journeys Across the Borders of the Mind. Keynote lecture: Your world, my world: exploring global issues through children's literature. University of London, 3 February.

Rosen, B. (1988) *And None of it Was Nonsense*. London: Mary Glasgow Publications.

Wells, G. (1986) *The Meaning Makers: Children Learning Language and Using Language to Learn*. London: Heinneman.

Zipes, J. (1995) *Creative Storytelling: Building Community, Changing Lives*. London: Routledge.

Suggested further reading (traditional story collections)

East, H. (1989) *The Singing Sack: 28 Song-Stories from Around the World*. London: A and C Black.

Garner, A. (1993) *Once upon a Time, Though It Wasn't in Your Time, and It Wasn't in My Time and It Wasn't in Anybody Else's Time ...* London: Dorling Kindersley.

Lupton, H. (1998) *Tales of Wisdom and Wonder*. Bath: Barefoot Books.

Mayo, M. (1993) *The Orchard Book of Magical Tales*. London: Orchard Books.

Medlicott, M. (1991) *Tales for the Telling: A Collection of Stories from Around the World*. London: Kingfisher.

Milord, S. (1995) *Tales Alive! Ten Multicultural Folk Tales with Activities*. Charlotte, VT: Williamson (contains story from Turkey about three gifts).

Riordan, R. (1998) *Stories from the Sea*. Bath: Barefoot Books.

9 Mummy's face is green! Developing thinking and skills in art

Gillian Robinson

Cameo 1

Head down, and in a world of his own Martin, a 6-year-old is drawing a picture. He has set the scene and now he wants to include some buried bones. Motivated by his knowledge and love of dinosaurs he knows exactly what these fossil bones are going to look like and where he is going to draw them. Crayon poised, he is about to create a site for the first bone when the teacher interrupts. The time-table tells her that the session has come to an end. 'Pack away please' she instructs, 'We are now going to have a story.' The fossil picture is removed and placed in a pile along with all the other unfinished drawings. Martin is bewildered and devastated.

Cameo 2

Emma, a 6-year-old, is given a range of crayons and introduced to a reproduction of a picture by Paul Klée which includes a small figure divided into coloured geometric shapes. Later she returns having drawn a figure divided into all colours and shapes. 'Is this real?' she says. This presents Jenny the teacher with a dilemma. If she says 'Yes' and Emma knows it's not, then her answer is not appropriate and if she says 'No' and Emma is at the symbolist stage, then this is equally wrong for her. 'What do you think?' the teacher asks. Emma replies 'I know it is not real. I can draw real things if I want but drawings don't always have to look real do they?'

Cameo 3

The rain streams down outside: a typical wet playtime. Ten-year-old Sanjit is completely absorbed covering a sheet of paper with one small drawing after another, creating to all appearances a pictorial storyboarding effect. The bell goes and instructions are given to pack away. Automatically all traces of activity during the playtime period disappear. The series of sketched drawings vanishes into the bin. Only their small creator knows their significance and potential.

Introduction

As teachers we know that a vital part of our responsibility is the provision of a curriculum that is broad and balanced. Somewhere within this provision is children's entitlement to an art programme, which is rich and multifaceted, motivating and challenging, and which takes account of the individuality of each child. It involves, in a busy timetable, somehow finding ways of respecting the time that Martin (Cameo 1) needs in order to engage fully in the imaginary world that he has created, being aware of the strategies that he will use in art in the developing process of understanding his world. Importantly, too, we need to be aware of the reasoning behind Emma's understanding of reality in Cameo 2. Sanjit's spontaneous ability to think and create solutions pictorially (Cameo 3) also needs to be understood and harnessed. How do busy teachers achieve this? This chapter seeks to share some possible solutions.

Making time for art

In Cameo 1 there are two important issues. The first is that Martin needs time to finish his picture and the second is the importance of the teacher's awareness of the stage Martin is at and what motivates him to want to learn. Martin is interrupted and the world he is creating from his imagination is brought to an abrupt end. Naturally he is bewildered and disappointed. So how do we generate time for his art? As teachers we need to look carefully and critically at our planning, trying to build in flexibility wherever possible so that children like Martin are given opportunities to follow enthusiasms and complete work. A few strategies for approaching this might include the following:

Time allocation

Some schools manage scarce art time by the block timetabling of art rather than the drip feed experience of art every day. This might mean that half the term, the focus is on art and for the other half on design technology. This is not ideal but if it can provide more continuous time, it ultimately might make for a more coherent experience and greater opportunities to develop levels of understanding.

Planning meaningful cross-curricular links

Additionally, there is the possibility of art combining with, and stemming from, other subjects. This can be very positive if the relationship between the two subjects, and the relevance and meaning of the combination, are understood by the teacher and by the child.

Building process into the programme of work

Some of the most meaningful and rewarding work in art, results from an engagement with the process where children have been involved in first-hand experience and with experimenting and investigating prior to creating a piece of work. There is a danger that lack of time for art can sometimes result in 'one-off' or product-led work rather than process-generated pieces. The product-led approach can lead to superficial work and, at their worst – because they are easily administered and quickly completed – to the use of work sheets. This is to be avoided as the outcome can be lost excitement and the portrayal of art as a passive activity. It is most important that instead, children are given opportunities in art where they are encouraged to research and to explore and are given ownership of their work by being offered relevant choices. Time for experimentation and the use of sketchbooks should be built into the programme and there should be evidence of continuity and development, which is an important factor if the art experience is to have any meaning for the child (Robinson 1995).

Art is personal

What motivates Martin (Cameo 1) to learn in art? Martin is using drawing both as a means of understanding the world and as a way to create his own imaginary world. By interrupting his activity, the teacher is taking him out of this imaginary world. In order to be sensitive to the role that art plays for Martin, it is important to understand not just the stage he is at now in his drawing and what motivates him, but to be aware of the likely pattern of his future development. Children create their own vocabulary of images and most children go through a recognizable pattern of stages (for example, Cox 1997). First they enjoy motor movement through playing and experimenting with materials and tools; then they move on to working symbolically, developing and practising 'schema' and imaginative symbolic images. Martin is at that stage now. Nonetheless, with an increasing awareness of the way in which images are represented by the media, and of the expectations of parents and friends that images should be representational, as time goes on Martin, who is a symbolist at heart, will begin to feel that he needs to make images that are representational. Soon he may feel that he can't draw. This feeling will be partly to do with natural development but will also possibly be due to a misconception about the purposes of drawing, rather than any inadequacy on Martin's part (Beetlestone 1998). However, the stages through which children are thought to pass are not entirely discrete. Rather they tend to overlap or operate simultaneously and older children, and adults, continue to experiment and work symbolically throughout their lives (Morgan 1993).

Looking back at Cameo 2, we can address the notion of Emma's view of reality. Here it is necessary to understand that even the experience of looking and seeing is not only about drawing observationally in a visually real way, for the image is seen through the eyes of each individual and therefore should be a personal response. Seen through Emma's eyes it will bear the marks of her experiences that shape her view of the world. Without this realization and understanding there can be a danger of opening children's eyes, without opening their minds and extending their vision to realize that new realities can be created through art (Duffy 1998). Clearly, even at this age, Emma realizes that there are different ways of drawing. Therefore, we as teachers should not be afraid to teach children that there are different but equally acceptable ways of making art. If the child has a very narrow expectation of drawing it may well lead to the child feeling that they cannot draw.

Fortunately there are ways to overcome this problem:

1 Use a sketchbook in which to experiment and explore. At times this might be used prior to the main activity. This places the emphasis on the process rather than on the end product and provides a particular challenge and an unthreatening exploration space where it is acceptable to 'make mistakes' and try things out, as we see later in the chapter.

2 Explore a range of tools and materials, for example, pencil, charcoal, chalk pastel, oil pastel, paint, collage materials and clay.

3 Challenge children to respond to natural and made stimuli.

4 Offer sensory and tactile challenges that provide opportunities to make things in three dimensions using tactile and observational response to stimuli.

5 Isolate small areas of things to look at by means of small view finders cut out of card or use magnifying glasses to emphasize and focus on specific detail.

6 Introduce children to examples of drawing by artists using a range of media from different cultures.

7 Use unusual tools. For example, make your own brushes or use sharpened sticks dipped in ink (Morgan 1993).

'My mummy's face is green'

A parallel situation can be seen in painting. A wide range, variety and nuance of colour are also really exciting to a child. Young children first use colour freely and not representationally, and colours are chosen for their appeal rather than for the ways in which they might relate to reality. For example, you might see several small children clad in

Figure 9.1 'Mummy's face is green!'

yellow plastic aprons busily painting at easels. Jars of ready mixed brightly coloured paint, each supplied with its own brush, stand in a row. Jack reaches forward for the pink and paints a strip across the top of the page, the nearest colour to him is pale green and with this he paints a circle for a face. He is painting 'mummy'.

There is no doubt that if challenged, Jack could tell you that the sky is blue and that mummy's face is pink, so why does he choose pink and green? The answer is that for this picture he is possibly choosing colours for reasons other than naturalistic representation. It could be because green is his favourite colour, because he intuitively knows that it will look 'right', or merely because it is the colour nearest to him and for the moment, if another child is reaching across, the most easily available. The solution is not to tell the child that they are wrong but, rather to engage with him in conversations about colour and present opportunities for mixing colours as early as possible. Previous colour mixing experiments can then be built on and both imagination and first-hand experience used as starting points for colour work. Older children use general descriptive colours and, later on, they use colour for matching, but we still need to nurture and encourage imaginative approaches to a colour response.

Celebrate the process

How do we as teachers promote and nurture creative and imaginative approaches? Look again at Cameo 3. Perhaps we should stop to think what might have happened if Sanjit's drawings had been made into a sketchbook and therefore stored, so that they could have been saved, talked about and possibly developed further.

One of the important ways in which we can encourage Sanjit's individual response, creativity and ideas is by giving him the skills, the stimulus and the opportunity to have something to say, and somewhere to record his experiences. This can happen in a number of ways. First, we can introduce him to the basic elements with which art is made – line, tone, colour, texture, pattern, form – essential to art in the same way that vocabulary is important in writing. Similarly it is important that he is introduced to a range of materials and techniques in art. For Sanjit, sketchbooks are an ideal place in which to explore the elements of art and sketchbooks can provide a space in which experimentations with techniques can be stored and revisited.

Ultimately, art education is not just about the teaching of skills. Along with the development of skills and hand control, there is also a need for the development of feelings and responses. Sketchbooks and notebooks are the ideal tools for this, offering a forum for feeding and developing ideas. Those of us who have already established them as a way of working will know how significant they can be in generating a situation where one thing leads to another, building up a sequence of work. Because they focus on and store processes, they are also an effective way of generating creative thinking. Sketchbooks enable children to see the pattern of their thinking as it emerges and are therefore a forum for promoting thinking skills and metacognition. Sketchbook content might include drawing and annotation, graphic tools, paint, collage, experimentation with materials, brainstorming of ideas, observational drawing, recording of a technique (Robinson 1995).

The world needs divergent thinkers and art has the capacity to challenge individuals and create thinking minds if the opportunities are there to question, experiment, explore and reflect. One of the hallmarks of art is that it promotes divergence, encourages children to ask questions and to look for different ways of developing ideas, to explore and experiment. In many other subjects we are encouraging children to search for 'right' answers. Art above all subjects nourishes the unconventional and nurtures the unexpected by:

- respecting children's imagination;
- developing their creativity;
- encouraging adventurous and lateral thinking;
- recognizing the validity of a personal response.

Artists' work in the classroom

Additionally, we can introduce Martin, Emma and Sanjit as young artists to the multi-faceted world of artists and craftspeople. One of the objectives for doing this is to ex-emplify the variety of responses that art activity fosters, and it is vital to offer as wide a selection of images as possible from different periods and cultures and created in different ways using a range of materials. In this way we open up their minds to new freedoms and new possibilities in art. This has particular relevance for any child who has reached the stage where they feel that they can't draw, because no two artists have the same vision or make the same image in response to an idea or a stimulus. By observing this children can learn that there is no 'right way to draw', just a range of different ways of looking and responding.

However, there is a caveat: if all that Martin, Emma and Sanjit see is the Van Gogh or Monet, then their experience will be severely limited, so a wide range of examples should be made available. These do not have to involve huge expense. Postcards can be collected and stored in a photo album, many shops now sell remaindered art books at reasonable prices, out of date 'art' calendars can be used and pictures can be downloaded and printed from the Internet.

Teachers may not be artists or experts but it is, nevertheless, necessary to get the facts right. Our knowledge about art must be solid before we discuss an artist or a particular painting with the children. This does not mean, however, that we necessarily need to tell children these facts. Sometimes far more learning takes place if the children are able to talk freely and openly to us about what they see in front of them, offering their own perceptions and ideas. We as teachers can do the same! Adults seem to have more problems with abstract art than do children. It is unlikely that Martin, Emma and Sanjit will understand fully the process by which the artist arrived at an abstract painting or, indeed, the context in which the abstraction occurred. However, this does not prevent the picture from becoming a good starting point for the exploration of colour and shape and the ways in which they can create mood and affect feelings.

Encourage children to ask questions, to look for different ways of developing ideas. It is important for Martin, Emma and Sanjit to realize that to dislike a work of art is as valid as to like it. After all, most of us know clearly what we like and don't like! The important thing is for them to be able to say why. It is necessary that our questioning skills allow children to have an opportunity to offer their own opinions when they engage with a painting or artefact and to question their own preferences (see Chapter 7). This requires an atmosphere of freedom and trust so that each child feels that his or her opinion, however different, is welcomed and respected.

Assessment

As art involves personal response, there is no doubt that the issue of assessment in art can be full of dilemmas and questions concerning what can be assessed, how it can be identified and the means by which it can be appropriately assessed. However, evidence of learning in art comes in many ways and there are very powerful means of assessment. Willingness to experiment, competence with new techniques and the development of ideas can all be assessed, especially when examining a sequence of children's work (see Chapter 17). Collecting selections of children's work or analysing the sequence of work in their sketchbooks, offers two immediately accessible contexts. It is crucial to note that, while looking at both the successful and the unsuccessful to see where the problems lie, we always view whatever the child has produced for its positive qualities. One way to achieve a productive class discussion about a challenge and to encourage children to look for positive qualities in each other's work is through a 'pavement show'. This happens when, immediately after the lesson or even during the session, while the objectives are still fresh in people's minds, the children's work is laid out on a large surface, for ex-ample, desks or the floor. Questions can then be asked related to the learning objectives, for example, 'Who can point to a picture where there is colour mixing and/or imaginative use of collage?' Of course, children's work should be respected and the questions should always be couched in positive terms to promote confidence and self-esteem. In addition, analysing the sequence of work in children's sketchbooks is a powerful means of assessment.

Consider the following assessment opportunities:

- consulting with children about selecting work for a record folder in art;
- talking to individual children while they are working and after they have fin-ished about what they have done, why they did it that way and what they might do next;
- sketchbooks in order to be able to observe and discuss the process and to identify the thinking skills that have been used;
- discussing outcomes with the class at the end of an activity to draw out teaching points and lesson objectives;
- displaying work and celebrating achievement.

Other opportunities are suggested in Chapters 17 and 18 which would link well to the art curriculum.

Display

From the minute we walk into a school, it is possible to see if it is alive and if what is displayed shows real exploration and celebration of learning. It is important that what is mounted on the walls represents what children have been working on and thinking about. Think how stimulating it is for the children, other members of staff and parents alike to see children's written work, painting, computer work, model making, maths books and photographs, all as part of the display.

Unfortunately, many schools will have a policy of displaying only finished results. The stimulus or starting point, the process of learning, the thinking and questioning that went into achieving the displayed items are seldom visible. This needs redressing. It is vital for us to realize that the finished result is only a part of the working process. There should be evidence of starting points and stimulus. There is an excellent example in a project that involved observational drawing of a mother and child where initially, the children explored what charcoal would do (Morgan and Robinson 1997). It was not scribble: it was exploration. The attempts were all put on the wall and underneath the teacher wrote 'We are exploring the marks which these tools will make.' Sometimes small flaps with hidden questions can make the display more interactive and encourage the child to be more involved in, and more aware of, the display.

It is also good for children like Martin, Emma and Sanjit to know why their work is being displayed on the walls. At its best, display has to be about celebration and communication. Display speaks volumes and when it shows not only the product but, through draft material and annotation, the process by which it was achieved, it can be a means of explaining to the child and to a parent or casual visitor the nature and the quality of the learning that is occurring in school.

Conclusion

To ensure that our children enjoy and maximize opportunities in art we, as teachers, should consider carefully the time we allow for art, how we structure that time and what kind of experience we are offering. A sound art education can be offered if the points mentioned above are taken into consideration. There can be no way round direct practical involvement and the build-up of personal confidence.

Questions to set you thinking

1   Can we positively say that what we offer children like Martin, Emma and Sanjit as an art experience is one that spans and informs the whole curriculum and at the same time is a way of learning in its own right?

2   Do we offer a stimulating environment? Creating a school resource, for example, shells, stones, bones, mechanical parts, toys, models, bringing exciting artefacts into the classroom, items from unusual places, a case full of exciting articles, taking children into the local environment, if possible organizing informative

and stimulating school trips, working from word stimuli – descriptions, poems or stories.

3   Do we provide an art experience that has a capacity to address visual and sensory learning and utilizes both the intuitive and logical operations of the brain? Do we provide experiences that are a means of working and thinking other than in words and are no less intellectual for that? Do we provide experiences that:

   (a) Embrace feeling and personal expression in common with the other arts that are a unique way of observing, imagining, interpreting, recording and making sense of the world?

   (b) Challenge children to be aware of process as well as product?

   (c) Provide a forum in which to think creatively and divergently?

   (d) Form valuable partnerships with other areas of the curriculum?

4   Do you offer a really stimulating environment?

References

Beetlestone, F. (1998) *Creative Children: Imaginative Teaching*. Buckingham: Open University Press.

Cox, M. (1997) *Drawings of People by the Under 5s*. London: Falmer Press.

Duffy, B. (1998) *Supporting Creativity and Imagination in the Early Years*. Buckingham: Open University Press.

Morgan, M. (1993) *Art in Practice*. Oxford: Nash Pollock.

Morgan, M. and Robinson, G. (1997) *Developing Art Experience 4–13*. Oxford: Nash Pollock.

Robinson, G. (1995) *Sketchbooks: Explore and Store*. London: Hodder and Stoughton.

Suggested further reading

Beetlestone, F. (1998) *Creative Children: Imaginative Teaching*. Buckingham: Open University Press.

Calloway, G. (2000) *Improving Teaching and Learning in the Arts*. London: Falmer Press.

Morgan, M. and Robinson, G. (1997) *Developing Art Experience 4–13*. Oxford: Nash Pollock.

Robinson, G. (1995) *Sketchbooks: Explore and Store*. London: Hodder and Stoughton.

10 ICT in the primary school

Nick Easingwood

Cameo 1

Alison is a Newly Qualified Teacher (NQT) in a small village primary school. She is a confident and capable user of Information and Communication Technology (ICT). The school is extremely well resourced, having made a significant recent investment in Interactive Whiteboards. This represents the first opportunity for her to use one extensively but also causes her concerns. Will it work in the same way as ones she's used before? As an NQT she is essentially 'on her own' so there is nobody immediately to hand if anything goes wrong. Quite apart from the technicalities, she is concerned about the pedagogy of using Interactive Whiteboards with her Foundation Stage class. She wants to ensure that it is a resource that enhances both her teaching and the pupils' learning and that she is not restricted to using it purely as a 'show and tell' resource.

During work on 'Money', she has been using Interactive Teaching Programs (ITPs) extensively with the children. *More Coins* [available as a free download from the *Schoolzone* website] enables the children to move coins around the screen and sort them. Although it is always preferable to use real or plastic money, for the purposes of an input or a plenary session, this is ideal. The board acts as a natural focal point, and the 'coins' are large enough to be easily seen, identified and discussed. At other times the children engage in group reading activities by using a talking Story Book (CD-ROM) in which they can turn the pages or access the multimedia features, such as the spoken text, or sound effects!

Cameo 2

Claire is a trainee teacher with a Year 5 class in the ICT suite of her one form a year entry primary school. The children are working in pairs on a LOGO task, where they have been asked to produce a repeating pattern using procedures. Emma and Dipesh are drawing a flower – it has a stem, and the repeating pattern has produced a complex geometric shape for the flower at the top. Claire stops to listen to the discussion. The children like the idea of the repeating pattern, but they are not quite satisfied with the finished graphic:

Emma:	I don't think that we turned the turtle far enough . . .
Dipesh:	We turned it 140 degrees . . .
Emma:	How far should we turn it?
Dipesh:	(*Placing his hand on the screen in the direction of the turtle*) Another 20 degrees, I think . . .
Emma:	I'm not sure. That will make 170 degrees.
Dipesh:	No, it won't, it'll be 160 degrees.
Emma:	So what will it look like?
Dipesh:	Let's try it and see!
	(*Emma types in the command. The turtle produces a much more pleasing result.*)
Emma:	That's cool!

Claire is delighted. She can see that real learning has taken place, and not only was the outcome good but more importantly the process by which they reached their outcome was excellent. They discussed what they thought they needed to do to reach their intended outcome, they wrote a procedure (program) for it, which in turn produced an excellent turtle graphic. Not getting it exactly right first time, they then had to correct it.

Although she included assessment in her planning, Claire is not exactly sure what to assess. Does she assess the outcome (the flower)? Does she assess the process (the discussion)? Does she assess the ICT skills that the children use (the typing and the pointing and clicking)? One of the potential 'difficulties' with LOGO is that it is a process-based, rather than an outcome-based activity; the finished drawings are not great art, although the process to get them might have been quite complex.

Cameo 3

Alan is a newly qualified teacher who has just joined the staff of a large primary school. Although he has access to an ICT suite for one hour a week, this doesn't bother him too much as he had plenty of experience in teaching in an ICT suite during his initial teacher training course. However, he has been presented with a new challenge – a class set of laptops which are wireless networked. This means that there is no longer any need to be physically connected to a cable for Internet and email access, or even located in specialist teaching space. He just needs to be near a 'base station' fixed to a wall somewhere in the school. At long last, ICT is back where it should be – with the children in their normal learning environment – their classroom, the library, the hall, school grounds or even out of school on educational visits. But where does he begin? How does he incorporate these mobile ICT resources into his everyday work?

Having identified the ICT resources that are available to him, he then has to complete his planning. He needs to look at the long-term planning for his year group which will indicate what curriculum content will be taught over the course of the whole year. Then he needs to produce the medium-term plans to identify what he is going to teach over the course of that all important first term. However, he discovers a difficulty – what does he need to plan and to assess? The very existence of an ICT document in the National Curriculum for England appears to give ICT the status of a subject in its own right, but the document itself clearly indicates that ICT should be used to support subjects, especially the core ones of English, Mathematics and Science. Does he plan for the ICT or the subject? And how does he organize and manage it?

Introduction

These cameo stories show there are natural concerns for beginning teachers, but there is little need to worry. All new teachers have the essential ingredients for teaching with ICT – in fact, teaching in general – great enthusiasm and a willingness to learn. The new teachers in the cameos understand that ICT makes a significant impact on teaching and learning and they are willing to use and incorporate it into their everyday teaching. They are asking exactly the sort of questions that they should be asking, not only as far as ICT is concerned, but for all aspects of their teaching. This reflection upon their own practice is essential if they are to develop as effective teachers (see Chapter 21), especially the consideration of pedagogical implications for incorporating ICT into their work. Too often in the past ICT was used simply because it was there, or because there was a feeling in schools that society needed people who could operate computers, rather than genuinely to enhance the teaching and learning process. There must be a value-added component to using ICT in a school; every school has made a significant financial investment in this equipment and as such it must offer something extra to both teacher and learner; it must not simply offer an electronic version of traditional teaching and learning methods and ideas. There is no point in using ICT to teach something that could just as easily – or indeed more easily – be taught with a set of plastic counters costing just a few pence.

It is the 'C' of ICT that is critical here. This stands for Communication, emphasizing the two-way, interactive nature of ICT. Interactivity is the most crucial aspect of using ICT: children must not be reduced to being passive recipients of information displayed on the screen, but must have control of the computer. Email illustrates this perfectly, although this interactivity could just as easily involve any application program. These involve the pupils in using the computer to help them to respond to, create, sort, refine and interrogate data and process it into information; all these are interactive activities which require the children actively to control the computer in order to achieve something. Additionally, these activities can be embellished by the integrated use of appropriate peripherals such as still and digital video cameras, scanners and programmable toys, such as floor turtles.

The use of ICT can create and extend genuine opportunities for collaborative and enquiry-based learning. The interactive use of ICT requires collaborative learning involving discussion and group interaction, where the computer and the peripherals form the focal point of activities (Crook 1994). Additionally, children are highly motivated when using ICT.

The power, potential and pedagogy of ICT

From a purely technical perspective, the main advantage of computers is that they are very good at handling large amounts of different types of information quickly and simultaneously, including text, numbers, tables, graphics, images and sound. The automatic functions of the hardware and the software, and the ability to sort, filter and order information instantly enables the user to spend more time on higher-order thinking skills, such as the analysis and interpretation of information. The teacher's role is to plan, prepare and deliver activities that ensure that children use these functions to analyse the information and interpret it before developing it further. This provisionality or semi-permanence is a powerful tool, and in itself provides the teacher and child with another reason to use ICT.

An example of this might involve the manipulation of a piece of word-processed text. This can be changed as part of the drafting or redrafting processes, either by editing the writing through the cutting and pasting of blocks of text or adding images, clipart, word-art or borders. Word-processing can frequently be changed and saved, leaving no trace of the many alterations that may have occurred, and if a new file name is used, the evolution of a piece of work can be tracked. This will be particularly helpful to Alan when he assesses the children's work, as he has a clear record of how it evolved. This will have a professional look to it – there is no rubbing out and the children won't be tired or demotivated from having to keep rewriting the same piece of work. This activity could then be taken several steps further, with the text being easily and quickly amended to meet the varying needs of a range of audiences. An example of this power might involve the transformation of a story into a newspaper article, a play or even a poem (Monteith 1998).

The children's work could then be shared and/or collaboratively developed by posting it on to the Internet or by emailing it to partner schools in other towns or counties, either in the same country or in different parts of the world.

ICT can also be used as a gateway to information via the Internet. When carrying out research projects, the children can find material from remote (international) locations, from sites specially designed for children or from 'real' sites, such as museums or art galleries. Modern Foreign Languages or Geographical work involving distant environments can be enhanced in this way. Class work could be enhanced by getting up-to-date news, sport or weather information, or preparatory work for a class trip could be covered by visiting a museum website. This might involve taking a virtual tour to discover the kind of things that will be seen, or by finding out such mundane minutiae as costs, opening times and whether there is a shop. Like all good teachers, Alison, Alan and Claire know that this could not and should not replace the experience of a real, focused and first-hand visit, but can certainly ensure that maximum value is gained from the day by careful forward planning. Expert questions could be posed and emailed to individuals either at the museum to be visited, or elsewhere, in advance of the visit.

The computer is also a very useful tool for modelling the real world through the use of simulation software, especially from CD-ROMs or websites. This is particularly useful where doing the 'real' thing would be too impractical on the grounds of health and safety, expense or time. The growing of a plant or tree could be simulated, perhaps through the use of a speeded-up animation, or conversely, the flapping of a bird's wings could be illustrated by slowing the process down. Learning can be extended through asking open-ended questions of the 'What would happen if …?' type (see Chapter 7).

Harnessing the power and potential of ICT

The National Curriculum for England (DfEE 1999) recognizes and reflects this wide range of possibilities. The ICT document is concerned with developing ICT capability, which is the combination of knowledge, skills and understanding of how and when to use ICT rather than teaching isolated key skills.

The main headings for KS1 and KS2 are 'Finding things out', 'Developing ideas and making things happen', 'Exchanging and sharing information', and 'Reviewing, modifying and evaluating work as it progresses'. This is reinforced by the frequent use of words and phrases, such as 'gather, enter and store, retrieve information, try things out and explore' (at KS1) and 'prepare information, select, classifying, checking, interpreting, organizing, reorganizing, create, test, improve and refine, answer "what if …?" questions, to investigate and evaluate …' (KS2).

So the answer for Claire is that she needs to assess the process, rather than the outcome of the LOGO project, as the pupils are preparing information and are responding to 'what if …?' questions, as well as investigating and evaluating their work.

The effective use of ICT demands a careful consideration of planning, preparation, organization and management and the application and promotion of a clear underlying pedagogy. Modern hardware and software have no inherent intelligence of their own; every operation performed is the result of a command of a user accessing given functions: effective teaching and learning with ICT are utterly dependent on teacher involvement at all stages of the process.

The new teachers in the cameos appreciate that whenever ICT is to be used, it must be used to enhance teaching and learning, not just because it is their class's turn in the ICT suite. The computer should be used because it is the most effective way to achieve teaching and learning objectives (DfEE 1998).

Planning and assessing for ICT

When planning to use ICT there are several key points that these three new teachers must consider. As ICT is a discrete National Curriculum subject there is a legal requirement for it to be taught so consequently there is an entitlement for all pupils to have access. From the outset they need to be clear what is to be taught and why. There needs to be continuity and progression in their planning and this means that the lesson plan will usually come from their schools' scheme of work (see Chapter 13). This is an important document, detailing exactly what should be taught to each class/year group during the course of the year. It ensures that content builds upon, that was covered in previous years, with no gaps or repetitions. This helps our three teachers greatly as they now have a clear vision of not only what their classes need to be taught but also why. The QCA Schemes of

Work for ICT can help here. These are a series of documents which are laid out in year groups, each of which has a number of units that tackle a particular aspect of ICT. Although the units tend to take a more prescriptive ICT key skills approach than the corresponding National Curriculum document, they also incorporate a more cross-curricular, computer-as-a-tool approach. Although non-compulsory, the units provide teachers with many good ideas in a logical structure where continuity and progression is assured. Increasingly, the National Primary Strategy is according importance to 'Themes', where Schemes of Work are replaced by topics, such as 'Weather' and appropriate ICT tasks, such as data logging of environmental conditions, are identified and employed.

When planning a lesson where ICT is to be used, consideration should be given to the following, educational, organizational and managerial aspects:

- The ICT must be relevant to the teaching and learning objectives for that particular lesson, so if it is a data handling lesson, the objectives are directly related to this.
- ICT should be overtly and obviously present in planning, but should not dominate it, (unless it is a discrete ICT lesson). Subject objectives come first, ICT objectives second.
- Planned content should be appropriate to the capabilities of the children: the subject content needs to be appropriately differentiated, but so does the ICT content. Time will be wasted if the program cannot be accessed because the children do not have appropriate mouse or keyboard skills, or because they cannot read what is on the screen.
- Teaching should be interactive and engaging: tasks should be short, focused and capture the children's interest throughout. Interactive teaching involves asking key questions throughout the lesson and remaining actively involved.
- The ways in which ICT is used – what opportunities are being made available for collaborative learning? Opportunities for discussion and shared effort are very important for extending children's learning.
- The key questions to be asked. If questions are sharply focused yet sufficiently open-ended, this will enable the children to think carefully about their answer and provide the reasons underlying it. This extends children's thinking and thus their learning. This also provides the opportunity to provide positive feedback at the same time, thus raising self-esteem and reinforcing learning.
- Deciding against which criteria assessments are being made to ensure that true progress has been made. Assessment needs to be made against the objectives for the subject, and must be considered at the planning stage. It is not appropriate to plan a lesson and then decide to 'do some assessment'. If this happens, it runs the risk of not addressing the key teaching and learning points as described in the lesson plan.

Organizing teaching and learning with ICT

Teaching with ICT is not difficult but it is different, as both the subject and ICT components need to be considered. Even if the teacher has access to an ICT suite, it is often advantageous to deliver the input in the classroom as this ensures that the valuable time in the ICT suite will be utilized with the children 'hands-on' the hardware.

The lesson should normally be in three parts:

1   A starter, usually consisting of a very short 'warm-up' activity to engage the children and to capture their interest and attention, and the main input for the lesson. This will be directly linked to the objectives for the lesson and these will be signalled to the children. This may be presented as WALT (We Are Learning To . . .), WILF (What I'm Looking For . . .) and TIB (This Is Because . . .). This might also include revision of work covered in the previous lesson in the sequence.
2   The work phase, where the children complete their tasks related to the objectives for the lesson.
3   The plenary, where learning in the lesson is summarized and related back to the objectives for the lesson; the children also share their work with the teacher and the other members of the class and also provide a link to the next lesson in the sequence.

With classes of younger children, or with groups of children who find concentrating for any length of time difficult, it might be better to 'chunk' the lesson. This involves dividing the lesson into even smaller sections, so there is a small amount of teaching followed by a small amount of the children working. This is repeated several times in the lesson, perhaps with an individual skill being taught each time. When introducing new material, it is usual for the teacher to demonstrate a new skill with an image being projected on to a screen or an interactive whiteboard. The pupils then acquire the skill, then reinforce what has been learned using the relevant hardware and software.

There are several advantages to using a collaborative learning approach: the child has a critical friend to help with their work, and the development and refining of ideas, the classification and analysis of data and the use of the hardware and software. Working in pairs is the best means of organization as it allows for pupil interaction, discussion and shared activity, yet enables the teacher to ensure that input and effort are equally balanced. Pairs can be arranged according to ability or gender, and should be changed frequently.

The interactive whiteboard

One of the most exciting recent technological developments is the interactive whiteboard. This is a board which is connected to a computer and enables the teacher to point and click, or even to write electronically on it, and to display key features as part of a lesson. However, the point needs to be made from the outset that the teacher demonstrating on the board is *not* a good use of ICT from a pedagogical aspect. It only becomes a good use of ICT when the pupils become actively involved in the lesson. This will occur when the children respond to what the teacher is doing or displaying interactively, or preferably, where they themselves use the board either to demonstrate something to the rest of the class or as part of their class work.

When Alison teaches the children, she is involving them though the effective use of active teaching. They are freely contributing, responding to her and her questions and they are using the board themselves. To these young children it is just another piece of ICT hardware to be utilized and enjoyed.

There are basically three types of interactive whiteboard currently available and although they have some differences, they are all essentially the same when it comes to using them. They all enable the user to write on them electronically, they allow the writing to be converted into a known font, and they have a series of resources. These include shapes, lines, arrows, maps, flags and pictures which can be displayed either on a plain white screen or on background screens, such as clock faces, music and handwriting paper, tables and charts. The interactive whiteboard is very easy to learn how to use.

Assessing teaching and learning with ICT

The main purpose of assessment is to ascertain whether the objectives of the lesson have been achieved and whether the children have learnt what the teacher intended them to learn. This indicates what the children have learnt during the course of the lesson; the next steps to be taken and may signal any potential problems which might need 'catch up' activities. In order for Claire to do this, she will need to use formative assessment (see Chapter 17), getting her evidence from listening to the children's discourse and getting them to record the commands they typed to control the turtle.

Claire can now see exactly what it is that needs to be assessed: the mathematical learning that is taking place, rather than the use of the ICT or in particular, the ICT key skills. She has specifically planned for this, as the objectives for the lesson were about developing the language of shape, space and direction. It should be noted though that if poor ICT key skills are hampering the activity, such as slow or inaccurate typing skills preventing an accurate completion of the task, then this is appropriate to mention in an assessment.

Once we have determined the nature and purpose of the assessment, we need to consider the form that the assessment will take. In the light of our cameos, one most likely type of assessment where ICT is used will be by task.

Conclusion

This chapter has provided some insights into the contribution that ICT can make to teaching and learning. ICT offers both a tool for learning and can help children to think as well as change the way they think. The ability to record and edit digital video, or compose and arrange different elements, perhaps text, sound icons and graphics on a page, perhaps hyperlinked to other pages or parts of text, rather than the more traditional linear way, requires a way of thinking that has not always been part of the primary school curriculum. The ability to make a floor or screen turtle draw a shape by moving a certain number of turtle steps or turn through a certain number of degrees, or the need to synthesize information ready for data analysis, offers genuine opportunities for the kind of higher-order intellectual development that was largely inaccessible to previous generations of primary age children.

Questions to set you thinking

1 How is ICT in its broadest form relevant to the lives of the children both outside and inside school?
2 How can the use of an interactive whiteboard help you to develop your teaching? What pedagogical aspects do you need to consider?
3 How might the use of wireless network laptops enable you to take ICT to the heart of children's work?
4 How much should you intervene when a group of children are working collaboratively to make the floor turtle move? How do you know when to lead the questioning and when to let them work it out for themselves?
5 How can you encourage children to synthesize data to a form that the computer can handle, and then how do you get the children to draw meaningful and appropriate conclusions from what they have discovered?

References

Crook, C. (1994) *Computers and the Collaborative Experience of Learning.* London: Routledge.
Department for Education and Employment (1998) *The National Literacy Strategy Framework for Teaching.* London: DfEE.
Department for Education and Employment (1999) *The National Curriculum for England.* London: HMSO.
Monteith, M. (1998) Peer group editing and redrafting, in *Focus on Literacy* pack. Nottingham: MAPE.

Suggested further reading

Loveless, A. and Dore, B. (eds) (2002) *ICT in the Primary School*, Open University Press.
Wheeler, S. (2005) *Transforming Primary ICT*. Exeter: Learning Matters.
Williams, J. and Easingwood, N. (2004) *ICT and Primary Mathematics: A Teacher's Guide.* London: RoutledgeFalmer.

Websites

Department for Education and Skills, ICT and Mathematics resources at: http://www.standards.dfes.gov.uk/primary/publications/mathematics/itps/, accessed July 2006.
Schoolzone, ICT resources at: http://www.schoolzone.co.uk, accessed July 2006.

11 Learning through physical activity

Wendy Schiller and Jeff Meiners

Cameo 1

Lani teaches in an outer city suburb with a culturally diverse population. Many families are from Vietnam, China, the Middle East and India. Parents work in local markets, small businesses or local food outlets. The 23 children in Lani's Reception/Year 1/Year 2 class can access the Centre for Communication Difficulties. Local education policy supports integration, and Lani has a Year 1 student who has been diagnosed with mild autism and is in a wheelchair. The school has a large open playground with tarmac surface and trees. A sports field is available for school use and the school assembly hall is timetabled for two 30-minute sessions per class per week. Resources and equipment are available for school sports (cricket, football, netball), tabloid activities (hoops, traffic cones, buckets, balls, skipping ropes) and obstacle courses (climbing trestles, balancing boards and supports, a parachute). There is an intensive three-week swimming programme, which is conducted by a qualified instructor, for children at the school. Children are encouraged to extend their aquatic skills to survival level.

Cameo 2

James teaches a Year R class (15 children) in an old, inner city school situated between two very busy roads. Most children live nearby and walk to school. Parents work in city-based information technology, banking or arts occupations. Several families are refugees from troubled zones in Africa or the Middle East and participate in the school's 'new arrival' programme. Outdoors, children have access to a small grassed play space at school and a large marked playing field nearby, also used for the school's 'sports carnival' once a year. A large tarmac area has designated areas for handball, modified cricket and basketball, and brightly painted circles, targets and grids for games. Indoors, there are two large halls with wooden floors, one with a stage, the other with wooden wall bars and ropes. Large and small balls, ropes, hoops and beanbags are available and several large mats for gymnastics.

Introduction

As part of professional preparation, Lani and James will have successfully completed a basic course in Physical Education (PE) and teaching practice in relevant settings with young children. They also bring personal life experiences, skills, knowledge and attitudes to teaching. Valuing physical activity impacts on how beginning teachers approach children's learning in PE. Lani and James must consider competencies, skills, knowledge, understanding, values and attitudes young learners bring to school, because families and communities are important in actively supporting children's positive engagement in physical activity.

Lani and James will be required to work with the physical environment, education policies, curriculum and established school traditions to support young children's positive participation in physical activity. Acknowledging and working with the established culture is vital when you arrive in a school as a new staff member. Lani and James should link with an experienced staff member as a mentor or 'buddy' to ask about the PE routines, procedures and school rules.

Children move to learn and learn to move!

Physical activity is important for the health and well-being of young learners. Children enjoy physical play so it would be foolish to ignore this. Because children's physical needs and motor development are as important as cognitive, social and emotional aspects, Lani and James' professional responsibilities involve planning for each child's needs in implementing a health and physical education curriculum. This means that regular, planned physical activity sessions are part of the weekly class timetable, and essential for assessing children's progress and reporting their achievements.

The rights of children as competent learners

The way educators 'perceive childhood and the status of children in society influences how children and childhood are understood' (Punch 2002: 321) and has implications for curriculum processes. The new sociology of childhood recognizes children as socially competent and able to express their own views and ideas (James *et al.* 1998) and is based on the *United Nations Convention for the Rights of the Child* (1989) where nations agreed to advocate for a better life for children globally. Specifically, Article 29 refers to education and 'development of the child's personality, talents and mental and physical abilities to their fullest potential', and Article 31 recognizes 'the right of the child to rest and leisure, to engage in play and recreational activities appropriate to the age of the child and to participate freely in cultural life and the arts'.

Issues relating to the power imbalance between adults and children in schools can be addressed in the PE curriculum (Brown 2003) by teachers using participatory techniques and listening to 'children's voices' (Punch 2002: 334). When children use images, words, pictures and actions to communicate their ideas, the diversity and plurality of their experiences and skills emerge (Mouritsen 2002; Morrow 2003; Darbyshire *et al.* 2005).

Through physical activity children can acquire agency by initiating ideas and co-constructing their learning with their teacher. Lani and James will each need to be a leader, bridge, motivator, and challenger of mass-produced cultures that see children as passive recipients or exploit them as consumers. Children can contribute their ideas for physical activities which are culturally appropriate and thereby the teacher–learner relationship becomes authentic, reciprocal and democratic. Such approaches encourage the positive valuing of cooperative physical activity by teachers and children.

Collaborative problem-solving approaches in physical activity by children and teachers use children's ideas, encourage sharing, negotiation, and acceptance of different perspectives and provide social cohesion (Schiller and Meiners 2003). Education departments internationally reflect these developments by producing curriculum documents that embrace socially constructive approaches and recognize schools as flexible learning environments in the broader community.

'New times, new kids, new spaces'

Given international concerns about increasing childhood obesity and diabetes, there is a danger of physical activity in schools being seen as a way to solve a nation's health problems (Tinning *et al.* 2006: 112). Tinning *et al.* consider that we are looking at 'new times, new kids, new spaces' and suggest that the children of today are reading trends from a variety of sources including media. They may look at life from a global perspective but are often coping with mobility and changing family circumstances (including changes of home) which may cause a sense of dislocation and impede social relationships. Hence, the teacher's role includes planning for socialization as part of PE curriculum implementation to support children's well-being. Careful planning, team work and cooperation in physical activity can promote harmony and peaceful interaction between young people.

Children often have access to multiple technologies and may use a computer in a separate space from adults (see Chapter 10). The computer space is private, individual, international and allows immediate access. Use of the web is part of everyday life. It is a stimulating and materialistic world full of images of bodies, lifestyles and commodities which are desirable, particularly for younger children who may not have well-developed critical skills. It is therefore part of the teacher's role to elicit children's perspectives on how they see and construct their own bodies as healthy and active. Do they see themselves engaging in physical activity which is like a TV advertisement for the latest running shoes? What sense do they make of all this? Teachers have a responsibility to encourage children to become informed and discerning in making choices available to them which affect their bodies. This is part of the PE curriculum and requires thoughtful approaches by beginner teachers like you.

Nurturing diversity

Recent curriculum documents emphasize the need for consultation with community members to ensure that appropriate provision is made for students with specific religious and cultural beliefs. Lani and James will need to consider the complex demands that differing contexts for physical activity present for children from certain communities. Cultural practices include approaches to specific clothing and appropriate activity at times of feasting and fasting so they need to be aware of particular restrictions placed by ethnic communities on girls or boys participation in PE. For example, some Muslim families require children to go without food or water from sunrise to sunset during Ramadan, so activities, such as swimming, are problematic for children because water must not enter their mouths. Also strenuous physical activity can cause fatigue and dehydration at this time. Communities who specify certain requirements for their children have suggested that teachers talk to them about possibilities for creating a more inviting physical activity culture while still respecting cultural boundaries. Tinning *et al.* (2006) suggest that teachers confront discriminatory practices or stereotypical assumptions about children's engagement and skills.

Specifically, beginner teachers can:

- Use what children know and can do as a starting point for sharing and encouraging caring interaction to foster honest and respectful acceptance of individual differences.
- Show respect for diversity by including games and physical activities valued by different cultures.
- Eradicate harassment and racism by engaging in dialogue about understanding difference, sensitivity and 'safe' environments for children.

Access, equity and inclusion in physical activity

Movement and physical activity should be inclusive experiences in which each child can participate and feel empowered by the experience. Current thinking focuses on what children *can do* while 'maintaining the integrity' of the activity (Australian Sports Commission 2001) without stress to a child with identified special needs.

In working with Reception/Year 1 and 2 children, Lani must plan carefully to provide suitable activities to ensure that her wheelchair user and children from culturally diverse backgrounds are included and feel empowered as valued members of the class. For example, all children can participate in a chair-based activity, such as a warm-up in PE, enabling them to become more understanding and respectful of differences in people's abilities (North and Carruthers 2005).

Beginner teachers can use the following strategies to work with children with language difficulty or other specific needs. Inclusive activities for young children are copying/mirroring in pairs, multi-sensory activities, hearing, touch and sight games, strengthening activities, body awareness, obstacle courses and relaxation (Downs 1995; Australian Sports Commission 2001).

With body perception linked closely to self-esteem, self-concept, self-confidence and gender identity (Gallahue and Ozmun 2006), movement can contribute to young children's sense of self. All children can enjoy movement as everyone has a body and can move and activities need to be child-centred and individualized. Physical activity can positively contribute to questioning stereotypical male or female movement which can limit the behaviour and achievements of young boys and girls.

Pre-planning for physical activity: reflecting on children's perspectives

Drawing

Children trace around each other making life size body outlines which can be used to discuss how much space they occupy, body parts, surfaces, proportions, shapes and actions. Drawing can be grouped into partnerships, friendships, or project teams to increase social awareness and interaction.

Play-maps

Play-maps graphically present children's perspectives on play (what and where they play and who with) and information about what they see as important in the home/ community.

Talking

Children interview each other with three key questions about health and physical activity, e.g. what they think: (1) about their body; (2) they *should* eat and *do* eat; and (3) how they look or want to look.

Writing

Children choose magazine or home photographs of physically fit and healthy adults they aspire to be like and write about why they admire them (e.g. family members, sports and dance personalities).

Journals

Individual journals are kept for a week including everything children eat, what physical activities they do each day (including jobs undertaken) and how they relax. They then share their thoughts in groups to develop individual and class goals.

Construction

Children use clay, play dough or pipe cleaners to sculpt and construct figures in action emphasizing body parts and body awareness.

Quality learning experiences for physical activity – what do they look like?

For beginner teachers being able quickly to manage a class for physical activity is a vital skill. Children respond positively to well-organized and stimulating opportunities to move as part of the daily programme. As well as providing respite from sedentary learning, daily physical activity in and beyond the classroom walls stimulates and invigorates the brain, enhances personal fitness and becomes part of a balanced and progressive programme for physical skill development. Providing daily physical activity motivates young learners and helps build positive student/teacher relationships, and a sense of autonomy, competence and confidence (Kilpatrick *et al.* 2002). Effective learning is experiential and harnesses energy through positive engagement (Laevers 2000).

Imagine the future culture of each school . . .

A quality programme includes a range of physical activities and may include a local swimming programme. This will require you to look beyond the immediate and setting long-term goals which need to be negotiated with children so they are relevant and meaningful. Goals also need to be realistic and achievable, taking account of the school context for teaching and learning priorities such as those described in the two cameos. Imagine what the big picture might look like if a high quality programme for physical activity is implemented in Lani and James' schools (see below).

Indicators of a quality physical activity programme

- Children are motivated participants in a wide range of physical activities.
- Programmes are built on the physical competencies of the children so that as they progress through the school they become confident, skilful motivated movers.
- Well-planned movement programmes are implemented on a daily basis as part of a balanced curriculum.
- Current theory and research informs programmes, taking account of inclusive practices for all children with differing abilities and culturally diverse backgrounds.
- All teachers motivate children enhancing enjoyment of functional and expressive movement.
- Parents work with class teachers to support and offer expertise, thereby enhancing their own participation as role models for their children.
- Children's physical interests, abilities and special talents are recognized by teachers and enhanced through well-planned programming.
- Children's experience of physical activity is developed beyond the pre-school or school by participating in opportunities provided by the wider community.
- Children's understanding of their personal responsibility for regular participation in physical activity develops progressively as part of an ongoing healthy lifestyle.

Key content areas for physical activity in the curriculum

Gallahue and Ozmun (2006) specify three key content areas for physical activity in the school curriculum. Beginner teachers need to draw upon basic movement experiences to support children's development of skills and concepts in each of the key content areas:

- *Games* are used to enhance movement abilities and are often classified into sub-categories that proceed from the simple to the complex (e.g. low level games which are simple or modified games and provide a basis for specialized activities and sport).
- *Dance* is an important part of the movement programme and involves co-ordinated movements, is rhythmical and involves temporal sequencing of events and synchronizing of actions.
- *Gymnastics* represents a wide variety of activities in which individuals work on their own and can improve their performances through individual effort. Generally gymnastics includes fitness activities (muscular strength/endurance and joint flexibility), stunts and tumbling (which include individual and partner activities), mat activities and apparatus activities (hand apparatus and large equipment).

Each area includes *fundamental movement skills*, such as *stability, manipulation* and *locomotion* as well as *movement concepts*, commonly described as *action* (what the body does), *effort* (how the body moves), *space* (where the body moves) and *relationships* (with whom or what the body moves) (Sanders 2002).

To develop movement skill themes and concepts, each lesson should include a warm-up to help children to stretch and exercise muscles which will be used in the movement experience; opportunities for skill and concept development (explore, discover, refine, practise) and cool down to relax and stretch muscles and settle children before returning to class or the next activity. Therefore, planned movement experiences/ lessons should be timetabled for three to five times per week to allow games, dance and gymnastics to be included in the PE curriculum. The main content of each lesson should contain three segments which provide opportunities for:

1 *free movement play* to allow free exploration of equipment, particular movements or skills by children;
2 *skill development* where the teacher concentrates on demonstrating new skills or further developing and refining children's existing skills using indirect and direct teaching styles; and
3 *'leading from behind'* encourages children to learn something about a skill for themselves. The teacher guides children by structuring the environment and through selection of equipment, but allows children to discover skills individually or in pairs.

As a beginner teacher planning physical activity lessons, you will need to clarify movement terms so that children develop a movement vocabulary and an understanding of different qualities of movement (Sanders 2002; Schiller and Meiners 2003).

Teaching styles for physical activity

Gallahue and Cleland-Donnelly (2003) divide teaching/learning into various styles useful for conceptualizing physical activity (Table 11.1).

Table 11.1   Conceptualizing physical education

Indirect teaching	Direct teaching
Indirect Style focuses on the *learner* rather than the *method*, allows for individual differences but is difficult for teachers to control or provide challenging movement problems	**Direct Style** is teacher-centred, efficient, focused, contributes to good class control *but* individual differences, inventiveness or creativity may be less evident
Exploratory Style sets movement problems (questions, challenges) without requiring a specific solution. The teacher does not demonstrate or give verbal descriptions. This style focuses on process not product – form and precision are not emphasized	**Command Style** involves teacher's short explanation and demonstration of the skills which children will perform. The teacher controls what is to be practised, how and when
Guided Discovery Style permits plenty of expression, creativity and experimentation *but* restricts how the learner may respond by setting movement problems for children to solve	**Task Style** facilitates individualization, with the teacher controlling what is to be practised and how, and structuring the environment so children can practise at their own pace
Indirect Combination Style is a *transitional* category combining movement exploration and guided discovery	
Combining Direct and Indirect Styles – The teacher continually structures and restructures using movement questions. This is useful for refining movement patterns or learning new game skills	

Teaching strategies

Beginner teachers will need specific strategies for managing the class, to motivate children and encourage creative responses, to ensure attention to task, shared decision-making and ownership which will lead to high quality movement (Schiller and Meiners 2003). Strategies should include the following:

- move around the space to change children's focus and to involve yourself in the activity;
- plan differentiated tasks for a range of children's abilities;
- model simple movements to support skill and concept development;
- use demonstration strategies (e.g. half the class at a time or partner observation);
- share good ideas developed by children working individually, in pairs, small and large groups;

- encourage positive, honest feedback and fair play;
- vary strategies for formation of groups/teams and ensure equity in participation and assessment.

Encouraging safety

Safety in PE is a prime concern for the beginner teacher. It is important to become aware of local arrangements for occupational health and safety, First Aid and a teacher's duty of care including local child protection policy. Some local authorities require teachers to have a current First Aid qualification so it is important to check local requirements and identify the First Aid contact for the school in cases of emergency. Classroom teachers need to be aware of children's special health circumstances, such as allergies, asthma, diabetes, and work with families so they are informed of any special requirements which may need to be accommodated in the planning of a programme.

For outdoor activity, sun safety is essential. This includes awareness of skin protection for *all* children, which may require protective sun screen and the use of hats which shade the eyes and the back of the neck. In Australia, the rule is 'no hat, no sun screen, no outdoor play'. Time has to be allowed for children to drink water regularly and vigorous activity should not be for prolonged periods without a rest or refreshment.

To cater for children's physical needs, beginner teachers will need to plan for use of equipment which is child-sized, skill-appropriate and provides sufficient activity for engagement of all children. It is vital to establish a safe environment with clear pathways free of obstacles for ease of movement (Figure 11.1). Enlisting help from teaching assistants, other teachers and parent volunteers in PE lessons can support the teacher by providing extra hands and eyes to assist with encouragement, participation, skill development and constructive feedback. Carefully planned movement content and use of a specific floor plan for equipment will ensure that all needs are met and skills are developed sequentially. This will allow new teachers like Lani and James to evaluate each child's progress as well as completing group assessments of children's ability levels to guide future planning.

Moving to the activity space

When moving to undertake physical activity outdoors or indoors in a large space, teachers need to establish clear ground rules to ensure that all children are safe and understand what is expected of their behaviour and responsibilities to take care of themselves and each other. There is a perception that when classes move outdoors, there is a licence to engage in activities that would not be acceptable in the classroom.

Attention needs to be given to the careful transition from classroom to the designated space for physical activity. Transitions can be fun by using 'follow-the-leader' games and task-setting challenges for arrival in the space, such as 'practice jumping lightly on the spot' or 'make a shape balancing on three body parts' or 'make a shape to show a letter of the alphabet', to engage the children immediately.

Large spaces provide opportunities for excitement with physical activity. This needs

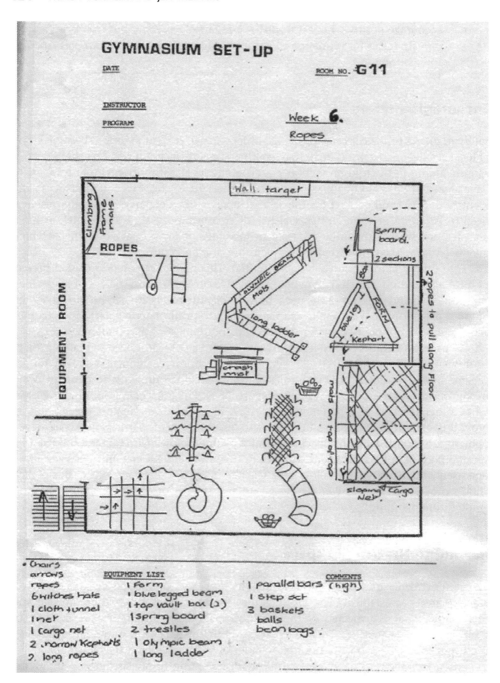

Figure 11.1 Obstacle course floor plan

to be acknowledged and utilized in planning. In fast-moving chase games, noise is natural as the voice is part of the body. Outdoor play can involve elements of what is known as 'rough and tumble' play and children enjoy using energy and opportunities to explore speed, body weight, space and control. Stop and go activities are vital beginning activities for establishing body control. Physical activity also provides opportunities for use of sensitivity to moving with others. Dance particularly offers ways of working carefully and with control, keeping in time, to a beat and moving closely with others in shared space using sequences and movement patterns.

Safe touch

The PE curriculum is one area in which safe touch is part of the programme and requires a considered approach by all teachers. Checking local policy and guidelines for appropriate physical contact is essential for the beginning teacher.

Children relate to each other in many different ways, by working individually, in pairs and small or large groups. Tasks may require children to work in close proximity as they explore working with the body, how it moves and what it can do. Developing awareness of personal space and general space shared with others is part of all movement lessons so children will be defining how comfortable they are with various groupings and formations. Content areas (such as games, gymnastics and dance) require differing use of space and physical contact. For example, some games may include spontaneous contact (such as chasing games or relays) while gymnastics and dance may focus on exploration of contact (such as hand-holding, weight transference or weight-taking). Tasks may include partner or group work with intertwining shapes, rhythmic sequences or supporting others by taking weight.

Beginner teachers need to be aware of suitable physical contact between themselves and a child, considering cultural attitudes and traditions regarding touch. This can include:

- providing non-intrusive gestures for comfort and reassurance;
- making contact with a child's hand, arm, shoulder or upper back rather than other parts of the body;
- being aware of signs that a child is not comfortable with touch;
- giving encouragement by using a conventional hand-shake;
- using positive verbal feedback and verbal cues.

Advice with particular instructions in aquatic, dance or gymnastic activity includes telling the child that you need to hold them in a certain way and seeking their permission.

Healthy lifestyles and healthy eating habits

Current research on obesity and healthy lifestyles indicates that playing outside keeps children thinner and that play in natural spaces may be the vital link that experts have

Figure 11.2 A play-map of physical activity places and spaces

been searching for to increase children's physical activity and sense of well-being. The combination of good nutrition, adequate sleep, suitable levels of active physical play outdoors and opportunities for social interaction contributes to a healthy lifestyle for young children. Beginner teachers like Lani and James can encourage children in their class to keep a health diary for a week, to make a play-map of physical activity places, spaces at home and in the local community, (Figure 11.2) and to describe their own involvement in physical activity and play through Photovoice using disposable or digital cameras (Darbyshire *et al.* 2005).

Conclusion

In summary, it is the teacher's role to educate children and work towards a school culture that moves beyond tolerating difference to accepting, understanding and ultimately celebrating diverse features of the learning community. This requires teachers to collaborate with the community, avoid social exclusion and advocate for the rights of all individuals. The emphasis is on the young child as a social and active learner, on thinking with the body and how you, as a teacher, can act as a catalyst for children to be enthusiastic participants in diverse physical activities and a healthy lifestyle.

Questions to set you thinking

1   What do you personally value about physical activity as part of your life? How does this impact on your teaching?
2   What is your skill level, knowledge base and attitude to physical activity in the curriculum?
3   How might you involve parents and the wider community in supporting young children's positive engagement in physical activity at school, at home and in the community?
4   How can you go beyond the slogans about healthy lifestyle and eating to promote children's understanding and encourage continued involvement in enjoyable physical activity?

References

Australian Sports Commission (2001) *Give it a go: Including People with Disabilities in Sport and Physical Activity*. Canberra: Australian Sports Commission.

Brown, S. (2003) Celebrating childhood. Keynote address, 13th Annual *European Early Childhood Research Association* conference, University of Strathclyde, Glasgow, Scotland, 3–6 September.

Darbyshire, P., MacDougall, C. and Schiller, W. (2005) Multiple methods in qualitative research with children: more insight or just more? *Qualitative Research*, 5(4): 417–36.

Downs, P. (1995) *Introduction to Inclusive Practices*. Canberra: Australian Sports Commission.

Gallahue, D. and Cleland-Donnelly, F. (2003) *Developmental Physical Education for All Children*. Champaign, IL: Human Kinetics.

Gallahue, D. and Ozmun, J.C. (2006) *Understanding Motor Development: Infants, Children, Adolescents, Adults* (6th edn). Boston MA: McGraw-Hill.

James, A., Jenks, C. and Prout, A. (1996) *Theorizing Childhood*. Cambridge: Polity Press.

Kilpatrick, M. Hebert, E. and Jacobsen, D. (2002) Physical activity motivation: a practitioner's guide to self-determination theory, *Journal of Physical Education, Recreation and Dance*, 73(4): 36–41.

Laevers, F. (2000) Forward to basics! Deep-level-learning and the experiential approach, *Early Years*, 20(2): 15–7.

Morrow, V. (2003) No ball games: children's views of their urban environments, *Journal of Epidemiology and Community Health*, 57(4): 234.

Mouritsen, F. (2002) Child culture-play culture, in F. Mouritsen and J. Qvortrup (eds) *Childhood and Children's Culture*. Odense: University Press of Southern Denmark, 14–42.

North, J. and Carruthers, A. (2005) Inclusion in early childhood, in P. Foreman (ed.) *Inclusion in Action*. Canberra: Thomson Publishing.

Punch, S. (2002) Research with children: the same or different from adults? *Childhood*, 9(3): 321–41.

Sanders, S.W. (2002) *Active for Life. Developmentally Appropriate Movement Programs for Young Children*. Washington, DC: National Association for the Education of Young Children.

Schiller, W. and Meiners, J. (2003) Dance: moving beyond steps to ideas, in S. Wright (ed.) *Children, Meaning-making and the Arts*. Sydney: Pearson Education Australia.

Tinning, R., McCuaig, L. and Lisahunter, K. (2006) *Teaching Health and Physical Education in Australian Schools*. Frenchs Forest, NSW: Pearson Education.

United Nations (1989) *Convention for the Rights of the Child*. New York NY: United Nations.

Suggested further reading

Australian Sports Commission (2001) *Give it a Go: Including People with Disabilities in Sport and Physical Activity*. Canberra: Australian Sports Commission.

Downs, P. (1995) *Introduction to Inclusive Practices*. Canberra: Australian Sports Commission.

Gallahue, D. and Cleland-Donnelly, F. (2003) *Developmental Physical Education for All Children*. Champaign, IL: Human Kinetics.

Gallahue, D.L. and Ozmun, J.C. (2006) *Understanding Motor Development: Infants, Children, Adolescents, Adults* (6th edn). Boston MA: McGraw-Hill.

Sanders, S.W. (2002) *Active for life. Developmentally Appropriate Movement Programs for Young Children*. Washington, DC: National Association for the Education of Young Children.

PART 3
ORGANIZING FOR TEACHING AND LEARNING

12 'It's my birthday bridge': multi-modal meanings through play

Maulfry Worthington

Cameo 1

Olaf (5 years 6 months) has an open egg box on the table. Drawing a face on a small circle of paper, he carefully places it into one of the six compartments. He repeats this five times until each compartment has a paper circle in it and then opens and shuts the lid several times. Looking up and smiling, he explains 'The horses are tired and they're in the stable now.'

Cameo 2

Alice (4 years 11 months) has been talking a lot about her coming birthday. Today she has glued some pieces of wooden dowelling of different lengths together to make a capital 'A'. She decorates her 'A' with glitter and tinsel, telling us 'It's my birthday bridge.'

Introduction

The observation notes above reveal two young children intent on making meanings as they freely explore their own ideas:

- Olaf used resources to stand for (or 'mean') tired horses in a stable. Opening and shutting the lid suggested a door to him: closing the 'door' allowed the horses to sleep;
- Alice had spent time exploring symbols during previous weeks. Her 3-D letter 'A' meant both the first letter of her name and 'like a bridge' (shape). Once decorated, it also carried meanings of 'celebration', 'birthday', or more specifically '*my* birthday'.

Other children would use such materials in very different ways in their play and assign different personal meanings to the same resources.

Meaning-making

Observing children's spontaneous play, we can see they are thinking deeply about what gestures, movements, sounds and words, objects, marks and symbols 'mean'. Infants and young children continually struggle to make personal sense of everything they encounter in the world and this sort of 'struggle' is a natural part of learning (see Chapter 6).

In this *socio-cultural* view of learning, children are recognized as active learners who construct meanings (Rogoff 2003). Children's meaning-making has been explored in recent years by researchers including Athey (1990) and Nutbrown (2006) who focus on schemas; and by Kress (1997) and Pahl (1999) who explore multi-modal play. Other researchers focus on children's meanings explored through their drawings, emergent writing and children's mathematical graphics (see Chapter 9). Play offers rich contexts within which children can explore all of these interconnected aspects of learning as they make meanings.

Multi-modality

The sort of play in which young children freely engage is highly significant, not only in a general sense for their well-being and social development but also to support their intellectual development. Genuine child-initiated play is spontaneous and belongs to the child: it has a quality of 'free-flow' (Bruce 2005) and provides a 'non-threatening way to cope with new learning and still retain self-esteem and self-image' (Moyles 1994: 7).

This chapter focuses on young children's play and representations from a 'multi-modal' perspective (Kress 1997). Kress argues that meaning-making develops through children's active engagement with 'lots of different stuff': the term 'multi-modality' simply means many modes or forms; many different ways of representing meaning. Young children interact with people and explore meanings through different media including gesture, talk, piles of things, dens they build, role play, cutting out, junk models and drawings.

Symbol use develops from infant behaviours when children pretend that one object stands for something else. When an infant waves one hand to 'say' goodbye, or when she holds a banana to her ear and pretends that it is a telephone, she understands that she can use her hand or the banana to *mean* something else (see Chapter 21). This ability is at the heart of understanding all symbolic systems and 'written' communication and was identified by Vygotsky in the 1930s (Vygotsky in Cole *et al.* 1978). Understanding and using different symbol systems, such as writing grow from multi-modal play and explorations (Kress 1997).

Symbolic systems include written languages, such as English, Arabic and Spanish; Morse code; musical scores; maps; diagrams; numerals and algebra. Even cultures that have no written alphabets often leave complex messages for each other with abstract 'signs' which may be made from twisted leaves, stones and twigs arranged in certain ways and understood by members of their community. It is the *meanings* that humans attach to the marks and signs of these languages and systems that allow us to become skilled symbol users.

Young children have an amazing ability to make personal meanings in various materials and contexts (see Chapter 9). It is important that they have space where they can play and explore freely indoors and out: classrooms that are full of tables and chairs do not offer the best environments.

The richest opportunities for children to make and explore meanings are provided within open-ended contexts which provide opportunities for *representing* meanings in some way (Bruce 2005). Essential play areas to support children's meaning-making include:

- role play, small-world play (and perhaps somewhere to make dens);
- junk modelling and cutting out;
- drawing and painting;
- mark-making (graphics area).

While this chapter focuses on these four contexts, other important areas that help children construct meanings include block play, malleable materials, such as clay, dance and music, and it is no coincidence that these contexts are often related to creativity. The thread that links these contexts and media is the open-ended possibilities they offer for making meaning. Creative and imaginative play is easily restricted when children's learning environments are *over*-planned with elaborate play-spaces and bought resources inside and out. It is difficult for children to construct their own meanings with something that is already a shop, with plastic fruit, a worksheet or a nurse's uniform.

The *Curriculum Guidance for the Foundation Stage* emphasizes that creativity 'begins with curiosity and involves children in exploration and experimentation . . . they make decisions, take risks and play with ideas' (DfEE/QCA 2000: 118). 'Creativity' is likely to continue to be a distinct area within the *Early Years Foundation Stage* (DfES 2006), but is also clear that children need to go beyond making creative things (*products*) and develop creative thinking and problem-solving, or *processes* (see Chapter 7). Teachers need to understand that children need opportunities to be creative in all curriculum areas, something that is also emphasized in the *Primary Strategy* (DfES 2003: 12).

Play should be at the heart of each day for young children. The *Curriculum Guidance for the Foundation Stage* (DfEE/QCA 2000) signalled a return to a play-based approach although is has been in schools that play has often been marginalized. This has sometimes led to play being almost a 'reward' and permitted only after children completed their work or left to Friday afternoons. In many Year R classes, adults often each work with a group while one group plays: unfortunately this creates a false divide between 'work' and 'play' and gives an unintended message to children, that adults value 'work' in adult-led groups more than their play. It also means that there are unlikely to be any adults free to support or observe children's play.

Contexts for meaning-making

Dens and role play

Some of the very richest play I have observed was children choosing to paint and draw; making things with junk materials and spontaneous role play. Resources do not always have to be elaborate or expensive to support creative and imaginative play and their personal meanings.

Making dens provides rich contexts for imaginative play and often represents spontaneous constructions, using whatever children find to hand. In the playground Frances and Yoko loved playing beneath the steps to their 'hut' classroom (see

Figure 12.1). Each day they laid out blankets and covers on the ground, sometimes adding drapes to create a small enclosed space. Although on occasions they dressed up, they seldom assumed other roles: it was their special den that was the focus of their interest.

Figure 12.1 Playing in the den

Kress describes a 'car' which two 6-year-olds made on the bedroom floor, using drawers, a pillow, toolbox and other items. Because their car was to sit in, wheels were unnecessary. Kress argues that such play is a form of 'complex sign ... and is just one more element in a much more complex meaning-making structure' (Kress 1997: 32).

In my own classroom, opening up a space next to the big wooden blocks triggered some very rich role play. The children extended their building with blocks, using them for many different props or pieces of furniture in their own role play, or constructions (Carruthers and Worthington 2006).

Pat Broadhead writes about role play areas that became the 'whatever you want it to be place' (Broadhead 2004: 70–83). Research suggests that rather than focusing too much on planning the *content* for role play, we should concentrate rather on the *processes* of play and children's learning and how we might best support these.

Small world play is closely related to role play and children will often create elaborate imaginary contexts with few and found resources. At home in the garden 6-year-old Louise created a make-believe 'town' on the rockery with numerous 'homes' for tiny dolls. She spent a long time carefully making tiny props, such as newspapers, utensils and furniture, made of natural things (twigs, seedpods and stones) that she found in the garden, and over a period of several weeks complex stories grew around the lives of the various 'families' who lived there.

Junk models and cutting-out

The examples of Olaf and Alice show how young children love making things with junk materials. They also build layers of meanings through paper which they then transform by cutting; or adding marks, drawings, sticking things on to the surface. Cutting-out changes the piece of paper into an object with which they play (Kress 1997). In her study of children's meaning-making in nursery education, Pahl (1999) has highlighted the ways in which children *transform* aspects of their play or things they make.

Sometimes children add their own symbols to the cut-outs and to models they make. Their meanings are contained in the object itself, the marks on it and the evolving ways in which they use it within their play. In my Year R/1 class, there had been a spate of interest in children making 'kites'. Some of these began as something else – such as a 'picture', or coloured tissue paper stuck on to white paper: later by the addition of wool or string the children transformed its function and offered new possibilities for play with what they had made.

Dragging her kite along the floor one day, Melanie saw its potential as a 'dog' she could take for a walk: the string of the kite now became the dog's lead. At the same time, Amritha removed the wool from her kite and replaced it with a stick to change her kite to a flag that she could wave.

Nadia (Figure 12.2) took a piece of paper and began making marks and symbols and a drawing of herself. Adding a few scraps of tissue paper and a circle of gold foil, she then attached a 'handle'. Nadia explained that she'd made a 'bag' and enjoyed walking around carrying it by the handle. Aware that her bag could not hold anything, she adapting it by adding a paper 'pocket' and delighted in finding tiny things to put in it. Later she played with her bag in her role play as a 'big sister'.

Figure 12.2 Nadia's bag with marks and symbols

These lovely examples are rich with young children's personal intentions and meanings and have a 'fluid quality' (Pahl 1999): they point to the sort of experiences children should be able to explore throughout the FS and into KS1.

Drawing and painting

From an early age infants discover that they can make marks, for example, with spilt milk or water. Exploring paint, pens and other media on steamed-up windows, in sand or the surface of the playground, they soon understand that their marks leave a trace on paper or other surfaces. Computers, tablet PCs and interactive whiteboards that allow children to make meanings (see Chapter 10) through their own marks on blank screens can extend possibilities.

Very young infants wallow in the *experience* of moving the pen or brush and the marks they leave, but at some point some of their marks may begin to make meanings to a child. Matthews's important research (1999, 2003) has identified three *generations* of marks that begin with arcs and 'push–pull' marks and originate within babies' 'conversations' with adults, and within their gestures and movements. These significant findings reveal the relationship between actions and meanings and highlight the depth and importance of children's thinking, visual marks and representations.

At 3 years 2 months, Ben described the arrangement of lines he drew within a partly enclosed space as 'a man fighting snakes in a snake pit' (Matthews 2003: 85). Kress recounts how another 3-year-old described the seven circular shapes he drew, saying, 'I'll make a car ... got two wheels and two wheels at the back ... and two wheels here ... that's a funny wheel.' Kress observed that this was the first time that the child had named a drawing and that he represented 'those features of *car*, namely wheels, or "wheelness"' (Kress 1997: 10–1).

Some of children's marks are made for the pure pleasure of exploring actions and exploring the quality of the paint. We cannot always know if these early marks 'mean' something since children may not always want (or be able to) explain what their marks are about. We need to be cautious about saying what we think we can see, or asking children to tell us about their 'picture'.

Sometimes young children will notice their marks and attach meanings *after* they have made them. At other times children set out with an *intention* or idea of what they might represent and both are important for the child. At around the age of 3 years, Matt began to separate out the different purposes of his marks as drawings, writing and some with mathematical meanings (Carruthers and Worthington 2006).

It is also very clear that different symbols, drawings and meanings are often combined at one time on one surface, each contributing to the whole. Marks that may appear to be a picture often include letter- or number-like symbols. Children do not simply learn in neat 'subjects' and the ways in which they represent and explore their thinking in multi-modal ways suggest complex thinking. Anning and Ring argue that 'we need a society that can listen to children and recognize that perhaps their drawings may tell us much more about children that we ever imagined' (Anning and Ring 2004: 124).

Early writing

Since the 1970s there has been growing interest in the development of young children's own early marks as writing. Research in the 1930s by the Russian psychologists Vygotsky (Vygotsky 1978) and Luria (1983) uncovered the beginnings of what we now know as emergent writing, although their work was not published in the West until much later. For many teachers Clay's (1975) book on emergent writing was a significant publication and was followed by numerous other books on this important subject.

There is no distinct point at which children begin to write or explore symbolic languages, such as writing or 'written' mathematics, since multi-modal explorations are also 'paths into literacy' (Kress 1997). From 3 or 4-years of age children begin to understand that they can attach their own meanings to their marks. The strength of emergent writing is that children choose the marks and symbols to think about and sometimes communicate their meanings to others. This allows children to build on what they already know and to construct deep understandings.

Matthews's work (1999, 2003) suggests a strong relationship between the *generational marks*, such as *horizontal and vertical arcs*, that young children explore in their early drawing and early symbolic (written) languages. The research on patterns of behaviour or *schemas*, suggests that there may be a link with the marks Matthews identifies: both appear to support children's early written symbols, such as letters and numerals (Carruthers and Worthington 2006). Once again, the thread that links all these aspects of learning is children's meaning-making: without opportunities to 'construct' meaning, it is unlikely that learning will go beyond superficial understanding.

Recent research into 'new literacy studies' now provides a focus on literacy as a social practice, exploring the dominance of the screen over printed text and using a multi-modal framework, (Pahl and Rowsell 2005; Kress 2003). Meanings are always co-constructed through interaction with others and within children's socio-cultural contexts of home, culture (community) and school.

Children's mathematical graphics

Until recently it was almost as though young children never make mathematical marks: while early marks may sometimes be valued as the beginning of drawing and writing, their early mathematical graphics are rarely acknowledged (Matthews 1999: 85). Hughes's (1986) research revealed some of the ways in which children could use their own informal marks to represent their mathematical thinking and these early mathematical marks became known as 'emergent mathematics'.

The extensive research we have carried out with children in the home and through our teaching with 3- to 8-year-olds, shows children's amazing ability to make, explore and communicate their mathematical thinking through their visual representations, in (at first) non-standard ways. We term such mathematical mark-making *children's mathematical graphics* (Carruthers and Worthington 2006).

Analysis of hundreds of examples we collected from our own teaching revealed some significant features and highlighted the development of early 'written' mathematics from birth to 8 years. It has also shown how children's own visual representations help them explore their understanding of quantities, written numerals, number operations and all areas of mathematics. It shows how using personal ways of representing their thinking also helps them to understand the standard symbols and algorithms that they will sub-sequently meet in school. Mathematical graphics enable young learners to 'bridge the gap' between their informal marks and personal mathematical meanings, and the standard, abstract written language of mathematics.

Figure 12.3 is a drawing that Catherine chose to do on her first day of school: it shows her sister who was two-and-a-half-years-old on that day. Catherine used approximately half of the numeral '2' (reversed here) to represent the fraction '½'. Her understanding appeared to be confirmed the following day when she wrote that she was '4½' in a similar way (writing a half of the numeral '4'): she had developed a personal symbol to convey the meaning of the fraction in this context.

Figure 12.3   Catherine's numbers and figures

Music, meanings and new media

Children may also make personal meanings with their own 'written' music when com-posing or listening to music. They may represent beats, pitch, duration of notes and different instruments; a particular instrument or the meaning of the composition, such as the sound of rain. They can be very skilled at then 'reading' their scores and playing their music from their notation.

Programmable computerized toys, such as 'Roamer', 'Pip' and 'Pixie', often arrive with worksheets for children to complete to write their own program. But when children can choose how they will represent instructions for the toy to move, they consider the layout and the meanings of the marks and symbols they choose to use.

Pedagogy

Above all, it is the ethos that you create, your own interest in what the children do and the way you use your knowledge of young children's development and learning that will be most significant in supporting powerful young thinkers: young children also need to know that their 'voice' (what they say and do) will be heard and that adults are genuinely interested and understand.

In their recent study of Year R classes, Adams *et al.* (2004) emphasize that 'perhaps our most worrying finding: the limited opportunities . . . for complex, imaginative play; and for authentic, engaging, first-hand experiences'. The researchers stress that such opportunities (with 'sustained, shared, purposeful talk' identified in the EPPE project (Sylva *et al.* 2004)) are the 'real "basics" of the early childhood curriculum'. The authors recommend that teachers 'review the balance of time allocated to these crucial aspects of children's lives' (Adams *et al.* 2004: 27).

The *Early Years Foundation Stage* (DfES 2006) emphasizes the 'central role of play . . . very young children learn by doing, rather than by being told' (2006: 11), and the curriculum is viewed as 'rich, play-based' (2006: 15). In recent years teachers and educators have raised concerns about the contrasting experiences children have when they move into Year 1, with its focus on subjects, lengthy periods of time sitting and listening and a fully timetabled day. The Inset materials 'Continuing the Learning Journey' were developed in response to such concerns and emphasize that in both Year R and Year 1, key elements should include similar play areas, such as role play, writing, sand and water, and that children should learn through first-hand experiences and 'high-quality play' (QCA 2005: 30).

This chapter is written with the understanding that all teachers in Year R and Year 1 will make frequent observations of child-initiated play. This need not take huge amounts of time or require lengthy screeds of writing. However, it is important to recognize that 'tick-boxes' will tell you little (unless they tell you what children *cannot* do). Effective observations will provide you with windows on children's thinking and understanding and add to your knowledge of how children learn through play (see Chapter 18).

Assessment needs to be from a positive perspective, focusing on what children *can* do (Drummond 2003; Carruthers and Worthington 2006; Chapter 17). Your plans for play will be best informed by your observations and planning from what you know about children's learning will enable you to build on their strengths and interests. It is important to involve Learning Support Assistants in making observations and planning for play so that you work as a team (see Chapter 16). You should both also share your observations and insights with parents and carers – and importantly, really listen to what they can tell you about their child (see Chapter 4).

Conclusion

These are exciting times to be working with young learners and, as your own understandings develop, your practice will also grow. Documents, such as the *Early Years Foundation Stage* and the *Primary Strategy*, promote many aspects of good practice but it is down to you, the teacher, to understand children's play and to decide how best to support their learning and development. Young children need adults who understand and value their play so that they can support and further extend their understanding. They need the sort of adults who are interested and willing to listen; who tune into their thinking and share in the magic of children's worlds and meanings.

Olaf, Alice and the other children in this chapter, indicate some of the many ways in which children create powerful personal meanings through play enabling them to 'cross boundaries' and link all areas of learning. Spontaneous, child-initiated play in which children explore their personal ideas provides the richest seed-bed for them to build personal meanings in multi-modal ways.

Questions to set you thinking

1   *Planning*: how can you ensure play is given significant, designated time each day? Consider how all adults in the class are available to support and observe children's play.
2   *Observations*: how will you involve all adults in your class in making informal (formative) observations of children's play? How will you use your observations to inform your planning and extend children's learning?
3   *Understanding development*: how much do you know about the development of drawing, writing and children's mathematical graphics? Think about how you can collect and annotate visual representations from children in your class so that you can develop your understanding and professional knowledge.

References

Adams, S., Alexander, E., Drummond, M.J. and Moyles, J. (2004) *Inside the Foundation Stage: Recreating the Reception Year*. London: Association of Teachers and Lecturers.

Anning, A. and Ring, K. (2004) *Making Sense of Children's Drawings*. Maidenhead: Open University Press.

Athey, C. (1990) *Extending Thought in Young Children*. London: Paul Chapman.

Broadhead, P. (2004) *Early Years Play and Learning: Developing Social Skills and Co-operation*. London: RoutledgeFalmer.

Bruce, T. (2005) *Early Childhood Education* (3rd edn). Abingdon: Hodder Education.

Carruthers, E. and Worthington, M. (2006) *Children's Mathematics: Making Marks, Making Meaning* (2nd edn). London: Sage Publications.

Clay, M. (1975) *What Did I Write?* London: Heinemann.

Department for Education and Skills (2003) *Excellence and Enjoyment: A Strategy for Primary Schools*. London: Department for Education and Skills.

Department for Education and Skills (DfES) (2006) *The Early Years Foundation Stage: Consultation on a Single Quality Framework for Services to Children from Birth to Five*. London: DfES.

Drummond, M.J. (2003) *Assessing Children's Learning*. London: David Fulton.

Hughes, M. (1986) *Children and Number: Difficulties in Learning Mathematics*. Oxford: Blackwell.

Kress, G. (1997) *Before Writing: Re-thinking the Paths to Literacy*. London: Routledge.

Kress, G. (2003) *Literacy in the New Media Age*. London: Routledge.

Luria, A. (1983) The development of writing in the child, in M. Martlew (ed.) *The Psychology of Written Language*. New York, NY: Wiley.

Matthews, J. (1999) *The Art of Childhood and Adolescence: The Construction of Meaning*. London: Falmer Press.

Matthews, J. (2003) *Drawing and Painting: Children and Visual Representation*. London: Paul Chapman.

Moyles, J. (1994) *The Excellence of Play*. Buckingham: Open University Press.

Nutbrown, C. (2006) *Threads of Thinking: Young Children Learning and the Role of Early Education*. London: Paul Chapman Publishing.

Pahl, K. (1999) *Transformations: Meaning-making in Nursery Education*. Stoke-on-Trent: Trentham Books.

Pahl, K. and Rowsell, J. (2005) *Literacy and Education: Understanding the New Literacy Studies in the Classroom*. London: Paul Chapman Publishing.

Qualifications and Curriculum Authority (2005) *Continuing the Learning Journey*. London: QCA.

Qualifications and Curriculum Authority/Department for Education and Employment (2000) *Curriculum Guidance for the Foundation Stage*. London: DfEE.

Rogoff, B. (2003) *The Cultural Nature of Human Development*. Oxford: Oxford University Press.

Sylva, K., Melhuish, E., Sammons, P., Siraj-Blatchford, I. and Taggart, B. (2004) *The Effective Provision of Pre-School Education (EPPE) Project. Technical Paper 12. The Final Report*. London: DfES/Institute of Education, University of London.

Vygotsky, L.S. (1930) The pre-history of written language, in M. Cole, V. John-Steiner, S. Scribner and E. Souberman (eds) (1978) *Mind in Society*, Cambridge, MA: Harvard University Press.

Vygotsky, L.S. (1978) *Mind in Society*. Cambridge, MA: Harvard University Press.

Suggested further reading

Carruthers, E. and Worthington, M. (2006) *Children's Mathematics: Making Marks, Making Meaning* (2nd edn). London: Sage Publications.

Kress, G. (1997) *Before Writing: Re-thinking the Paths to Literacy*. London: Routledge.

Matthews, J. (2003) *Drawing and Painting: Children and Visual Representation*. London: Paul Chapman.

Pahl, K. (1999) *Transformations: Meaning-making in Nursery Education*. Stoke-on-Trent: Trentham Books.

13 Planning for learning – children and teachers

Janet Moyles

Cameo 1

(Response from a newly qualified teacher when asked by students what had been her most successful strategy for dealing with children's learning.)

'Planning lessons thoroughly in writing over the day, week and half-term. This gave me the confidence to know where I was heading. It also meant I could let the children in on what they're supposed to learn and that made it all much easier. I could give the children some information to start with and then add details later in the lesson – otherwise they would have got swamped and switched off.'

Cameo 2

Pip, a student teacher working with a class of 5-year-olds, is dreading today's plenary session. Yesterday, the children all shouted out at once and the whole thing ended in disarray. Worse still, the teacher had tried to be nice to her and tell her that everyone has 'failures' and it was 'not too bad'. The trouble is that she can't think of any other way to plan the plenary. To save a bit of time, Pip uses history as the focus of the literacy work and has been relieved to see that this appears to have worked well and the children have enjoyed describing, drawing and labelling the artifacts. Now comes the plenary and three pairs of children are given the opportunity to explain what they did. Pip notices that the second of the pairs treats the descriptive task rather like a quiz and the children give the rest of the class clues like 'I'm thinking of a word that begins with B' and 'The word sounds like red and you go to sleep in it'. All the children are entranced by this presentation and the plenary goes smoothly. This becomes planned into the plenary session as a key feature solving Pip's earlier problem.

Introduction

It may seem that the legislated curriculum determines all children's learning and our teaching in the Foundation and Key Stages. In reality the curriculum is really an overview of what should be taught in general during a term or year: it is the teacher's job to translate it into learning activities for the particular children in a class, bearing in mind what they already know and can do. This applies whether the children are subject to the *National Curriculum* or to the *Early Years Foundation Stage* (EYFS: DfES 2006). The results are what are usually called medium- to short-term written plans which break down what it is possible to cover in a week or two and then daily (Woodward 2001). These are the nuts and bolts of teaching and learning and hold together the relationship between what is taught, what is learned and the required curriculum. They build on what has gone before and allow teachers to link the assessment of aspects of learning with the next set of teaching and learning activities (see Chapter 17).

Campbell and Neill (1994) reported that primary teachers spend on average 10.5 hours a week on planning (out of a 52.6 hour week) – a lot of time so it's worthwhile getting it 'right'. Although time-consuming, written planning is eminently worthwhile for the teacher and children (see Cameo 1) it means that we think through clearly what is needed and correlate our own and the children's interests and dispositions to the overall curriculum. As we saw in Cameo 2, all planning should be flexible so that new ideas can be absorbed and used when something triggers a useful change. But as Woodward (2001: 1) suggests 'plans are just plans. They're not legally binding. We don't have to stick to them come hell or high water. They are there to help us shape the space, time and learning.'

Primary teachers usually plan the programme of activities (or lessons) with three specific things in mind:

- children's existing (individual and collective) knowledge and interests (often specific to the age group);
- curriculum intentions (the legislated curriculum, EYFS and schools' guidelines);
- the teacher's own interests, strengths, motivations and professional responsibilities.

Each operates to both support and yet equally constrain the others. For example, whatever the teacher's curriculum intentions, the children often have their own agenda (as Cameo 2 shows) and making as good a match as possible between them is a crucial yet challenging planning feat. It involves teachers in:

- having a good knowledge of a particular class of children as well as an understanding of children's development (including cognitive as discussed in Chapter 6 and Dean 2005);
- detailed and thoughtful planning and implementation of activities based on knowledge of children and curriculum;
- undertaking interpretation and analysis of children's experiences and responses and evaluating outcomes, often occurring through observation (see Chapter 6).

These three areas are the focus of this chapter and they are approached from the practical angle of offering a range of different kinds of thinking about curriculum planning. First, we need to clarify what is meant by 'curriculum'.

Curriculum

Very broadly, it could be said that the curriculum is everything the child experiences in the context of schooling which is intended to foster learning. But 'everything' is a very tall order and clearly there is a wealth of knowledge in the world which it would be impossible to transmit to every child everywhere. The school curriculum tends to operate first on thinking about subjects, such as English, science, geography, technology, art and the rest, and then within these certain concepts are apparent, e.g. form and structure, grammar, change, and so on. The 'subject' curriculum, therefore, is only a part of a broader overall curriculum intended to ensure that children are required to think about and understand some of the major influences we experience, and have experienced, in the everyday world.

Schools also have a 'hidden' curriculum, which centres around those aspects which children and teachers cultivate within their more informal relationships but which contribute to the general ethos of the school and through which incidental learning often occurs, for example, children learning games from each other in the playground (Bishop and Curtis 2001).

Curriculum processes should involve the children in many learning experiences of which knowing, thinking, doing, communicating and remembering are some main features. We know that any curriculum 'works' when, as Bennett *et al.* (1984) suggest, children can give evidence that they are:

- acquiring new knowledge and skills;
- using their existing knowledge and skills in different contexts;
- recognizing and solving problems;
- practising what they know;
- revising and replaying what they know in order to remember it.

What we attempt to do as teachers is to ensure through our planning that all of these processes are engaged in by children during most of the school day in balanced proportions. This will be achieved through planning activities to develop particular skills, e.g. around individual subjects, such as science, or around predetermined structures like the NLS and NNS. The balance comes through ensuring, for example, that children don't spend all day practising something they can already do, which is often the case with activities like worksheets – investigating a problem will be a better way of exploring a concept. Bennett *et al.*'s five-point list is a very useful checklist for examining a day's or week's plans in relation to the quality of children's experiences.

Planning for learning

In some schools, planning is undertaken strictly in relation to the subject being taught, something which tends to happen most in the final two years of KS2. In other settings, particularly Foundation Stage settings, a number of subjects or areas of learning can be incorporated into 'themes', such as 'Weather', 'Travel Agents' or 'Light'. With activities planned in this way, close attention needs to be paid to ensuring that children understand fully the key concepts involved and can apply their understanding to new situations.

Of course, there is similarly the danger that with ten curriculum subjects, general curriculum aspects, such as citizenship, personal/social education and assessment procedures, will mean that the children's understanding will be shallow and superficial as we rush them and ourselves into the next focus. This only emphasizes the need for medium- and short-term planning to be clear and realistic with consideration of the key concepts which need to be taught and learned (Kenyon 2004).

There are a few 'golden rules' for planning medium- and short-term curriculum experiences whatever the basis of the planning:

1   Start with something from which children can have an immediate experience – something to DO. (Torches and a darkened area of the room, or a 'Colour Walk' around the local area could lead into much useful science teaching with older children and coverage of knowledge and understanding of the world with younger children.)

2   Children must be given opportunities to offer their suggestions to the planning – it gives them some responsibility from the outset and the teacher has the security of knowing that activities will be within the children's interests and experiences. For example, knowing that your quiz approach to the plenary has been taken up by the teacher (Cameo 2) will both motivate the children and enhance their self-esteem.

3   Relate the activities to children's lives and experiences. It is well known that children learn from a basis of things which have meaning to them and make 'human sense' (Donaldson 1992). Teaching about the Aztecs or Ancient Egypt will require a great deal of work *from the teacher*, yet who is it who is supposed to be learning? At the very least children need to access relevant sites on the Internet, see plenty of pictures or CD/DVDs of people and places, handle artefacts and have drama/role play opportunities. These are not frills but key ingredients to effective learning.

4   Include within curriculum plans:

- content – subject and wider curriculum, including reference to attainment and outcomes;
- skills and processes children should use and develop (and cross-curricular links);
- the main concepts to be covered;
- timings, what will happen when;
- resources, practical and human;
- points at which assessment will be undertaken;
- assessment procedures/practices;
- health and safety considerations;
- evaluation.

(See also Butt 2003: 6–7 for other detailed ideas.)

These may be done all on one large plan, or different smaller plans showing how subjects or concepts integrate with each other. One example of this would be something like 'time' which is integral to history, mathematics, geography and the science curriculum.

5 Pin weekly and daily plans on the wall – this constant reminder to children and others who enter the classroom, often prompts the appearance of relevant books, websites, pictures, objects, and so on. It allows children the opportunity for prediction and gives an indication of what they are intended to learn.

6 Try to introduce the focus of any new plans at the end of a week, then spend time talking over the potential learning with the children. Children may well use the weekend to seek out useful books or Internet resources or talk it over with adults and older siblings. It is also your starting point for what children already know and can save a lot of unnecessary time and planning in teaching aspects which are already within the children's existing understanding.

7 Involve the children in constantly *reviewing* progress: what they have learned and what more there is to do and understand in the time available. This not only ensures everyone remains focused but means that planning each day's activities is done on the basis of what children already know.

8 Allow children with specific interests to follow these within the planned work and mark these on your overall plan. This is particularly important where some children's interest may be waning and personal motivation is required.

An example of a medium-term plan is given in Figure 13.1. How far does it appear to meet the requirement of the list above? What might be added in order to make is more comprehensive?

Support staff and specialist teaching

Needless to say, it is important to use the human resources available to support your teaching. Teaching assistants (TAs), some with specialized knowledge, have burgeoned in our primary schools over the last few years (Moyles and Suschitzky 1997 and Chapter 16).

Some schools are now operating specialist teaching time, when the school's subject specialists work with different classes or groups of children. Many primary schools operate practices, such as 'setting' for maths, English or Science, which is a way of ensuring that children of different abilities receive teaching focused on their specific needs. However, many primary schools still operate a one-teacher/one-class system with teachers being required to teach all subjects to all abilities.

Detailed planning and implementation

The emphasis on children 'doing' and playing, is particularly vital with 3–7-year-olds and for older children should only gradually be replaced by more 'formal' learning approaches (Moyles 2005 and Chapter 12).

Primary children who occupy too much time being instructed or working at pencil and paper activities will soon get bored and may, at best, simply not learn and, at worst,

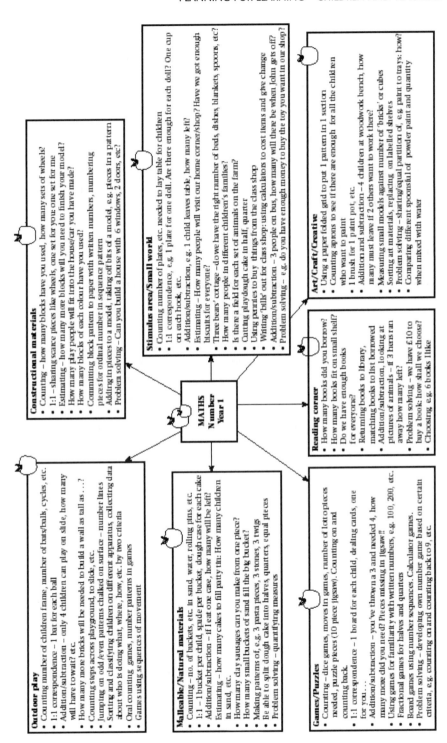

Constructional materials
- Counting – how many blocks have you used, how many sets of wheels?
- 1:1 correspondence – 1 bat for one ball, one set for me
- Addition/subtraction – how many more blocks will you need to finish your model?
- How many play people will fit into the house/car you have made?
- How many blocks of each colour have you used?
- Committing block pattern to paper with written numbers, numbering pieces for ordinal number in sequence pattern
- Adding in places to a model, taking off bits of a pattern, e.g. pieces in a pattern
- Problem solving – Can you build a house with 6 windows, 2 doors, etc?

Stimulus area/Small world
- Counting number of plates, etc. needed to lay table for children
- 1:1 correspondence, e.g. 1 plate for one doll. Are there enough for each doll? One cup on each bed, etc.
- Addition/subtraction, e.g. 1 child leaves table, how many left?
- Estimating – How many people will visit our home corner/shop? Have we got enough biscuits for everyone?
- Three bears' cottage – do we have the right number of beds, dishes, blankets, spoons, etc?
- How many people in different children's families?
- Is there a field for each set of animals on the farm?
- Cutting playdough cake in half, quarter
- Using pennies to buy things from the class shop
- Writing 'bills' out for class shop: using calculators to cost items and give change
- Addition/subtraction – 3 people on bus, how many will there be when John gets off?
- Problem solving – e.g. do you have enough money to buy the toy you want in our shop?

Art/Craft/Creative
- Using a paper folded grid to put 1 pattern in 1 section
- Counting aprons to see if there are enough for all the children who want to paint
- 1 brush for 1 paint pot, etc.
- Addition and subtraction – 4 children at woodwork bench, how many must leave if 2 others want to work there?
- Measuring small models against number of 'bricks' or cubes
- Sorting art materials, replacing on labelled shelves
- Problem solving – sharing/equal partition of, e.g. paint or trays: how?
- Comparing different spoonsful of powder paint and quantity when mixed with water

Outdoor play
- Counting number of children frame, number of bats/balls, cycles, etc.
- 1:1 correspondence – 1 bat for each ball
- Addition/subtraction – only 4 children can play on slide, how many will have to wait? etc.
- How many more bricks will be needed to build a wall as tall as ...?
- Counting steps across playground, to slide, etc.
- Jumping on odd /even patterns chalked on surface – number lines
- Sorting and classifying children on different apparatus, collecting data about who is doing what, where, how, etc. by two criteria
- Oral counting games, number patterns in games
- Games using sequences of movement

Malleable/Natural materials
- Counting – no. of buckets, etc. in sand, water, rolling pins, etc.
- 1:1 – 1 bucket per child, spade per bucket, dough case for each cake
- Addition/subtraction – if I eat one cake, how many will be left?
- Estimating – how many cakes will fit patty tin: How many children in sand, etc.
- How many clay sausages can you make from one piece?
- How many small buckets of sand fill the big bucket?
- Making patterns of, e.g. 3 pasta pieces, 3 stones, 3 twigs
- Be able to split dough cake into halves, quarters, equal pieces
- Problem solving – quantifying measures

Games/Puzzles
- Counting – dice games, moves in games, number of lotto pieces needed, puzzle pieces (10 piece jigsaw). Counting on and counting back.
- 1:1 correspondence – 1 board for each child, dealing cards, one for you...
- Addition/subtraction – you've thrown a 3 and needed 4, how many more did you need? Pieces missing in jigsaw?
- Using games for familiarity with written numbers, e.g. 100, 200, etc.
- Fractional games for halves and quarters
- Board games using number sequences. Calculator games.
- Problem solving – developing own number game based on certain criteria, e.g. counting on and counting back to 9, etc.

Reading corner
- How many books did you borrow?
- How many books fit on small shelf?
- Do we have enough books for everyone?
- Returning books to library, matching books to list borrowed
- Addition/subtraction, looking at pictures of animals – if 3 hens ran away how many left?
- Problem solving – we have £10 to buy a book: how shall we choose?
- Choosing, e.g. 6 books I like

MATHS
Number
Year 1

Figure 13.1 Medium-term plan

may generate discipline problems (see Chapter 19). Children presented with too much too soon may be so busy exploring new materials that the teacher's intentions are lost and the children's dispositions to learning affected adversely. Worksheet activities and continual exposition rarely enable children to be engaged actively in their own learning processes.

Long-term plans offer information about subjects or themes and include the concepts, processes and skills we are aiming for, but the heart of day-to-day teaching is to undertake some quite detailed planning of each particular activity to be carried out by the children. The chart shown in Figure 13.2 is one found helpful by beginner teachers to structure their activities, giving as it does opportunity to comment on both the children's activities and also on what the teacher or other adults will be doing. Students often need to recognize that children *can* learn without a continual adult presence (see Chapter 14) but that if you do want to work with individuals or groups this must be incorporated into the planning. As indicated in the Bennett *et al.* model earlier, activities will need different levels of teacher attention:

- *teacher intensive* – when children are undertaking new learning or the teacher is assessing existing learning;
- *teacher in attendance* – when children are engaged in applying knowledge and may need occasional teacher support;
- *teacher monitoring* – when children are practising skills and knowledge in relatively familiar situations requiring little teacher involvement;
- *teacher available* – when children are engaged in absorbing their own mastery and may need the teacher to tell or show an outcome at some stage.

The planning chart also ensures that each activity will need a specific introduction, something which develops it further, and a conclusion. The evaluation gives the basis for making decisions as to who has learned what and what is needed for progression to the next stage.

Remember with such planning charts that your AIMS are related to things you wish to achieve in the *slightly longer-term*, for example, 'Children should enjoy science and learn a

Session:		Date:	Time:	Curriculum Area:
Plan	**Comment**			
Aim				
Objectives				
NC links				
Resources				
Activity structure	**Timing**	**Teacher activity**	**Children's activity**	
Introduction				
Development				
Conclusion				
Evaluation – continued overleaf				

Figure 13.2 Chart for structuring activities

number of key concepts.' In contrast, OBJECTIVES are *short-term* related to what the children should have learned and done by the end of that activity – 'Children should be able to use their knowledge of light in order to explain how the beam falls on an object.'

Ready to teach?

The final level of planning is how you and the children are actually going to work together in the learning context. There are several phases in this interaction, summed up under the following headings and questions:

1 ENTERING STRATEGY
   What will be your starting point(s)? Introduction?
2 EXPLORATION MODE
   What exploration will the children undertake? What materials/resources will be available? How/by whom will they be set up?
3 CONTENT
   This will be as in your planning, but how will you tell the children what you intend them to learn as well as to do?
4 OWNERSHIP AND RESPONSIBILITY
   What level of ownership will the children have? What responsibilities? How will the children know what they are supposed to learn? How will these aspects be conveyed?
5 TEACHER STRATEGIES
   What will your role be? What will the role of TAs be? How will you and your TA interact/intervene in the activities and sustain/extend them?
6 EVALUATION AND ANALYSIS
   How/when/who will you observe to see what children were learning in relation to concepts covered and the objectives set? Will other adults be involved in observation and recording? Who? When during the activities?
7 REFLECTION/REVIEW/PLENARY MODE
   What opportunities will you provide for children to reflect on their learning and be part of its review/evaluation/analysis?
8 JUSTIFICATION
   What quality and standard of outcomes will you expect? How will the value of these be communicated to others (e.g. through display, website, records)?

It is necessary to consider different kinds of organizational strategies, for example, whether you introduce something to the whole class, give tasks to groups or pairs, or allow children free choice to explore materials for themselves.

It is vital that you and the children reflect on what you did and the success or otherwise of the outcomes (see Chapter 21).

Interpreting, analysing and evaluating children's experiences

What we are essentially assessing is to what extent the children (and we as teachers) have been able to do the following:

- reach the objectives set in planning;
- develop appropriate attitudes and opinions;
- reach high standards and offer quality outcomes;
- deal with the rates at which children learn;
- find out about children's strengths and weaknesses;
- understand what learning should take place next for children to progress;
- know what activities or experiences should now be provided or repeated and what differentiated experiences are needed for individual, or groups of, children.

These are then evaluated against longer-term aims to see what adjustments are required in planning. This process involves much interpretation of evidence and collection of data for written evaluations and records (see Chapter 17). Be careful that interpretations are as value-free and objective as possible (see Chapter 18).

Finding out about children's learning

Another main strategy for finding out about children's learning has to be through talking to them or getting them to write down what they did and what they think they learned. However, in analysing, interpreting and evaluating learning capabilities in this way, we need to remember that children's ability to understand it is not always matched in their written or oral performance. Children who can *give* an extensive oral explanation of an exciting science experiment often then write 'I put it in the cup and it disappeared. the end' [*sic*]. This happens right across the primary school particularly where fine motor development is slow and a child actually finds writing difficult if not actually physically painful. Just those very processes of *active learning* discussed in detail above, are nearly always more important to primary children than writing about tasks! After all, would you always want to write about what you had done, or would you rather move on to the next exciting learning adventure?

Finding other ways of analysing and evaluating what children know is vital, not least through planning classroom activities in such a way that you have time to *observe and record* (Edgington 2004 and Chapters 17 and 18). It is in active situations that children frequently illustrate more of their knowledge. For example, I well remember a boy who stood on the edge of a group of children attempting in a design technology lesson to make a pulley out of various items of 'found' materials. He chose to watch, and flatly refused to explain his reticence to become involved. After half-an-hour the group had still not managed to produce a pulley. Almost at the end of the session, the boy walked up to the table, picked up three or four items and rapidly and ingeniously made a working pulley. It would have been easy to have thought of him as dull, lazy, insecure, sullen or downright obstinate. This is just one example of how we must be sensitive to the different ways in which pupils' learn and perform (Hayes 2003).

Other ways in which children can demonstrate learning

As well as oral and written language outcomes, children could be expected to show different aspects of their learning in several other ways:

- drawings;
- poems (and other different forms of writing, e.g. acrostics);
- diagrams and charts;
- mind maps (Buzan 2003);
- composing lists;
- digital photographs, with or without children's captions;
- making booklets about different activities – 'This is what we learned when we worked with the sand … '; 'This is what we found out about Ancient Egypt';
- explaining to other children what to do;
- developing web-based communications;
- digital camera/video/audio recordings of activities;
- undertaking drama/role play;
- doing demonstrations for others.

However assessment is undertaken, you need to ensure that children are given opportunities:

- to *make their own ideas explicit*. Starting from what children know is vital in on-going planning (see Chapters 1 and 2);
- to produce *an end result* in different ways and *with several* alternative solutions. Investigations and problem-solving activities allow children to show physically what they 'know' (see Chapter 7);
- to explore ideas with peers – it is much easier to argue your points with peers than with adults particularly as children get older;
- *actively* to question their own thinking and undertake explorations in order to learn about their own misconceptions (see Chapter 6);
- to challenge their own outcomes through open-ended questioning 'What would happen if …?';
- to be part of situations in which they need to *generalize* in order to use and develop concepts;
- to *observe* rather than simply *look at* objects and artefacts and raise questions. Help children to detect relevant similarities as well as differences;
- to *achieve* by setting *goals for children* which are attainable with just the right amount of effort – this means knowing individual children's capabilities well – and telling them what they are intended to learn;
- to explore materials before expecting children to do something specific with them (Drake 2005);
- to apply their knowledge in a situation where they can succeed;
- to learn and use the appropriate vocabulary for each topic so that they have the means to explain their activities to you;
- to gather all the information they need in order to fulfil the demands of the

activity. We don't have to wait for children to re-invent the wheel every time but, having been told, children *must* be allowed to 'prove' whatever the concept is for themselves (Sotto 1994);

- to be part of the planning process;
- to be praised genuinely for achieving real learning.

The teacher's role

Teachers should give themselves plenty of opportunity for interpreting, analysing and assessing what their role has been in the children's learning and reflecting on it (see Chapter 21). The following questions will act as a conclusion to this chapter and also serve as a reminder of the importance of planning for children's learning on a daily and weekly basis.

Questions to set you thinking

1   How positive or otherwise do you feel about the curriculum activities you provided?
2   Did you present activities with enthusiasm and vigour?
3   In what ways did the teaching and learning appear successful/unsuccessful to you?
4   What did you learn – about planning, curriculum, children …?
5   Was the atmosphere generated in the classroom pleasant, task-oriented and positive?
6   How did you handle any challenges?
7   Were you more involved with the children in relation to supervision of *activities* or the management of *learning*?
8   Were your teaching strategies congruent with the objectives you set? Did you offer a structured sequence of experiences?
9   Were your interactions with children 'professional' and did you give and receive appropriate feedback?
10 How well did you communicate with children? Did you pace your talk appropriately and were your instructions (verbal and non-verbal) clear?
11 Did you make effective use of your time and energy?
12 Did you use a variety of teaching styles and strategies – exposition, different groupings, discussion, play and active learning, practice tasks, problem-solving, investigations …?
13 Have you marked, analysed and diagnosed children's learning errors and noted those who need support?
14 Have you made appropriate observations and evaluations of children's learning?
15 Have you and the children used the physical space and resources effectively, including ICT?
16 Would you have enjoyed the activities if you had been one of the children?
17 Have you discussed your progress with a mentor and noted points for professional development?
18 Have you enjoyed the experience of teaching – and learning?

References

Bennett, N., Desforge, G., Cockburn, A. and Wilkinson, B. (1984) *The Quality of Pupil Learning Experiences*. London: Lawrence Erlbaum.

Bishop, J. and Curtis, M. (2001) *Play Today in the Primary School Playground: Life, Learning and Creativity*. Buckingham: Open University Press.

Butt, G. (2003) *Lesson Planning*. London: Continuum.

Buzan, T. (2003) *The Mind Map Book: Radiant Thinking – Major Evolution in Human Thought*. London: BBC Active.

Campbell, R. and Neill, S. St.J. (1994) *Thirteen Hundred and Thirty Days: Final Report of a Pilot Study of Teacher Time in Key Stage 1*. Commissioned by the Assistant Masters and Mistresses Association. Coventry: University of Warwick.

Dean, J. (2005) *The Effective Primary School Classroom*. London: RoutledgeFalmer.

Department for Education and Skills (DfES) (2006) *The Early Years Foundation Stage: Consultation on a Single Quality Framework for Services to Children from Birth to Five*. London: DfES.

Donaldson, M. (1992) *Human Minds: An Exploration*. Glasgow: Penguin.

Drake, J. (2005) *Planning Children's Play and Learning in the Foundation Stage*. London: David Fulton.

Edgington, M. (2004) *The Foundation Stage Teacher in Action: Teaching 3-, 4-, and 5-Year-Olds* (3rd edn). London: Paul Chapman.

Hayes, D. (2003) *Planning, Teaching and Class Management in the Primary School*. London: David Fulton.

Kenyon, P. (2004) *Planning, Assessing and Record-Keeping*. Leamington Spa: Scholastic.

Moyles, J. (ed.) (2005) *The Excellence of Play* (2nd edn). Maidenhead: Open University Press.

Moyles, J. and Suschitzky, W. (1997) *Jills of All Trades: Teachers and Classroom Assistants Working Together in KS1*. London: University of Leicester/Association of Teachers and Lecturers.

Sotto, E. (1994) *When Teaching Becomes Learning: A Theory and Practice of Teaching*. London: Cassells.

Woodward, T. (2001) *Planning Lessons and Courses: Designing Sequences of work for the Language Classroom*. Cambridge: Cambridge University Press.

Suggested further reading

Drake, J. (2005) *Planning Children's Play and Learning in the Foundation Stage*. London: David Fulton. Particularly useful for those teachers of FS and KS1 children.

Kenyon, P. (2004) *Planning, Assessing and Record-Keeping*. Leamington Spa: Scholastic. A short, concise introduction to the key issues.

Woodward, T. (2001) *Planning Lessons and Courses: Designing Sequences of work for the Language Classroom*. Cambridge: Cambridge University Press. This is an excellent and very comprehensive book which should be read by all novice teachers. It offers clear explanations about the teacher's key principles.

14 Developing young children as self-regulating learners

David Whitebread and Penny Coltman

Cameo 1

In a Year R class, a group of children work together to solve a jigsaw puzzle. Initially the children all begin tackling the task separately, competing for pieces and hoarding. As the puzzle remains incomplete the children begin to co-operate, using non-verbal communication as they offer pieces to each other. Eventually the children begin to talk to each other about the task. One child takes charge of the picture on the lid of the puzzle box, indicating to others where key elements of the picture should be located. Other children check these instructions, comparing the picture with the puzzle on the floor. As the puzzle reaches completion children negotiate the correct positions of pieces, supporting each other as they reach a shared goal.

Cameo 2

A group of children in a Year R class are working independently on individual writing tasks, when Polly pokes Rosie with a pencil. Rosie asks Polly to stop. When the poking continues, Rosie turns to Adam, who is sitting to the other side of her, for support. Adam prefers not to tackle Polly directly, but instead approaches another child Angela, asking her whether or not she thinks that it would help the situation if he swapped seats with Rosie. Angela merely turns to Polly, explaining that poking with a pencil can hurt and that she should stop doing this to Rosie. Her calm approach successfully diffuses the situation and the children return to their writing.

Introduction

The aim of good teachers should be to make themselves redundant. If we are effectively to educate our young children, we must enable them to become independent, or what might more properly be termed self-regulating learners. There is currently widespread interest in fostering 'independent learning' among young children, as attested by a number of publications (Featherstone and Bayley 2001; Williams 2003) and by recent official government guidelines. In this chapter, we examine the psychological research literature concerning the nature of independent or self-regulated learning and report the findings of a two-year research project.

What is meant by 'independent learning'?

The education policy context

Recent initiatives, circulars and curriculum documents from various UK government agencies have offered a range of suggestions as to what independent or self-regulated learning might involve. In the revised QTS Standards entitled Qualifying to Teach (TDA 2006), for example, teacher trainees are required, under Standard S3.3.3, to 'teach clearly structured lessons or sequences of work which interest and motivate pupils and which make learning objectives clear to pupils ... [and] promote active and independent learning that enables pupils to think for themselves, and to plan and manage their own learning'.

In the *Curriculum Guidance for the Foundation Stage* (DfEE/QCA 2000), one of the stated 'Principles for early years education' (2000: 3) is that there should be 'opportunities for children to engage in activities planned by adults and also those that they plan and initiate themselves'.

It is clear from these and other governmental policy statements that there is currently a strong commitment to the area of independent learning. However, there is also a need for clear definition. In some policy guidelines, e.g. the recent *Early Years Foundation Stage* (DfES 2006), the emphasis is more on helping children with personal independence skills and becoming an independent *pupil*, i.e. being able to function in a classroom without being overly dependent on adult help. This is very distinct, however, from the concern to help children to develop as independent *learners*, that is, being able to take control of and responsibility for their own learning. It is for this reason that the term 'self-regulation' is preferred, with its emphasis on the learner taking control and ownership of their own learning.

The context of the classroom

While a commitment to encouraging children to become self-regulating learners is very common among primary school teachers, at the level of everyday classroom realities there are a number of problematic issues. The need to maintain an orderly classroom, combined with the pressures of time and resources, and teachers' perceptions of external expectations from headteachers, parents and government agencies, can often militate against the support of children's independence.

Evidence from a study across the FS and KS1 conducted by one of the present authors (Hendy and Whitebread 2000) very much supported this view. The early years teachers interviewed shared a commitment to encouraging greater independence in learning among young children, but held a wide spectrum of views about the essential key elements within it, and of their role in fostering the necessary skills and dispositions. There was a dominant concern, nevertheless, with the *organizational* element of children's independence, as opposed to any concern with cognitive or emotional areas. Perhaps most significant, however, was the finding that the children appeared to become more, rather than less, dependent on their teachers during their first few years in school.

Galton (1989) has argued that the situation is not unresolvable. Tension in relation to independence arises, he claims, when teachers expect the children to negotiate their learning, but are not willing to allow any negotiation in relation to control. He cites examples of teachers who have successfully opened up the rules of classroom behaviour to shared decision-making, with a consequent higher level of independent thinking and working becoming apparent.

What is also clear, however, is that if primary school teachers are successfully to foster independent learning in their classrooms, a clear understanding needs to be developed of the skills and dispositions involved in self-regulated learning, and of the pedagogical practices which are most likely to foster these.

Psychological approaches to self-regulated learning

Within cognitive developmental psychology in the past 30 years or so, there has been a very considerable body of research evidence related to the development of children as independent learners. Within the psychological literature this has been variously characterized as 'learning how to learn' (Nisbet and Shucksmith 1986), 'reflection' (Yussen 1985), 'self-regulation' (Schunk and Zimmerman 1994), and 'metacognition' (Metcalfe and Shimamura 1994), all of which are concerned with children's developing self-awareness and control of their own mental processing. What has emerged is a body of research and theory that suggests that it is this aspect of development which is crucially responsible for individual differences in children's development as learners. Certainly, it is well established that metacognitive deficits are common among children with learning difficulties (Sugden 1989).

This work has been inspired by two traditions within developmental psychology. First, is the socio-cultural tradition founded on the work of the Russian psychologist, Vygotsky (1978, 1986). For Vygotsky, the development of children's learning was a process of moving from other-regulation (or performing a task while supported by an adult or peer) to self-regulation (performing a task on one's own). A considerable body of research work in recent years has investigated the processes by which adults support children's learning. This research has largely endorsed Vygotsky's approach (see Chapter 6). Crucially, research has shown that a key characteristic of a good scaffolder is the ability sensitively to withdraw support as the child becomes able to carry out the task more independently, or to take over more of the regulatory role for themselves (Schaffer 2004).

Learning for Vygotsky can therefore be characterized as a process of internalization, whereby the procedures for successful completion of a task are initially modelled and articulated by an adult or more experienced peer, with the child then gradually becoming able to talk themselves through the task (the common phenomenon of child self-commentary thus takes on particular significance!). Finally, the child can fully self-regulate using internal speech or abstract thought.

The second tradition is the information processing approach and specifically, the early work in the 1960s and 1970s of Flavell *et al.* (1966) on the development of children's memory abilities. Young children under the age of 7 were found to be capable of carrying out a taught memory strategy, but incapable of producing that strategy for use spontaneously (or independently!). This led to Flavell's (1979) development of a model of 'metamemory' and Brown's (1987) model of metacognition, which was characterized as consisting of three related elements:

- *'metacognitive experience'*: the on-line monitoring or self-awareness of mental processing, and reflections upon it;
- *'metacognitive knowledge'*: the knowledge which is gradually accumulated about one's own mental processing, tasks and cognitive strategies for dealing with tasks;
- *'self-regulation'*: the metacognitive control of mental processing, so that strategies are developed and used appropriately in relation to tasks.

There have been two significant later developments in this area of research. First, there has been a broadening of notions of self-regulation from the purely cognitive concerns of Vygotsky, Flavell and Brown to include emotional, social and motivational aspects. The work of Goleman (1995) on emotional intelligence, for example, is part of this trend. Understandings emerging from neuroscience also support a model that integrates emotional and cognitive aspects of self-regulation. The development of metacognitive and self-regulatory functions appears to be related to developments in the frontal lobes (Barkley 1997).

Second, there has been the recognition of metacognitive processes in very young children. In a recent and very comprehensive overview, Bronson (2000) demonstrates that the development of metacognitive and self-regulatory processes is fundamental to the whole range of young children's psychological growth. She describes in detail extensive research which has explored the emotional, prosocial, cognitive and motivational developments in self-regulation throughout the different phases of early childhood.

In our own recent research (the Cambridgeshire Independent Learning, or CIndLe, project;[1] Whitebread *et al.* 2005), we worked with 32 Foundation Stage teachers over two years and collected approximately 100 hours of video, and numerous other occasional observations. From this data, 705 events have been recorded and documented which show evidence of self-regulatory and metacognitive behaviour. As the average duration of these events is a number of minutes, and in some cases as much as 20–30 minutes, this average rate of incidence of around seven events per hour is a striking testimony of the pervasiveness of self-regulatory and metacognitive behaviours in children in the 3–5 age range.

As part of this project a checklist of self-regulatory behaviours (CHecklist of Independent Learning Development, or CHILD 3–5) was developed consisting of 22 statements describing the most common and significant achievements in cognitive, motivational, emotional and social areas of development within the 3–5 age group (see Table 14.1). A number of the statements from the checklist were evidenced with considerable frequency, some being present in as many as a third of all the recorded events. For example, the statements of abilities for which the most numerous observations were recorded included the following:

- can control attention and resist distraction;
- can speak about how they have done something or what they have learnt;
- can make reasoned choices and decisions;
- develops own ways of carrying out tasks.

Of these 705 self-regulatory events documented in the project, 582 (i.e. 82.6 per cent) contained an element of specifically metacognitive activity. This provides initial and substantial evidence of the clear ability of young children to engage in a wide range of metacognitive and self-regulatory activities.

The pedagogy of self-regulation

Collins *et al.* (1989) provided an extensive review of approaches which they termed 'cognitive apprenticeship' models of teaching and learning whereby, using various techniques, adults help to make the processes of learning explicit to children, and encourage their self-regulation.

Several other useful pedagogical techniques deriving from this broad tradition have been investigated and developed with Primary-aged children. These include:

- 'co-operative groupwork' (Forman and Cazden 1985): a range of techniques involving children in collaborative activities which oblige them to articulate their own understandings, evaluate their own performance and be reflective about their own learning. (See Figure 14.1 for an example from the CIndLe project);
- 'reciprocal teaching' (Palincsar and Brown 1984): a structured procedure which involves teachers modelling the teaching of a particular task to children who are then asked to teach the activity to their peers;
- 'self-explanations' (Siegler 2002): an instructional practice which requires children to give 'how' and 'why' explanations about, for example, scientific phenomena or the events in a story, and then asks children to give explanations of their own and an adult's reasoning;
- 'self-assessment' (Black and Wiliam 1998): a range of pedagogical ideas involving children's self-assessment of their own learning, including, for example, children making their own choices about the level of difficulty of tasks to be undertaken, and selecting their best work for reflective portfolios;
- 'debriefing' (Leat and Lin 2003): a range of techniques for reflecting upon an activity or piece of learning including 'encouraging pupils to ask questions', 'making pupils explain themselves' and 'communicating the purpose of lessons'.

Within the UK, Brooker's (1996) analysis of her work with a Reception class over a year provides an excellent example of this kind of work. She began, before the start of the school year and during the first term, by interviewing the children on a number of occasions, asking them, among other things, 'Why do children go to school?, 'What are you good at?', 'What do you like doing best?' and 'How do you think you learn things?' In the spring term she moved on to develop the habit of self-assessment, training herself to withhold the usual excessive praise bestowed on children of this age and instead asking them 'How do you think you got on then?' At the end of the second term she asked the children 'What would you like to learn next term, after the holidays?' and this began a final phase during which, by a process of constant discussion and negotiation, the children gradually acquired more and more ownership of the curriculum and procedures of the classroom. Progressively, as the year went on, their views influenced the content and organization of their school day.

Table 14.1 Checklist of Independent Learning Development 3-5

Statement	Exemplar event	Description
		Emotional elements of independent learning
Can speak about others behaviour and consequences	Warning about paper clips	Three children are playing in the workshop area. A girl that appears to be leading the game is explaining to the rest of the group how dangerous paper clips can be, modelling the correct way of using them
Tackles new tasks confidently	Counting to a 100 Making big sums Counting backwards Counting forever	A sequence of events representing a clear progression in the way children spontaneously set up and solve increasingly more challenging mathematical tasks after being provided with enough cognitive structuring by the teacher
Can control attention and resist distraction	Fixing a bike	A child has entered the workshop area and has decided that he is going to fix the bike that has been placed as part of the setting. The child remains on task for an extended period of time using different tools and checking the outcomes of his actions.
Monitors progress and seeks help appropriately	Building a bridge	A group of children have decided to build a bridge to get to a castle but the bridge keeps falling down. The 'builders' actively seek the advice of other children that stop in front of the construction to see what is happening
Persists in the face of difficulties	Finding the screwdriver	A girl has entered Santa's workshop area. She is looking for the screwdriver to make some toys. She actively looks for it and asks for the other children's help. After 15 minutes where she appears to have been engaged in other activities, she finally finds it. 'I found the screwdriver!'
		Prosocial elements of independent learning
Negotiates when and how to carry out tasks	Planning the game Playing in small group	A group of children have been encouraged to create a game using a hoop and a ball. The children actively discuss who is going to hold the hoop and who is going to throw the ball. They all agree they have to take turns. 'Otherwise it wouldn't be fair', says one of the children. They try out the game before teaching it to the rest of the class
Can resolve social problems with peers	Negotiating number of children	Too many children are in the workshop area. A child becomes aware of the situation and acts as a negotiator trying to determine who can stay and who has to leave. He uses different questions to solve the problem: 'Who doesn't want to be here?', 'Who's been here the longest?'
Is aware of feelings of others; helps and comforts	Making cards	A girl helps a boy make a card. She doesn't 'do' it for him but has been asked to show him what to do. During the sequence she is very helpful and 'keeps an eye on him'. She does not take over, yet seems to take pride in the helping process
Engages in independent co-operative activities with peers	Three Little Pigs crisis	Children are playing Three Little Pigs in the role play area. A 'crisis' has been introduced. The Big Bad Wolf has stopped the electricity getting to the house. The children are exploring using torches and working out what to do

Statement	Exemplar event	Description
Shares and takes turns independently	Taking turns	A group of girls are playing a lottery game. They spontaneously take turns asking: 'Whose turn is it?' and reminding each other: 'It's your turn now!'
Cognitive elements of independent learning		
Is aware of own strengths and weaknesses	Counting beans with Jack	A girl is counting beans using a puppet (Jack). Being aware that there are too many beans to count, she decided to put some of the beans away so Jack can 'count them better'
Can speak about how they have done something or what they have learnt	Drawing a fire	Two boys sit side by side at the drawing table and discuss how to draw a fire. One says it is a zig-zag shape and draws an example, saying that his mummy told him it was like this. The other disputes this and says it goes little and then very big, drawing small downward lines and long vertical lines. They talk about how fire is spread and how the flames move
Can speak about planned activities	The castle	Two girls have decided that they want to make a castle in the play area. Being prompted by the teacher's questions they verbalize what they want to put in the castle, the materials they need and what to do first
Can make reasoned choices and decisions	Writing an animal story	Two boys collaborating on a story decide between them that they want it to feature a particular animal so send someone in search of a picture to copy
Asks questions and suggests answers	Skeletons	A group were interested in skeletons, and the Nursery Nurse helped them to draw around one another and copy pictures from books to fill in their skeletons. The children felt the bones in their bodies as they drew. They asked questions about the bones and in some cases one child answered another's question
Uses a strategy previously modelled	Peer support in writing	Two boys support another with his writing when they see him struggle. They communicate clearly, using strategies they have heard from their teacher, and are sensitive to his feelings.
Uses language previously heard for own purposes	Writing messages	Two girls help a boy who also wants to write. They track what he is doing and point to an example of a message (written by a child) on the wall and draw attention to the individual letters, naming them for the boy.
Motivational elements of independent learning		
Initiates activities	Making computers	Two children decide to make a computer out of a cardboard box. They work collaboratively together and persist when things don't go well e.g.: working out how to join the box (computer screen) to the table
Finds own resources without adult help	Goldilocks and the three bears	The children have decided to recreate the story of Goldilocks and the three bears. They have found three boxes of different sizes for the beds, three bowls and spoons for the bears and a pot to cook the porridge

Statement	Exemplar event	Description
Develops own ways of carrying out tasks	Making books	One child made a 'book' by sellotaping together three small sheets of computer paper. She drew simple illustrations and asked her teacher to scribe the story for her. It was a perfect story: 'The cat was lost. The flower was lonely. The dog had no friends. The sun came out and cheered them all up.' The book was read to the class and by four weeks later, half the class had made books using the same method
Plans own tasks, targets and goals	Christmas wrapping	A group of children have turned the play area into Santa's workshop. They have decided that they are going to wrap presents; they have found resources, and they have negotiated their roles.
Enjoys solving problems and challenges	Building a bridge	The teacher has set up a problem: the children need to get a treasure located at the other side of the room, crossing a river filled with crocodiles. The children decide to build a bridge and they co-operate to achieve their plan

Figure 14.1 Children's collaborative activities

Within the CIndLe project, we also explored effective pedagogies to encourage aspects of self-regulation. What became clear was that we needed to think broadly and look at the overall ethos of the classroom, and this led to organizing the classroom in ways which gave children access to resources, allowed them to make choices and gave them responsibility for the activities in particular areas of the classroom. We also needed to examine the ways in which we interacted with the children, making sure that we asked more genuine open-ended and challenging questions, that we explicitly discussed learning, emotions and self-regulation strategies and that we engaged in sustained conversations with the children within which we explored and developed their ideas (what Neil Mercer and colleagues have referred to as 'exploratory talk': Littleton *et al.* 2005).

Finally, from this work emerged four underlying principles which tied together all of these practices in ways which explained their importance when considered in the light of what we know about children as learners:

1   Emotional warmth and security – attachment.
2   Feelings of control.
3   Cognitive challenge.
4   Articulation of learning.

1 Emotional warmth and security – attachment

Secure emotional attachments in young children have been found to be associated with a range of positive emotional, social and cognitive outcomes. The evidence also suggests that this emotional security is the product of the child experiencing early relationships, which are emotionally warm, sensitive and predictable (see Durkin 1995, for a review).

> **Cameo 3**
>
> In a nursery setting, Zac is desperately keen to engage in some 'firemen' role play with his friend and clearly views the wearing of the fireman's outfit as essential.

He successfully puts on the helmet, but experiences much more difficulty with the jacket. Holding the coat upside down he attempts unsuccessfully to locate the sleeves. He twists the jacket this way and that, resulting in ever greater bodily contortions.

Zac's teacher does not intervene until he asks for help, as she is sensitive to his wish to persevere with the problems presented by the jacket. But she does offer encouragement through non-verbal interactions, remaining at hand to ensure he does not become distressed. Zac responds to the verbal encouragements of his teacher, maintaining determination and persistence.

At last the jacket is on, and Zac and his teacher enjoy a shared 'thumbs up' celebration of a goal achieved (Figure 14.2).

Figure 14.2 Thumbs up!

This cameo is an excellent example of a teacher providing emotional support which enables a child to learn that perseverance can be a pleasurable experience and lead to a successful outcome. Often in the absence of this kind of support, either the element of perseverance is lost as adults complete the task for the child or pleasure is replaced by frustration and the task is abandoned. More generally, to provide emotional warmth and security in the classroom environment, teachers can:

- provide a model of emotional self-regulation, talking through their own difficulties with the children;
- show that they appreciate effort at least as much as products;
- show an interest in the children as people, and share aspects of their own personal lives;
- negotiating frameworks for behaviour with the children which are seen to be fair and supportive.

2 Feelings of control

Feeling in control of their environment and their learning is fundamental to children developing confidence in their abilities, and the ability to respond positively to set-backs and challenges. Human beings are quite literally control freaks. An early experiment carried out in California by Watson and Ramey (1972) involved the parents of 8-month-old babies being given special cots which came complete with attractive and colourful 'mobiles'. The parents were asked to put their babies in the cots for specified periods each day for a few weeks. In some of the cots the mobiles either did not move, or moved around on a timed schedule. But in other cots the mobile was wired up to a pillow, so that the mobile would move whenever the baby exerted pressure on the pillow. At the end of the experiment, the parents of the babies who had experienced these 'contingency mobiles' wanted to pay the research team large amounts of money to keep the cots because their babies had enjoyed these so much. Here's another example.

Cameo 4

Thomas's nursery class is visited by a photographer. On returning to his classroom Thomas collects a digital camera and persuades a group of friends to act as subjects for his photography. He arranges his 'group' and uses the language of the photographer to encourage smiles. Some children are happy to comply and agree to sit as asked, waiting until Thomas has taken his photo, but others re-arrange themselves and wander off. Regardless of these varied responses the 'photographer' sticks to his task (see Figure 14.3).

Figure 14.3 After the photographer's visit

Here is a good example of a teacher allowing sufficient flexibility for a child who has been inspired by a particular experience to pursue this interest. Allowing opportunities for child-initiated activities enhances children's sense of ownership of and responsibility for their own learning. It is also important to give children opportunities to make real choices and decisions about classroom activities and procedures.

3 Cognitive challenge

The third underlying principle of good practice, which encourages self-regulatory and independent learning, is the presence of cognitive challenge. Children spontaneously set themselves challenges in their play and, given a choice, will often choose a task which is more challenging than the task which an adult might have thought was appropriate. Providing children with achievable challenges, and supporting them so they can meet them, is the most powerful way to encourage positive attitudes to learning and the children's independent ability to take on challenging tasks.

> **Cameo 5**
>
> As part of a Year R project on rainforests, a jungle role play area has been created by the teacher and children together. The area is used by the teacher to promote a number of problem-solving discussions and activities. A process is developed of children discussing and 'playing out' their suggested solutions, exploring consequences and evaluating strategies. One problem is that poachers have entered the jungle, killing and capturing the rainforest animals. What could be done to solve this problem?
>
> As children offer ideas, the class is encouraged to listen carefully to them and then to act upon them. Children make a range of suggestions, including dressing up like animals to frighten the poachers and making a helicopter to spot and trap them. The teacher values every suggestion, giving particular credit to ideas which develop those of other children.
>
> Here we see the teacher taking children's proposed solutions to a challenging and engaging set of problems and helping them to think through and develop their ideas. The activity is set up to be highly collaborative, with the children working in teams. The children are, therefore, encouraged to take intellectual risks in an emotionally supportive context. More generally, to promote this kind of cognitive challenge, it is helpful to require children to plan and organize activities themselves, avoiding too early adult intervention.

4 Articulation of learning

Finally, it is clear that if children are going to become increasingly aware of their own mental processing, thinking and learning needs to be made explicit by adults, and the children themselves need to learn to talk about and to represent their learning and thinking.

> **Cameo 6**
>
> A nursery practitioner takes an opportunity to photograph a group of children as they engage in a self-initiated role play, packing a rucksack with cameras,

binoculars and a map. The children explain that they are going outside to find a Giant's Castle.

Later the practitioner shows the children the photographs taken earlier encouraging them to talk about their memories, reliving a shared experience through conversation. 'How did you use the map to help you to find the Castle?', 'What did you see through the binoculars?'

In this episode the teacher is using the immediacy of the digital camera technology to stimulate an extended conversation with a group of children. As she was not an active participant in the children's imaginative play, she is able to ask genuine questions and stimulate the children to reflect upon their thinking and decision-making.

Conclusion

When independent learning has been advocated or discussed in education, often the focus has been on purely organizational issues to do with children being able to get on with their work without being over-dependent on the teacher. In this chapter, however, we have argued that encouraging children to become independent or self-regulated learners involves more than this and is fundamental to children developing as *learners*.

There are structural reasons why facilitating genuinely self-regulated learning in primary classrooms is not straightforward. However, we believe that it is possible and, certainly, the 32 teachers who worked with us in the CIndLe project, and other teachers involved in other projects, have managed to achieve outstanding results and have found ways of developing their practice which have been enormously beneficial.

Our experience has been that whenever a teacher moves to give young children more responsibility for their own learning, or allows them to be more involved in decisions regarding the running of the classroom, or the organization of the curriculum, these teachers have been deeply impressed by the responses from the children and have seen the benefits for the children's motivation and learning very quickly. When they enter school the vast majority of young children are voracious in their enthusiasm for life and for learning and, sadly, for many the experience of schooling diminishes rather than supports these appetites. Education has become, for too many of our children, something which is done to them, rather than with them. We hope that some of the ideas in this chapter will help beginner teachers to make the educational experience in their class-rooms one which genuinely supports young children's development as confident and self-regulated learners.

Note

1   If you would like to know more about the CIndLe project, you can access further details, downloadable versions of publications and an order form for the CD-based training re-source produced by the project team at: http://www.educ.cam.ac.uk/cindle/index.html

Questions to set you thinking

1 How can we involve primary school children in making decisions about their learning and the organization of learning in their classrooms?
2 How can we support and encourage the children in our classes to become risk-takers in learning, adopting a positive attitude to mistakes and enjoying taking on difficult challenges?
3 How can we encourage exploratory talk in our classrooms, and how can we organize ourselves as practitioners so that we spend more time in genuine discussions with children about their ideas?

References

Barkley, R.A. (1997) *ADHD and the Nature of Self-Control*. New York, NY: Guilford Press.

Black, P. and Wiliam, D. (1998) *Inside the Black Box: Raising Standards through Classroom Assessment*. London: Kings College School of Education.

Bronson, M.B. (2000) *Self-Regulation in Early Childhood*. New York, NY: Guilford Press.

Brooker, L. (1996) Why do children go to school? Consulting children in the Reception class, *Early Years*, 17(1): 12–6.

Brown, A.L. (1987) Metacognition, executive control, self-regulation and other more mysterious mechanisms, in F.E. Weinert and R.H. Kluwe (eds) *Metacognition, Motivation and Understanding*. Hillsdale, NJ: Lawrence Erlbaum.

Collins, A., Seely-Brown, J. and Newman, S.E (1989) Cognitive apprenticeship: teaching the crafts of reading, writing and mathematics, in L.B. Resnick, (ed.) *Knowing, Learning and Instruction*. Mahwah, NJ: Lawrence Erlbaum.

Department for Education and Skills (DfES) (2006) *The Early Years Foundation Stage: Consultation on a Single Quality Framework for Services to Children from Birth to Five*. London: DfES.

Durkin, K. (1995) *Developmental Social Psychology: From Infancy to Old Age*. Oxford: Blackwell.

Featherstone, S. and Bayley, R. (2001) *Foundations of Independence*. Husband's Bosworth: Featherstone Education.

Flavell, J.H. (1979) Metacognition and cognitive monitoring: a new area of cognitive developmental inquiry, *American Psychologist*, 34: 906–11.

Flavell, J.H., Beach, D.R. and Chinsky, J.M. (1966) Spontaneous verbal rehearsal in a memory task as a function of age, *Child Development*, 37: 283–99.

Forman, E.A. and Cazden, C.B. (1985) Exploring Vygotskian perspectives in education: the cognitive value of peer interaction, in J.V. Wertsch (ed.) *Culture, Communication and Cognition: Vygotskian Perspectives*. Cambridge: Cambridge University Press.

Galton, M. (1989) *Teaching in the Primary School*. London: David Fulton.

Goleman, D. (1995) *Emotional Intelligence*. New York, NY: Bantam Books.

Hendy, L. and Whitebread, D. (2000) Interpretations of independent learning in the Early Years, *International Journal of Early Years Education*, 8(3): 245–52.

Leat, D. and Lin, M. (2003) Developing a pedagogy of metacognition and transfer: some signposts for the generation and use of knowledge and the creation of research partnerships, *British Educational Research Journal*, 29(3): 383–416.

Littleton, K., Mercer, N., Dawes, L., Wegerif, R., Rowe, D. and Sams, C. (2005) Talking and thinking together at Key Stage 1, *Early Years*, 25(2): 167–82.

Metcalfe, J. and Shimamura, A.P. (eds) (1994) *Metacognition: Knowing about Knowing*. Cambridge, MA: MIT Press.

Nisbet, J. and Shucksmith J. (1986) *Learning Strategies*. London: Routledge and Kegan Paul.

Palincsar, A.S. and Brown, A.L. (1984) Reciprocal teaching of comprehension-fostering and comprehension-monitoring activities, *Cognition and Instruction*, 1: 117–75.

Schaffer, H.R. (2004) *Introducing Child Psychology*. Oxford: Blackwell.

Schunk, D.H. and Zimmerman, B.J. (1994) *Self-Regulation of Learning and Performance*. Hillsdale, NJ: Lawrence Erlbaum.

Siegler, R.S. (2002) Microgenetic studies of self-explanation, in N. Granott and J. Parziale (eds) *Microdevelopment: Transition Processes in Development and Learning*. Cambridge: Cambridge University Press.

Sugden, D.(1989) Skill generalization and children with learning difficulties, in D. Sugden (ed.) *Cognitive Approaches in Special Education*. London: Falmer Press.

Teacher Development Agency (2006) *Professional Standards for NQTs*. Available online http://www.tda.gov.uk (accessed 26 June 2006).

Vygotsky, L.S. (1978) *Mind in Society*. Cambridge, MA: Harvard University Press.

Vygotsky, L.S. (1986) *Thought and Language*. Cambridge, MA: MIT Press.

Watson, J. and Ramey, C.T. (1972) Reactions to response-contingent stimulation in early infancy, *Merrill-Palmer Quarterly*, 18: 219–27.

Whitebread, D., Anderson, H., Coltman, P., Page, C., Pasternak, D. and Mehta, S. (2005) Developing Independent Learning in the Early Years. *Education 3–13*. 33, 40–50.

Williams, J. (2003) *Promoting Independent Learning in the Primary Classroom*. Buckingham: Open University Press.

Yussen, S. (ed.) (1985) *The Growth of Reflection in Children*. New York, NY: Academic Press.

Suggested further reading

Bronson, M.B. (2000) *Self-Regulation in Early Childhood*. New York: Guildford Press.

Featherstone, S. and Bayley, R. (2001) *Foundations of Independence*. Husband's Bosworth: Featherstone Education.

Hendy, L. and Whitebread, D. (2000) Interpretations of independent learning in the Early Years, *International Journal of Early Years Education*, 8(3), 245–52.

Schaffer, H.R. (2004) *Introducing Child Psychology*. Oxford: Blackwell.

Williams, J. (2003) *Promoting Independent Learning in the Primary Classroom*. Buckingham: Open University Press.

15 Getting it sorted! Organizing the classroom environment

Janet Moyles

Cameo 1

The beginner teacher takes great trouble to set up a new 'travel agents' stimulus area in the classroom. It has an appropriate sign, brochures, pens and paper, telephone, maps of the world, travel posters for Disneyworld, a computer, a cash register and a furniture arrangement which, as far as possible, reflects a real travel agency. Next morning, when the class of 8-year-olds arrive, there is great delight in the area and everyone wants to be the first to play. There is much jostling, pushing, arguing and, eventually, a few tears as the shop ends up in a demolished heap. The young teacher is devastated by the quick demise of her hard work and vows never to set up such an area again.

Cameo 2

It is customary at the end of the day for the Year 1 children, in Jackie's class, to sit on the carpet for quiet reflection and a story. The children listen quietly and attentively to each other and to the teacher. However, there are always one or two children who constantly tug at the fraying edges of the carpet and set other children off pulling at the loose threads. Jackie asks them in a kindly but firm manner, several times, to 'Please stop making the carpet worse' but every day her story is interrupted, and eventually stopped, in order to remove the offending children.

Introduction

The cameos raise very different issues about the classroom as a context for teaching and learning. On the one hand, a primary teacher needs to be a very organized and aware person, with a clear rationale for managing such things as a broad curriculum, teaching and learning resources, mounds of paperwork while, on the other hand, being able to give maximum time and effort to managing children and their learning.

No doubt you are questioning why, in the first cameo, despite this teacher's care and effort, she apparently did not succeed? What more did she need to understand about the children and the learning context in order to achieve her intentions? Similarly, in the second cameo, why does this experienced teacher fail to pay attention to something relatively small which continually undermines her authority during story time and, worse still, causes interference to children's concentration, enjoyment of the occasion and potential learning? The answer to these and other questions lies in understanding some crucial factors which inextricably interrelate in the primary classroom and significantly affect its organization and management, namely:

- *teachers*: their beliefs and values and how these underpin all other elements of classroom organization and management;
- *children*: their family backgrounds, age phases and individual learning and behavioural needs which must be addressed.

In this chapter we will examine briefly these three issues and what they mean to the beginner teacher.

Beliefs that matter

All of us bring to teaching memories of our own lives in school, perceptions about what it is to 'teach' and beliefs about how classroom systems should be. You will, no doubt, have heard statements like:

> Children today are not as well behaved as they used to be.
> Children just don't listen these days.
> Literacy and Numeracy, the basics, are what really matter in primary school.

These beliefs about children, teachers and education may or may not reflect how *you* feel about these things but certainly echo others' perceptions. Holding such views would make a vast difference to the way each of these people might themselves teach children, organize the curriculum, or, in this case, manage the classroom. An added difficulty within teaching is that while the schooling system operates for all, ostensibly on the basis of equality of opportunity, each individual within the system – child and teacher – is different and has a differing level of expectation, capability, understanding and need.

As a beginner teacher, you must determine what YOU believe. Without this personal construct – of children, the teacher's role and the learning environment – it is an uphill struggle to establish yourself as a competent and confident class teacher.

People aged 3–11 years

When children enter early years settings at the age of 3 years, they already bring with them a wide range of experiences (see Chapters 1–4). Parents and other family members are their first 'educators' (Drury *et al.* 2000; Brooker 2002, and Chapter 5) and, as teachers, we must not ignore what children bring from their culture and their past (Kwhali 2006). From the time they enter early years settings, children are also developing greater and greater levels of independence in their actions and thinking – the very move from home to an early years setting represents the main beginnings of independence from the family (see Chapter 14). Whatever the new environment, children react to being in a different socio-cultural framework with a large number of (relatively unknown) other children and adults and this can significantly affect their behaviour and self-concept (Brooker 2002). If you doubt this, just think how you feel entering the new school in which you will spend your teaching practice or induction year.

Family background

An effective teacher will ensure that early experiences are endorsed within the classroom structures. For example, children from different ethnic backgrounds will have their cultures represented within home corner materials, and 'the family' will reflect a range of types of structures to be found in modern society (Kwhali 2006). The effective teacher will also want to *extend* children's experiences and offer them a range of broader options. One example might be the child who arrives with very stereotypical gender views (like the 3-year-old boy who told me it was women's work to pick up the jigsaw pieces from the floor!) or those who have not yet learned to cope with children different from themselves (see Chapter 20). Remember, we cannot change anything as fundamental as the child's background. What has to 'change' is the way adults respond on the basis of accepting the children's background as a starting point for managing learning and ensuring continuity and coherence.

Continued contact with parents is a specific feature of primary education and most parents want to work with teachers in achieving the best for their children (see Chapter 5) and in working with children with special needs (see Chapter 19). In primary classrooms, teachers are *in loco parentis*, replacing the parent as diligently as we can.

Managing learning with different age groups

Many primary ITE courses now specialize in either advanced early years courses, in which students learn to work with those aged birth/3–7 years or, in specialist KS1/KS2 courses (5–11 years). Courses will normally make some differentiation between phases but will emphasize the notions of continuity and progression across primary education. Throughout the primary years children are developing a wide range of skills and constructing knowledge and understanding through their interactions and, as they increasingly gain ability to work from more abstract concepts, their teaching and learning needs and the organization of these will gradually change. For example, older children may be expected to work more collaboratively and undertake more complex problem-solving tasks which will require a very different classroom organization and teaching style (Baines *et al.* 2003; Blatchford *et al.* 2003, and Chapter 7).

For younger children, it is not a question of 'watering down' the activities which would be given to junior children. Rather it is necessary to understand the distinct emphases required in focusing upon young children, in developing their learning effectively and in examining the particular classroom strategies (Moyles and Adams 2001; Edgington 2004).

The *Early Years Foundation Stage* has its own areas of learning and teachers of the youngest children still require a sound knowledge of the subject elements within these areas. Creating classroom structures which allow 'sustained shared thinking' opportunities (Sylva *et al.* 2003) and ongoing observations and assessments leading to planning for provision of learning experiences, are key areas for FS teachers (Moyles *et al.* 2002).

A sound understanding of child development and the process of learning is vital for all primary teachers if they are to organize and manage the classroom appropriately for different age groups (Merry 1998). Regrettably, this is one aspect which has received decreasing emphasis on primary ITE courses over the last few years. Beginner teachers must be prepared to ask appropriate searching questions related to children's development during curriculum sessions and to enhance their own understanding through reading and interpreting observations of children across the age phases (see Chapter 17).

Children's independence

Children across the primary school years are developing independence in a variety of ways, particularly in thinking, confidence, self-esteem and development (Whitebread *et al.* 2005, and Chapter 14).

- *Thinking*: Many children work out explanations for themselves about phenomena (see Chapter 7) based on prior experience. This trial and error way of working is very typical of primary age children and should be fostered, for we all learn a great deal by our mistakes and our guesses. The management of learning situations must allow children to raise serious, sensible questions which receive equally serious answers (de Boo 1999). Classroom structures need to allow opportunities for exploring open-ended questions, more appropriate in developing higher-order thinking skills to challenge understanding and ensure the teacher learns about the children's learning (Costello 2000).
- *Confidence*: The problem with labels is that people so often live up to the image the label suggests, so that being 'naughty', 'good' or 'difficult' leads to exactly that kind of behaviour being exhibited. In turn, being 'difficult' gains some children the level of attention they demand (inevitably meaning that other children get less) and generates a self-fulfilling prophecy on the part of teacher and child with the child becoming more difficult and the teaching continually reaffirming the label (see Chapter 19). As a consequence, classroom management is made more problematic in that much time and energy is taken up in dealing with difficult children rather than ensuring teacher time is more equitably distributed (Roffey 2006).
- *Development*: Children of birth to 8-years are gradually developing physical competence which allows greater independence of movement and actions. After 8-years, children tend to refine and hone existing skills through general maturity rather than making any great leaps in development (Maude 2001). Although the children in the second scenario appear to be 'naughty', children naturally manipulate things around them and increase control over their fine motor skills. Ironically, it may well be that fraying the carpet edge was actually helping one child to concentrate! It could equally be that one of the 'frayers' is still socially quite immature and finds sitting within a confined space in close proximity to others quite disconcerting. Perhaps one or both of the children have not yet acquired age appropriate levels of emotional stability, in which case fraying the

carpet may be a symptom of underlying anxiety about, for example, whether the parent or carer will turn up at the end of the day. The message is clear: *understand the children as individual people* and organize and manage the classroom with this knowledge in mind. Think of them as people with all the emotions and needs which you yourself have – though at a different phase in life. Make one-to-one as well as collective relationships with them. For the children who cannot physically sit still for any extended period, it may be more appropriate that they draw a picture during story time or are asked to make pictorial or written notes during periods of teacher exposition to the whole class. This kind of thinking is at the very heart of child-centred education, the provision of a differentiated curriculum and effective classroom management. Virtual learning environments make this eminently possible (Gibbs 1999: Gillespie *et al.* 2007).

Organizing and managing the teaching and learning environment

The classroom represents 'home' for five or more hours of each weekday during term times for children and teachers alike. Its prime function is to 'house' the teacher and the learners in a kind of 'workshop' (or playshop!) context which supports crucial interactions between them (Moyles *et al.* 2003). The teacher must translate knowledge of children and pedagogy into classroom organization and management structures to everyone's benefit, no mean feat given that few people will have been totally responsible for 30+ other people before! The vital elements which must be considered are:

- the physical environment, both indoors and out;
- structures (including routines), health and safety and resource management;
- rights, responsibilities and rules;
- communication.

Physical environment

The classroom or class base is part of a larger school building which was built in a particular time in history under the existing philosophies of education. Whatever the building, teachers must operate current ideologies and practices making the most of whatever they have to promote effective teaching and learning experiences.

Figure 15.1 immediately suggests a KS1 classroom, where children may be given some choice in their activities, albeit choosing from those learning experiences provided by the teacher in specific areas of the room, or be directed within specific sessions, e.g. the literacy hour. A teacher's ideology superimposes on any physical classroom space a way of working for that teacher and those children. During your next classroom visit, note whether the classroom has an arrangement of grouped tables, individual desks in rows facing the front, tables or desks arranged in 'work bays'.

There is much to learn from the ways in which teachers organize the seating arrangements. People whose ideology lies in a child-centred type of education can be quite horrified at the sight of rows of desks and chairs which tend to signify whole class

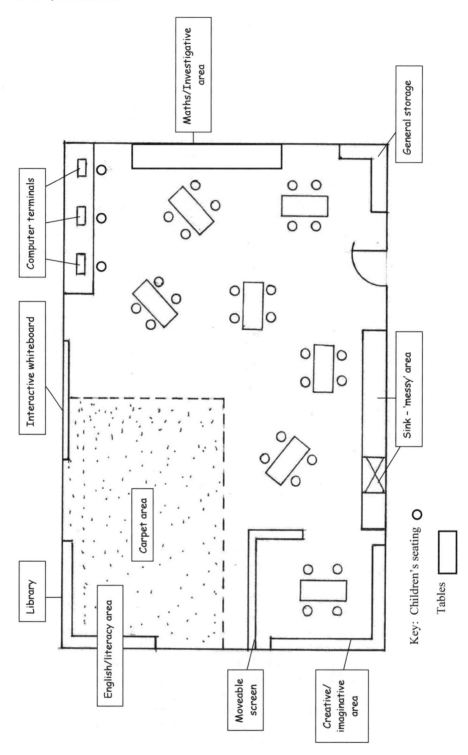

Key: Children's seating ◯

Tables ▭

Figure 15.1 Classroom Layout plan (KSI)

teaching. Collaborative group work requires tables to be organized in such a way that co-operation and interaction between children can take place, for example, that they can all see each other's faces and share resources. Such arrangements, however, can positively hinder children attempting to undertake concentrated, individual work or hamper the teacher in trying to demonstrate to the whole class. The organization of the desks or tables needs to be contingent upon the types of activities which are taking place (Dixie 2006).

Carpet areas are excellent for bringing a cosy 'togetherness' to shared events in the classroom, be it poetry or a story (as in Cameo 2), in plenary sessions, discussions or singing together. They may not be so useful for older children (physically large 11-year-olds can find sitting on a carpet cross-legged rather uncomfortable and demeaning) or for a teacher's detailed exposition on a special topic. It may be far more useful if the carpet area is detailed as a stimulus area, such as the travel agent in Cameo 1, so that children can follow up a teacher-directed session with more first-hand, direct experiences.

When entering a classroom in which you are going to work for the first time, it is advisable to make a plan as this helps to fix the area in your mind and offers the opportunity of rechecking when planning future learning activities are needed. It is also useful for observation purposes (see Chapter 18).

It is as well to remember that the 'outdoor classroom' is as important as the indoor environment when it comes to teaching and learning, especially with younger children (Bilton 2002; Carruthers in press). There is growing evidence that children need more physical activity than they currently have in school (Maude 2001; Andersen *et al.* 2006) and government and media alike constantly raise the issue of children's health, physical fitness and inclinations to sporting activities. Aspects of the science and geography curricular for older children, e.g. studying naturally occurring phenomena and identifying wildlife, have the advantage outside of being based on reality. With younger children, taking the 'Garden Centre' role play area outside, for example, means that mapping your journey to buy seeds and plants can cover a range of curriculum areas and offer opportunities for 'messy' water and soil activities.

Structures and routines

By structures, is meant the way the classroom operates so that children are clear what they are doing and do not need to expend time and energy in constantly finding out where things are and what they must do. Routines represent the order in which things happen and are often related to the daily and weekly timetable for the class.

Overall timetables are usually determined by the school with several sessions being 'fixed times', for example, hall periods or assemblies. Within the constraints of the required curriculum, teachers have the task of deciding on the best use of time within what is left either individually or in year groups. Making good use of teaching and learning time is vital as we must ensure that the 'whole child' is educated.

Making observations of our own classrooms can reveal that children are, for example, spending much of their time waiting for teacher attention (Adams *et al.* 2004) – this may be because the daily structures and routines are inappropriate and need reconsidering. Perhaps children are too dependent upon the teacher for resources or tasks, or are given insufficient guidance on what do when they are 'stuck'. A class discussion generating a set of ideas of what to do when you need help, such as ask another child, look in a book, do another task until the teacher can see you, can quickly alleviate this problem.

Routines are helpful though we should guard against them becoming 'routinous' and, therefore, boring. A little deviation from routine helps to keep children and teachers alert and interested, for example, try taking the children outside for story activities using a 'treasure hunt' idea – find words, read, do tasks from their reading, communicate with others and feedback in the plenary on their different experiences.

Such routines as those involved in children entering and leaving the classroom or in tidying up, need constant attention. Does it happen smoothly or do the children fidget and tussle with each other? Often, as in the carpet cameo above, children and teachers simply get overly familiar with a situation.

Demanding levels of responsibility from the children appropriate to their age by, for example, ensuring that they are responsible for the access/retrieval and upkeep/ maintenance of resources, ensures that they are not dependent upon the teacher or classroom assistants for every item of equipment. This also means that materials should be located and labelled appropriately; children can do this in negotiation with the teacher and especially labelling on the computer, though location may be the teacher's decision. Train and trust children. Expect them to behave appropriately in all matters and most of them will. A quality classroom is likely to be one where there is a place for everything and everything is mainly in its place. You should not spend precious time at the end of each day sorting out the classroom when there is marking, preparation, display, records and a wealth of other tasks upon which your time is more profitably spent.

Rights, responsibilities and rules

Children and teachers, whatever their race, gender or class, have the right to the best possible classroom experiences – and that also means behaving appropriately, and politely, towards each other. Issues should be discussed, responsibilities of each party determined and ground rules established. Both teachers and learners should feel able to raise issues which might stop them working effectively in the classroom, for example, both are likely to be affected by noise – constant shouting or nagging will usually make this situation worse, whereas discussion about alleviating the situation can result in a quiet, working atmosphere being maintained by the children. A sensible rule which children will readily accept is 'one at a time' in relation to toilet visits. Whatever the rule, it should be established quickly, with firmness and consistency (Yeomans and Arnold 2006). If, for any reason, changes to the rules are required, these should be communicated, renegotiated, written up and read out for all to see, hear, agree and put into effect as efficiently as possible.

Behaviour

It would be trite to suggest that if you get the classroom organization and management sorted out, there will be no behaviour problems. We have, however, only to think about the number of times there is a fuss and disagreement over quite minor incidents – a child tripping over another, arguments over resources – to realize that many behavioural issues are at least related to classroom structures (Dean 2004). Bored children also misbehave, so presenting work at an appropriate standard relieves some problems. Most primary children enjoy school, appreciate the relationship they have with teachers and want to be part of stimulating activities. Many behavioural problems can be contained within acceptable boundaries once teacher and child have 'got the measure of each other' and a working relationship agreed.

Communication

Primary teachers usually excel at explaining to children WHAT to do and HOW to do it. Communication, however, often breaks down because teachers fail to tell children WHY they are undertaking certain activities and what they are expected to KNOW and to DO as a result.

There will be many different levels at which we communicate with children requiring varied *classroom groupings*. Talking to them as a whole class to establish the groundwork for something to which all children will contribute or demonstrating a new technique are examples. Grouping by ability for some activities will mean that we can work to stretch the abler children or give closer attention to a group requiring additional help (Dean 2005). Grouping by task will be helpful where resources are perhaps limited and only a few children at a time can have access to practical equipment. With younger children, groupings are commonly by friendship and there may also be occasion where sex groupings might be used, particularly where the teacher is attempting to encourage boys to use the home-corner provision or girls to become more adventurous with the constructional materials. Sukhnandan (1998) is a useful research-based text on groupings (Baines *et al.* 2003).

Communication with other adults: Regular communication with a more experienced teacher, such as a mentor, can ensure that adversity is kept in perspective and the classroom runs as smoothly as possible. Becoming a teacher with full responsibility for the class can feel like an isolated job in a typical closed classroom situation, especially after a year or two of teaching. You may well have help from others, e.g. teaching assistants, parents, further and higher education students, sixth formers, and professionals whose advice in sought about particular children. As teachers, we really must help them to support us and the children, which means being clear before they arrive what their role is and what support we need. In the case of teaching assistants, unless it is vital to the activity that they sit and listen to the story, for example, request their help in preparing the next batch of materials, repairing books, labelling materials or, better still, working to provide extended learning opportunities for individual children (see Chapter 16).

One level of communication, which is often forgotten, is that of communicating with yourself – reflecting on your experiences and needs. What did YOU do today? How did you feel about it? What skills have you used and what needs do you have for tomorrow or next week? Take time to reflect upon your beliefs about teaching and learning and talk to others about your successes and occasional inevitable disasters.

Conclusion

The crucial aspect involved in classroom organization and management is what teachers believe – about themselves, children, the purposes of education and schooling, curriculum processes and the ethos of the particular school.

Having a clear rationale for organizing and managing a classroom in a particular way, needs to be explored by beginner teachers based on their own beliefs and developing ideology of effective pedagogy. Constant reflection on how it all works is crucial to continuing success and evolution of effective practice. The best primary classroom practitioners operate a wide range of skills (Gipps *et al.* 2000; Belvel and Jordan 2003).

To put all this in perspective, let us return to Cameo 1. This teacher felt that her course had taught her that children would learn much about the work of travel agents (as well as some geographical knowledge, multi-cultural understanding and opportunity to use literacy and numeracy skills) from having this first-hand experience presented to them in the classroom. However, this element was still not within her understanding of children's responses to such experiences. She had been taught on her ITE course, but had not yet absorbed it into her own value systems, that most children need exploration of new materials and contexts before being expected to deal in any depth with the concepts presented.

The student could have:

- given children the responsibility for setting up the travel agency in the classroom, so that, at each stage they were exploring the materials and the context;
- asked the children to present rules for use of the travel agency and to decide what was and was not acceptable behaviour;
- made her own rules as to how the travel agency should be used and put up an appropriate sign;
- allowed children to use the travel agency only when she was available to supervise their activities.

If your instinct is towards the first and second options, it is likely that you are a 'child-centred' person who puts thoughts about the children's learning experiences first. If you chose the final two options, these, on the whole, reflect a more 'teacher-centred' reaction.

Questions to set you thinking

1 Which of the above actions would you choose? Why?
2 How are these values and ideals likely to influence your classroom organization and management?
3 How might you complement your current thinking and broaden its range better to suit the children you teach?

References

Adams, S., Alexander, E., Drummond, M.J. and Moyles, J. (2004) *Inside the Foundation Stage: Recreating the Reception Year.* London: Association of Teachers and Lecturers.

Andersen, L.B., Harro, M., Sardinha, L., Froberg, K., Ekelund, L., Brage, S. and Anderssen, S. (2006) Physical activity and clustered cardiovascular risk in children: a cross-sectional study, *The Lancet*, 368: 299–304.

Baines, E., Blatchford, P. and Kutnick, P. (2003) Changes in grouping practices over primary and secondary school, *International Journal of Educational Research*, 39(1–2): 9–34.

Belvel, P. and Jordan, M. (2003) *Rethinking Classroom Management: Strategies for Prevention, Intervention and Problem Solving.* London: Corwin Press.

Bilton, H. (2002) *Outdoor Play in the Early Years: Management and Innovation.* London: David Fulton.

Blatchford, P., Kutnick, P., Baines, E. and Galton, M. (2003) Toward a social pedagogy of classroom group work, *International Journal of Educational Research*, 39(1–2): 153–72.

Brooker, L. (2002) *Starting School: Young Children Learning Cultures.* Buckingham: Open University Press.

Carruthers, E. (in press) Children's outdoor play – a sense of adventure? in J. Moyles, *Early Years: Issues and Challenges.* Maidenhead: Open University Press.

Costello, P. (2000) *Thinking Skills and Early Childhood Education.* London: David Fulton.

de Boo, M. (1999) *Enquiring Children: Challenging Teaching.* Buckingham: Open University Press.

Dean, J. (2004) *Organizing Learning in the Primary School Classroom* (4th edn). London: RoutledgeFalmer.

Dean, J. (2005) *The Effective Primary School Classroom.* London: RoutledgeFalmer.

Dixie, G. (2006) *Managing your Classroom.* London: Continuum.

Drury, R., Miller, L. and Campbell, R. (2000) *Looking at Early Years Education and Care.* London: David Fulton.

Edgington, M. (2004) *The Foundation Stage Teacher in Action: Teaching 3-, 4-, and 5-Year-Olds* (3rd edn). London: Paul Chapman.

Gibbs, G. (1999) Learning how to learn: using a virtual environment for philosophy, *Journal of Computer Assisted Learning*, 15(3): 221–31.

Gillespie, H., Boulton, H., Hramiak, A. and Williamson, R. (2007) *Using Virtual Learning Environments to Enhance Learning and Teaching in Schools.* Derbyshire: Learning Matters.

Gipps, C., McCallum, B. and Hargreaves, E. (2000) *What Makes a Good Primary School Teacher? Expert Classroom Strategies.* London: RoutledgeFalmer.

Kwhali, J. (2006) Colour neutral: the absence of black voices in early years, *Race Equality Teaching*, 24(2): 9–12.

Maude, P. (2001) *Physical Children: Active Teaching.* Buckingham: Open University Press.

Merry, R. (1998) *Successful Children, Successful Teaching.* Buckingham: Open University Press.

Moyles, J. and Adams, S. with others (2001) *StEPs: A Framework for Playful Teaching.* Buckingham: Open University Press.

Moyles, J., Adams, S. and Musgrove, A. (2002) *SPEEL: Study of Pedagogical Effectiveness in Early Learning.* London: DfES Research Report 363.

Moyles, J., Hargreaves, L., Merry, R., Paterson, A. and Esarte-Sarries, V. (2003) *Interactive*

Teaching in the Primary School: Digging Deeper into Meanings. Maidenhead: Open University Press/McGraw-Hill.

Roffey, S. (2006) *Helping with Behaviour: Establishing the Positive.* London: RoutledgeFalmer.

Sukhnandan, L. (1998) *Streaming, Setting and Grouping by Ability: A Review of the Literature.* Slough: NFER.

Sylva, K., Melhuish, E., Sammons, P., Siraj-Blatchford, I., Taggart, B. and Elliot, K. (2003) *The Effective Provision of Pre-School Education (EPPE) Project: Findings from the Pre-school Period.* London: Institute of Education, University of London.

Whitebread, D., Anderson, H., Coltman, P., Page, C., Pino Pasternak, D. and Mehta, S. (2005) Developing independent learning in the early years, *Education 3–13, 33*: 40–50.

Yeomans, J. and Arnold, H. (2006) *Teaching, Learning and Psychology.* London: David Fulton.

Suggested further reading

Belvel, P. and Jordan, M. (2003) *Rethinking Classroom Management: Strategies for Prevention, Intervention and Problem Solving.* London Corwin Press.

Dean, J. (2004) *Organizing Learning in the Primary School Classroom* (4th edn). London: Routledge/Falmer.

Dixie, G. (2006) *Managing your Classroom.* London: Continuum.

Gipps, C., McCallum, B. and Hargreaves, E. (2000) *What Makes a Good Primary School Teacher? Expert Classroom Strategies.* London: Routledge/Falmer.

16 Teamwork in the primary classroom

Wasyl Cajkler and Wendy Suschitzky

Cameo 1

Emma has just started her second teaching experience at a large inner city school. Her tutor has noticed that there are two other adults in the class working with the children. She asks Emma to tell her about these adults and why they are there. Emma looks rather worried and replies: 'I know that Jane works with the boy with a physical disability and Amena works with the Somali children, but I'm not sure of the times when they come into the class and what I am supposed to do when they arrive.'

Cameo 2

Peter is an NQT in a class with a high proportion of children with Special Educational Needs. He has regular help from a TA, Suzanne. He includes a section for her work in his lesson plans and discusses the children's achievements with her at the end of the lessons. When meeting with his induction tutor, Peter describes a typical exchange with the TA. The learning objective for this lesson was 'to describe and visualize 2-D and 3-D shapes'.

Suzanne: James and Selma managed to get all the shapes in the correct boxes but Kirsty needed lots of help to do it neatly.
Peter: But did they all meet the learning objective?
Suzanne: I think so, I'm sure they all know the shapes.

It is agreed that Peter needs to examine more thoroughly the contribution that the TA makes to the children's learning and to find better ways to communicate with his colleague.

Introduction

Teaching is no longer a stand-alone activity and in schools there is a wide range of staff. In January 2005 there were 147,400 full-time equivalent (FTE) teaching assistants in schools in England, with 431,700 FTE teachers, giving a ratio of 1 teaching assistant for each 2.9 teachers (DfES 2005). As a result, trainee teachers are required to 'Ensure that colleagues working with them are appropriately involved in supporting learning and understand the roles they are expected to fulfil' and by the end of the induction year they should 'Ensure that colleagues working together are clear about their role(s) and involved as appropriate, in lesson planning, setting objectives, managing learning and assessing progress' (TDA 2006: 13).

In this chapter we will use the term teaching assistant (TA) as we seek to provide guidance for new teachers sharing the challenges faced by Emma and Peter. Based on recent research, the chapter explores the workings of classroom partnerships. The more we understand teaching assistants' roles and contributions, the more effective may be the partnerships in classrooms.

Who are teaching assistants?

Emma (Cameo 1) works with two types of assistant. Amena is a multilingual TA assigned to support pupils with English as an additional language (EAL). Jane is a learning support, or special needs assistant, assigned to a pupil with a physical disability. Peter's case (Cameo 2) is different, as he works with one assistant, Suzanne, who supports pupils with special needs to help secure their inclusion and development within a mainstream classroom. TAs working in support of pupils with special needs account for at least a quarter of all TAs (Roaf 2003), but support staff have very varied roles. Hancock and Colloby (in Hancock and Collins 2005) identified eight titles for support staff that Emma and Peter might encounter as primary teachers: 'Learning Support Assistant; Classroom Assistant; Nursery assistant; Nursery nurse; Learning mentor; Parent helper/volunteer; Teaching assistant; Bilingual assistant' (Hancock and Colloby 2005: 6).

What do teaching assistants do?

Emma's first challenge is to find out what TAs do. This is not straightforward as there are many types of assistant with a range of descriptions (though some may have none at all). The National Agreement (DfES 2003, *Raising Standards and Tackling Workload: A National Agreement*) envisaged more use of support staff to 'remodel' the teaching workforce and relieve teachers of routine tasks, aiming to do the following:

- reduce (progressively) teacher workloads;
- remodel the workforce with redistribution of routine tasks;
- reform the roles of support staff;
- establish higher level teaching assistants (HLTAs) in all schools.

Higher Level Teaching Assistant status (accorded to TAs who demonstrate a range of professional competences) was developed by the Training and Development Agency for Schools (TDA) following consultation with support staff, headteachers, teachers, professional bodies, unions and employers. By the spring of 2006, 15,000 TAs had achieved HLTA status. These developments are transforming the way that some TAs work and it is essential for Emma and Peter to identify how the remodelling has been implemented in their schools. But, while support staff may provide welcome relief from administrative tasks, Collins and Simco (2006: 204) report that 'there are wide variations in the actual roles of TAs'. Indeed, there are numerous studies on the work of support staff and the variety of contributions that they make: for example, Wilson *et al.* (2002) on Scottish TAs, Farrell *et al.* (1999) on LSAs in England, Moyles and Suschitzky (1997) on English KS1 classrooms, Blatchford *et al.* (2002, 2004) on KS1 and KS2 respectively and Mortimore *et al.* (1994), a detailed study of associate staff in general (bursars, librarians, technicians and teaching assistants). It is impossible to list all relevant studies but from a detailed review, Cajkler *et al.* (2006) have listed contributions made by TAs under four headings. TAs (but also others) claimed that the first two categories took up most of a TA's time:

1   *Direct academic and socio-academic contributions to pupils*: TAs support learning by providing interaction opportunities, improving pupil motivation, promoting independence and interpreting and adapting teacher input. TAs engage with pupils on tasks set by the teacher, supporting the work of individuals and groups. They respond to the needs of one pupil or a group of pupils. They instruct, guide and support a small group away from the teacher but remain directed by the teacher in terms of focus and content, though some may modify materials. Despite this, they make decisions about pupils and seek solutions to their anxieties, whether they be social or academic.

2   *Contributions to inclusion*: TAs contribute to building pupils' self-esteem and confidence, by mediating social interaction with peers, 'bridging' between the pupils and the teachers and managing in-class behaviour. To be successful, such processes depend on the TA's ability to intervene when appropriate and to withdraw when appropriate. They may also offer pastoral or personal care for pupils with disabilities.

3   *Stakeholder relations*: TAs act as a link person between different stakeholders, for example, between parents and schools (in some cases as a cross-cultural link), and they claim to bridge between teachers and pupils, e.g. listening to pupil perspectives and feeding back to teachers, feeding back to teachers about pupil progress as in the second cameo. In short, they may oil the classroom wheels of communication and interaction in a range of critical ways.

4   *Contributions to teachers*: TAs perform routine tasks that enable teachers to focus on securing academic engagement, e.g. display work, registers, maintaining/ developing resources, giving feedback on pupil progress to teachers.

DfES expectations, mentioned above in the remodelling of the workforce agenda, include the delegation of 25 tasks to TAs. In addition, teachers are offered Planning, Preparation and Assessment time (PPA), that may be covered by a HLTA who acts as cover so that the teacher is able to plan, prepare and assess (DfES 2003).

In the past, TAs may well have mixed paints and scrubbed paint pots. Who does this and similar routine jobs now? In some schools, policy may determine that this remains the case, but recent publications (Campbell and Fairbairn 2005; Hancock and Collins 2005), confirm the pattern reported by Cajkler *et al.* (2006), i.e. that TAs are engaged in classroom practice in a range of teaching-related activities, for example:

(a) assisting the SENCO;

(b) supporting in mathemetics lessons;
(c) helping to manage behaviour;
(d) contributing to assessment;
(e) supporting literacy;
(f) working in the early years;
(g) developing pupils' use of ICT.

It is clear that direct support for pupils' learning takes up most of the time of TAs. In Year R and KS1 classes, TAs have been reported to be involved in direct one-to-one interactions with pupils (Blatchford *et al.* 2002) and Wilson *et al.* (2002) in Scotland estimated that at least 60 per cent of TA time was devoted to direct support for learning. While it is clear that they may fulfil important administrative support roles (e.g. taking the register, stock taking, preparing materials, maintaining displays, preparing and managing the distribution of playtime fruit, organizing resources), support for learning is held to be the most significant activity in which they engage.

Evolution of training for TAs

What should you, as a beginner teacher, know about the training of TAs? You need to know that there are different routes for TAs. It is still the case that some TAs may be in place purely on the basis of classroom experience, having begun as volunteers. However, the image of the TA as an untrained helper, casually employed, is beginning to be eroded. Nowadays, TA appointments involve assessment of skills against job descriptions, while in-service training for teaching assistants involves a range of opportunities, with both formal and/or informal outcomes. Knowing about these will assist the development of the student/TA/teacher partnership.

Sage and Wilkie (2004) describe a clear distinction among TAs prior to the 1990s. The distinction was between nursery nurses who held an NNEB or a BTEC Diploma qualification (both two-year, vocational courses) and those who had little or no training related to educational practices. Nursery nurses would have significant training in the observation of children's learning while STAs may have undergone training in teaching basic skills. 'Now there are a range of courses from level 2 (GCSE equivalent) to degree level, short-term and extended, in colleges and universities, or in school through NVQs' (Sage and Wilkie 2004: 19).

Opportunities for TAs in the UK include the following:

*   the Specialist Teaching Assistant (STA) programmes introduced by the DfE in 1994 in order to 'contribute more markedly to the teaching and learning of basic skills in support of qualified teachers' (DfE 1994, cited in Loxley and Swann 1998: 156);
*   a four-day induction programme (DfES 2000), used by LEAs with new TAs;
*   initiative-related training, for example, to teach supplementary programmes for National Strategies, such as Additional Literacy Support (ALS) (DfEE 1999);
*   Foundation Degrees for Teaching Assistants (FDA), available in a large number of HEIs since 2001.

Working together as a team

In Peter's class, one of the TA's roles is the assessment of learning by observation of the children. Peter needs to help Suzanne to appreciate that children often progress in small steps in their learning and that the progress should be noted and reported to him as the teacher with overall responsibility for all the children's learning. His instructions at the beginning of the lesson should take the form of a greater emphasis on the learning objectives rather than on helping children to complete the tasks. His plans should contain appropriate questions for Suzanne to ask the children. Perhaps Peter could model this, and then feed back to Suzanne so that she might learn observation skills from him. Another strategy could be that Suzanne works with the high attainers and/or monitors the rest of the class to leave Peter free to use his knowledge with the lower attainers in order to identify the steps they are taking with their learning.

Emma's knowledge about Amena, the assistant who works with Somali children, is thin and she needs to know in detail what multilingual teaching assistants offer. Amena may have significant linguistic, inter-cultural and social skills that enable her to work not only with Somali pupils bilingually but also with other children. Cable (2004) describes how three teaching assistants, described as bilingual (BTAs), spoke many languages. One spoke English, Gujarati, Panjabi and Urdu; another had English, Twi, Ga and Arabic, while the third was just trilingual in English, Bengali and Sylheti. The BTAs stressed their role as integrators of children, as their supporters, bridges to participation and learning, and their advocates. They were not merely translators. 'The BTAs in this study saw a key part of their role as developing children's confidence and ability to learn; in effect, developing their learning dispositions' (Cable 2004: 218). They acted as a cross-cultural bridge between home and school, explaining the school's mission and being the first port of call for bilingual parents. They explained school policy and practice to parents; providing reassurance and explanation about their children in school. This kind of exterior role may not apply in the case of Emma's school but the multi-faceted bridging role (to teachers, parents and pupils) is reported in other studies of TAs, e.g. when they seek clarification from the teacher on behalf of pupils (Shaw 2001: 23). Collins and Simco (2006: 206) report the BTA perception that pupils 'are happy that we know their language and then sometimes they will not go to their own teachers ... They come to us for help because they know they can speak to us in our own language and they can explain themselves better than they can to the teachers'.

However, it should not be assumed that knowing the language of pupils means that the TA has accompanying teaching or assessment skills. The teacher needs to probe this and advise accordingly. Both teacher and TA need knowledge of language acquisition, the assessment of language skills and how to promote the learning of English while maintaining the first language. Most importantly the teacher must fulfil her responsibilities to the EAL children and ensure that she spends sufficient time working with them and getting to know their achievements and needs.

Good practice: practical strategies for successful teaching and support work

Working with teaching assistants involves five principal activities: planning, consultation, communication, managing in the classroom and evaluation. However, Howes (2003: 152) warns against a model of the classroom which sees the teacher as the leader and the TA as the led. New classroom teams (Thomas 1987, 1991; Clayton 1993) are more complicated than that. Howes (2003) highlights the fund of knowledge and experience that TAs now bring to classroom teams, for example, knowledge about the pupils, their background, their concerns, their living conditions, their apprehensions about schools and their reactions to the curriculum. They often work with the most vulnerable or apprehensive members of the classroom. So, TAs may well have highly developed skills in communicating with pupils, observing pupils at work, and acting as advocates for marginalized or disaffected pupils.

The teacher and TA may have the same or different expectations of the children both intellectually and in dealing with social and emotional behaviour. When working with children with SEN, the quality of the collaboration between professionals ensures that everyone's expectations of the children and their understanding of their strengths and difficulties are the same (Soan 2005: 76). It is important that teachers know all the pupils in the class so they can plan for all. Special needs assistants are not there to act as a foil or barrier to the teacher, but to support inclusion by promoting independence in the classroom.

The key to successful teamwork lies in:

- preparing together (and time for this may not always be easy to find);
- sharing goals (pre-planning wherever possible, so TAs do not have to guess what you intend);
- communicating clearly with other classroom colleagues about the direction that learning should take, for the whole class and for individual pupils (sharing of plans and materials);
- listening to the TAs' perspectives;
- asking for advice about pupils and incorporating strategies that take account of feedback from TAs;
- gaining trust and understanding from TAs by showing genuine support and respect for what they do;
- reviewing the work of the classroom team and identifying approaches that draw on the strengths of each member of the team.

As part of the preparation for this chapter, we consulted two groups of TAs (23 in total) to ask what advice they would give to a beginning teacher on how to work together effectively. They expressed the following principles:

1   Clear, regular communication and consultation with TAs were critical.
2   Attitudes to TAs should be positive and respectful.
3   There should be acknowledgement of their skills, using TA knowledge and skills to help, e.g. not just using TAs to manage behaviour.

4   Sharing the planning and sharing the objectives were considered essential so that TAs understand how they are expected to support the learning.

It is a teacher's professional responsibility to find out what TAs bring to the classroom: linguistic, pedagogic, musical, technical and personal/social (understanding of pupils). If there is a curriculum area in which the teacher is less confident, such as music, then using the musical knowledge of the TA will enhance the learning for the children and build the professional relationship with the TA. Among TAs consulted for this chapter, it was not uncommon to identify a TA as one of the school's ICT 'experts'.

In addition, the TAs expressed concerns as follows:

1   How they were introduced to children and about being treated with respect in general.
2   Working with SEN pupils: the most vulnerable children may work predominantly with the TA. What can TAs offer? Should this be the role of the TA?
3   Understanding hierarchies: being clear what the TA role is, which may involve consulting the school's official expectations, but will certainly involve dialogue with the TA.

Dealing with drawbacks in classroom teams

Moyles and Suschitzky (1997) suggest that the presence of TAs can limit access to high quality teaching, a concern that gives food for thought when planning lessons and schemes of work. Lacey (2001: 166) found that 'the best LSAs were good at judging how much support to offer to individual pupils'. Teachers working with TAs need to be aware of the importance of listening to pupils and understanding when to encourage independent work and when to offer help as pupils want support to be given in as non-intrusive a way as possible, preferring not to have their needs highlighted (Bowers 1997; Farrell *et al.* 1999: 50). Possible negative outcomes have been reported in a range of studies about pupils with disabilities, for example, Broer *et al.* (2005) in which former pupils complained of the ways in which support staff acted as a barrier to inclusion and independence. While young pupils may see the TA as a helper, even a co-teacher, as pupils get older there is some evidence that TA attention is sometimes deemed unnecessary and intrusive (Bowers 1997). To what extent are Emma and Peter engaged with all learners in their classroom? Are some pupils shielded or hidden from them because they are left to the care of the assistant?

Avoiding this drawback again presupposes engagement with and understanding by all classroom staff of the aims, content, stages and outcomes of each lesson, a condition that Emma and Peter should facilitate and secure when planning with their classroom teams. This will ensure that TAs are not 'over-protective, thereby removing pupils' learning challenges' (Moran and Abbott 2002). There may be a need to discuss and agree classroom procedures so that both staff and pupils understand. Moran and Abbott's study found a primary school with explicit guidelines for the TA supporting the integration of a child in a mainstream class:

These included ensuring that the child brought all the necessary materials to class, that the TA arrived as unobtrusively as possible, and that duties were properly clarified with the mainstream class teacher. Such tasks and activities were likely to involve working with the special unit child either individually or in a small group as translator, scribe and supporter ... There were, additionally, explicit instructions as to what TAs must *not* do. First, they were not to talk to the child when the mainstream class teacher was talking, but to deliver any necessary explanation later; second, they were not to sit only with the unit child as this would cause both social and academic dependence; and third, they were not always to interpret everything for the child, but to encourage him or her to ask the teacher for clarification. (Moran and Abbott 2002: 166)

TAs are engaged in a range of support activities. As a beginner teacher, you might critically evaluate this approach against current practice in your school. Calder (2003) writes that teachers must be prepared to give guidance about the kind of support they want. They must advise TAs about their plans and about changes to their plans: the issue cannot be ducked. Reluctance to manage TAs led to stresses reported by TAs who 'have to guess what the teacher would like and accept' (Calder 2003: 35). Leaving TAs to try to interpret what you want from gestures or body language causes additional stress to the TA (Bradley and Roaf 2000, cited in Calder 2003). Both Emma and Peter could ask their mentors if they can be given some development time to talk with their TAs about professional issues instead of relying on brief conversations about organizational issues.

Conclusion

OfSTED claims that observable gains in pupils' learning result from the attention of a TA in particular lessons (OfSTED 2002: 10). TA presence may improve the quality of teaching, when the TA:

- has a close partnership with the teacher (who plans the TA's contribution);
- is clear about his/her role, including giving feedback to pupils on learning and behaviour;
- interacts in the classroom with the teacher to create more challenging discussion;
- deals with minor misdemeanours and manages pupils' behaviour effectively;
- has sufficient subject knowledge to be able to challenge pupils;
- has good questioning skills;
- helps the teacher use a wider range of methods, supporting him/her to cater for pupils with differing needs.

(OfSTED 2002: 9)

Some of the above may be missing in the cameos because Peter and Emma are uncertain about the contribution of support workers. Some of the OfSTED recommendations may be modified by experience of working in classroom teams, for example, the third point above, but the importance of reflective dialogue cannot be over-emphasized. Whenever possible, planning and review of lessons must involve TAs. The teacher should be aware of how the TA uses questions in the classroom or whether the TA can be entrusted to implement a behaviour policy following appropriate induction. With regard to classroom activities, at the very least, TAs should have copies of schemes of work and lesson plans as well as key curriculum documents, such as policies on literacy, spelling, marking and classroom behaviour. Ideally, they will have a role description and an understanding of how the classroom partnership works to include and value their contribution. The mere presence of additional adults in the classroom is not a guarantee of success or effectiveness. The team requires effective and continual management, a task now expected of teachers.

Questions to set you thinking

1 How is the TA introduced to the beginner teacher?
2 What is the level of 'teamness' in your classroom?
3 To what extent is the TA aware of the objectives of each lesson?
4 What is the quality of the TA's feedback to you on children's engagement, learning, interest and anxiety?
5 What contributions do you and your TAs make to teaching, learning and assessment?

References

Blatchford, P., Martin, C., Moriarty, V., Bassett, P. and Goldstein, H. (2002) *Pupil Ratio Differences and Educational Progress over Reception and Key Stage 1*. London: DfES.

Blatchford, P., Russell, A., Bassett, P., Brown, P. and Martin, C. (2004), *The Role and Effects of Teaching Assistants in English Primary Schools (Years 4 to 6) 2000–2003: Results from the Class Size and Pupil Ratios (CSPAR) KS2 Project*. London: Institute of Education, University of London.

Bowers, T. (1997) Supporting special needs in the mainstream classroom: children's perceptions of the adult role, *Child Care Health and Development*, 23(3): 217–32.

Bradley, C. and Roaf, C. (2000) Working effectively with learning support assistants (LSAs), in P. Benton and T. O'Brien (eds) *Special Needs and the Beginning Teacher*. London: Continuum.

Broer, S.M., Doyle, M.B. and Giangreco, M.F. (2005) Perspectives of students with intellectual disabilities about their experience with paraprofessional support, *Exceptional Children*, 71(4): 415–30.

Cable, C. (2004) 'I'm going to bring my sense of identity to this': the role and contribution of bilingual teaching assistants, *Westminster Studies in Education*, 27(2): 207–22.

Cajkler, W., Tennant, G., Tiknaz, Y., Sage R., Taylor C., Tucker S.A., Tansey, R. and Cooper, P.W. (2006) A systematic literature review on the perceptions of ways in which support staff work to support pupils' social and academic engagement in primary classrooms (1988—2003), in *Research Evidence in Education Library*. London: EPPI-Centre, Social Science Research Unit, Institute of Education, University of London.

Calder, I. (2003) Classroom assistants: how do they know what to do in the classroom? *Improving Schools.* 6(1): 27–38.

Campbell, A. and Fairbairn, G. (2005) *Working with Support in the Classroom.* London: Paul Chapman.

Clayton, T. (1993) From domestic helper to assistant teacher: the changing role of the British classroom assistant, *European Journal of Special Needs Education,* 8(1): 32–44.

Collins, J. and Simco, N. (2006) Teaching Assistants reflect: the way forward? *Reflective Practice,* 7(2): 197–214.

Department for Education (1994) *Notes of Guidance on the Training of Specialist Teacher Assistants.* London: DfE.

Department for Education and Employment (1999) *Additional Literacy Support (ALS).* London: DfEE.

Department for Education and Skills (2000) *Working with Teaching Assistants: A Good Practice Guide.* London: DfES.

Department for Education and Skills (2003) *Transforming the School Workforce.* London: DfES.

Department for Education and Skills STATISTICS (2005) *School Workforce in England.* London: HMSO.

Farrell, P., Balshaw, M. and Polat, F. (1999) *The Management, Role and Training of learning Support Assistants.* London: Department of Education and Employment.

Hancock, R. and Collins, J. (2005) *Primary Teaching Assistants: Learners and Learning.* London: David Fulton.

Hancock, R. and Colloby, J. (2005) Eight titles and roles, in R. Hancock and J. Collins (eds) *Primary Teaching Assistants: Learners and Learning.* London: David Fulton.

Howes, A. (2003) Teaching reforms and the impact of paid adult support on participation and learning in mainstream schools, *Support for Learning,* 18(4): 147–53.

Lacey, P. (2001) The role of learning support assistants in the inclusive learning of pupils with severe and profound learning difficulties, *Educational Review,* 53(2): 157–67.

Loxley, A. and Swann, W. (1998) The impact of school-based training on classroom assistants in primary schools, *Research Papers in Education,* 13(2): 141–60.

Moran, A. and Abbott, L. (2002) Developing inclusive schools: the pivotal role of teaching assistants in promoting inclusion in special and mainstream schools in Northern Ireland. *European Journal of Special Needs Education,* 17(2): 161–73.

Mortimore, P., Mortimore, J. with Thomas, H. (1994) *Managing Associate Staff in Schools.* London: Paul Chapman.

Moyles, J. and Suschitzky, W. (1997) *Jills of All Trades: Teachers and Classroom Assistants Working Together in KS1.* London: University of Leicester/Association of Teachers and Lecturers.

OfSTED (2002) *Teaching Assistants in Primary Schools: An Evaluation of the Quality and Impact of their Work.* London: HMSO.

Roaf, C. (2003). Learning support assistants talk about inclusion, in M. Nind, J. Rix, K. Sheehy and K. Simmons (eds) *Inclusive Education: Diverse Perspectives.* London: David Fulton in association with The Open University, 221–40.

Sage, R. and Wilkie, M. (2004) *Supporting Learning in Primary Schools.* Exeter: Learning Matters.

Shaw, L. (2001) *Learning Supporters and Inclusion: Roles, Rewards, Concerns, Challenges.* Bristol: Centre for Studies on Inclusive Education.

Soan, S. (2005) *Reflective Reader: Primary Special Educational Needs.* Exeter: Learning Matters.

Teacher Development Agency (2006) *Professional Standards for NQTs*. Available online http://www.tda.gov.uk (accessed 26 June 2006).

Thomas, G. (1987) Extra people in the primary classroom, *Educational Research*, 29(3): 173–81.

Thomas, G. (1991) Defining role in the new classroom teams, *Educational Research*, 33(3): 186–98.

Training and Development Agency for Schools (2006) *Draft Revised Professional Standards*. London: DfES, available online http://www.tda.gov.uk/teachers/currentconsultations/professional standards.aspx (accessed 30 May 2006).

Wilson, V., Schlapp, U. and Davidson, J. (2002) *More than an Extra Pair of Hands? SCRE Research Report*. Edinburgh: Scottish Council for Research in Education.

Suggested further reading

Campbell, A. and Fairbain, G. (2005) *Working with Support in the Classroom*. London: Paul Chapman Publishing.

Hancock, R. and Collins, J. (eds) (2005) *Primary Teaching Assistants: Learners and Learning*. London: David Fulton.

Hancock, R. and Colloby, J. (2005) Eight titles and roles, in R. Hancock, and J. Collins (eds) *Primary Teaching Assistants: Learners and Learning*. London: David Fulton, 7–13.

Sage, R. and Wilkie, M. (2004) *Supporting Learning in Primary Schools*. Exeter: Learning Matters.

Soan, S. (2005) *Reflective Reader: Primary Special Educational Needs*. Exeter: Learning Matters Ltd. (Section 2: Working with Others, Chapters 5–8, 51–96.)

PART 4
SUPPORTING AND ENHANCING LEARNING AND TEACHING

17 Assessing children's learning

Kathy Hall

Cameo 1

Amanda and Yasmin (Year 3), are looking through their 'literacy portfolios'. They are taking out pieces of work – poems, stories, non-fiction writing, illustrations and paintings they did in the past term. They share them, occasionally reading out some pieces along with the comments their teacher, Nathan, had written on their work. They laugh and talk as they reflect on their efforts and the circumstances in which they produced some of the work. They sometimes compare pieces. They recall why they chose to keep certain samples in their portfolios. Nathan sits down beside them and says to Amanda, 'What kind of a writer are you?' Amanda pauses for a moment, then says 'I'm a scary writer.' Before Nathan can respond to this, Yasmin says 'And I'm a poet.'

Cameo 2

The Year 6 children are working quietly and individually on number problems. One problem they are working on is as follows: the sign on a lift in an office block says 'This lift can carry up to 7 people' 136 people want to go up in the lift. How many times must the lift go up? Kate, the teacher, notices that the children are offering a range of answers for this. Some are simply dividing 136 by 7 on their calculators, getting 19.42857143 and then copying this down. Some realize it must be a whole number. Zillah rounds down and writes 19 in her copy. Jason rounds up, putting 20 in his copy. Kate sits with Zillah and asks her why she thinks the answer is 19. She says 'Well I reckon that by the time the lift goes up and down a few times at least 3 people will get fed up and will use the stairs, so that means it will be 133 divide by 7 which is 19.' Kate, realizing that Zillah is drawing on real-life experience here, explains to her that all the information that is needed to solve the problem is actually given and that you don't have to use your own experience of using lifts to help you. They discuss this for a while and then Zillah reconsiders her answer and decides it should be 20. In the whole class situation later they discuss rounding and the logic of 19.42857143 people!

Introduction

These two cameos raise key issues about what is assessment, what its purpose is, how to do it, and what the connection is between assessment and learning. As I address these themes I will come back to the two cameos of 'good assessment practice'. Are these cameos really examples of assessment? Do they really reflect good practice? Who is being assessed in each case? Who is the assessor in each case? What were they trying to find out? What kind of evidence is available? Is this evidence valid, reliable, trustworthy?

We are constantly assessing our own and others' actions in everyday life. We are who we are as a result of our own interpretations of others' reactions and evaluations of us over time and in many different situations. Our actions and reactions say something about who we are – our identities and sense of self – and are influenced by the feedback we get from other people about what seems to be a reasonable way to behave. Every conscious act we do involves some level of interpretation and assessment. On the basis of the evidence available to us and our changing circumstances we re-evaluate and modify our actions. Assessing, evaluating, judging, interpreting are integral to everyday life.

Everyday school life is the same. Teachers and children alike participate in school life in the light of expectations, interpretations, evaluations and judgements of situations. In this sense assessment is not the preserve of just teachers – a truism that teachers, parents and indeed policy makers sometimes forget. This chapter places considerable emphasis on interpretation, including the learner's interpretation. Acknowledging the learner's take is fundamental to good assessment practice in the primary school. The chapter is structured around the following key themes: assessment purposes, assessment evidence, formative assessment and feedback, national testing and prioritizing assessment for the promotion of learning.

Assessment purposes

There are many reasons to assess learning:

1 to plan the next topic or series of lessons;
2 to judge the effectiveness of teaching;
3 to group learners for teaching according to their attainment in a topic/subject;
4 to compare learners' attainment with others in the class, others of the same age;
5 to monitor learner's progress over time;
6 to obtain a better understanding of a learner's difficulties, say, strengths and weaknesses as a reader;
7 to provide evidence that learners themselves can use to improve;
8 to provide evidence of attainment for use as a basis of discussion with learners' parents/carers;
9 to provide evidence of standards for use by the school, by the local authority, by the government;
10 to compare standards of attainment at the level of the school, local authorities and nation over time;

11 to accredit learning by providing people with certificates that can be used in the next stage of education or by employers.

Many of these purposes overlap. For example, the first two on the list could be accommodated jointly in that the results of same assessment task or test and could be used to help the teacher make decisions about the next topic, as well as give an indication of how effective earlier teaching was. Similarly, the third and fourth purposes could be accommodated simultaneously. What about purposes 9 and 10? The evidence made available through assessments designed to address these purposes might be used to construct league tables so schools can be compared. It is unlikely that the assessment results furnished for such purposes would be sufficiently detailed to offer insights about a learner's strengths and weaknesses (purpose 6) or offer insights that might inform the next steps in learning (purposes 1 and 7). In order to construct league tables, the assessment methods used have to be comparable across all schools in the country. They are usually based on formal, end of year or key stage formal tests which are devised outside of the school.

On the other hand, assessments that are designed to inform teaching and learning are usually devised by the teacher and woven into day-to-day teaching. They are not usually carried out at set times and, since comparability is not an issue, they may be carried out in different ways by different teachers. The issue in this kind of assessments is getting information that teachers and learners can use to move forward. From the point of view of the learner this information is known as feedback: information that the learner uses to do better next time.

What assessment purposes from the list could be fulfilled in Cameo 1? The portfolio of work could be a useful source of evidence that might be shared at a parents' evening. Using the portfolio of work as an evidence base, the teacher might write a prose summary of a learner's writing attainment. To help with the production of such a summary the beginner teacher might draw on the programme of study (PoS) and the level descriptions (LDs) for writing – these provide details of the skills, knowledge and attitudes that are expected to be acquired in writing at various key stages. In sum, they offer a model of progression in learning and can be thought of milestones or destinations. The teacher's summary, together with the annotated evidence in the portfolio (see below), would be an excellent focus for a discussion with the learners themselves and/or with parents. It could also provide evidence of individual learner's progress over time.

In Cameo 1, the portfolios are providing an opportunity for learners to revisit their earlier work and to reflect on the feedback they were given by their teacher – the expectation being that learners benefit from talking about their achievement with each other, and with their teacher. How likely is it that league tables could be compiled from the evidence made available in such a portfolio of work? Do you think such portfolios of evidence would be comparable across classes in a school and across schools in the country? Usually such comparisons are not the purpose of assembling assessment evidence in this way. The evidence put into the portfolios will likely arise from day-to-day classroom work. The purpose is much more likely to be about celebrating and acknowledging achievement, promoting learning and monitoring achievement than enabling external agencies to hold the school or the nation to account.

To summarize so far: assessment serves many purposes, some of them overlapping.

There are four key purposes, however: (1) to promote learning; (2) to diagnose learning difficulties; (3) to hold the education system to account; and (4) to accredit learning. Here is an assessment example for each of these purposes respectively: a teacher-devised assessment task to determine learners' ability to identify and apply number operations in shopping situations; a reading test/task involving an analysis of a reader's mistakes or miscues: a test of a child's ability to read a passage of printed text aloud following which the assessor closely examines the nature of the errors made; the standard assessment tests and tasks at Key Stages 1 and 2; and A-level exams.

Assessment evidence

We are all familiar with marks, grades, levels, scores, degree classifications, and so on – measures that aim to capture or sum up attainment. These measures 'stand for' attainment in a particular area. We variously credit these measures with validity, reliability, in a word, trust. The level of trust we have in them depends on the context in which the assessment was carried out and the use to which we want to put the assessment information.

Assessment evidence can also be more direct – as well as (or, preferably, instead of) a level or a grade, we may have the actual evidence, such as the artifacts in the above portfolios. These artifacts might be annotated with teacher/assessor comments, such as the date on which the work was done, what the task was seeking to assess, how long it took to complete, whether the learner produced it working alone or with others or with support from the teacher or classroom assistant; a comment on the work linked to the criteria in the level descriptions; what the nature of the task was, and so on. It might also include a comment about how the learner rated their performance or felt about the task. Such annotations provide useful background information of the assessment context. Unlike mere levels and grades, which are often too deeply coded to be really helpful in informing teaching and learning, annotated artifacts provide concrete evidence that is meaningful, not just to the teacher, but crucially, to the learner. This kind of description might be very useful in understanding why a pupil performed well or badly. If the teacher comments are specific to the relevant success criteria, it can also be an excellent way of helping learners understand the criteria against which their work is judged. We will come back to this point again later.

Sometimes teachers use 'tick sheets' or inventories to sum up or describe a child's achievement. These can be useful for getting an overview of what a class of pupils can and can't do, but they are usually not sufficiently fine grained or detailed enough to guide teaching and learning.

Where does assessment evidence come from? All the following are legitimate sources of assessment evidence: what learners say, what learners do, what learners produce, what learners think and what learners feel. Not all these sources will be equally relevant for the four main purposes of assessment noted in the previous section but all sources will be relevant to the class teacher whose main assessment purpose is the promotion of learning.

Evidence of learning may come from different situations: the classroom, the play-ground, the assembly hall, the gym, i.e. wherever learning happens and can be observed.

Because assessment evidence is always partial, always open to negotiation and contestation, it is important to assess learning in a variety of situations (e.g. in a group or, individually) and using a variety of modes (e.g. writing, talking, making/constructing). It is especially helpful to invite learners to offer views on their performance and sometimes to record these views. Such an approach acknowledges the partiality of evidence and communicates to the learner that judging and assessing are about values and opinions and that there is no one infallible method (Hall and Burke 2004). This is acknowledged in Cameo 1 where we see learners having the opportunity to talk about the teacher's comments on their work.

Good assessment practice involves being attuned to how learners respond to situations and using this information in interaction with learners to develop their understanding (such as Cameo 2). These situations may be collaborative ones in which pupils are working together on a joint task or individual ones where learners are working on their own individualized tasks. Good assessment practice also involves designing tasks that will generate evidence of learning that matters. Here is how one writer (Nuttall 1987) in a classic study of assessment describes the kinds of task that validly assess learning:

- tasks that are concrete and within the experience of the individual;
- tasks that are presented clearly;
- tasks that learners perceive as relevant to their current concerns.

Such tasks, he suggests, invite pupils to show what they can do, as opposed to show up what they can't do. Such tasks also invite extended interaction between pupils and teacher, thus giving the teacher some access to the learner's thinking, attitudes and perhaps a glimpse of the learner's potential. Such tasks provide an opportunity for giving feedback.

Is Cameo 2, an example of good assessment practice? In my view, it is a good example of assessment designed to inform learning in the 'here and now' of classroom life. Here the teacher, Kate, is watchful of her pupils' responses. She appears to have the view that not only is what her learners do providing her with important evidence of their achievement, but deemed important also is the reasoning that lead them to act as they do. She is willing to probe what is salient to her learners. She is assuming that this offers vital clues about how she might help them. Kate tries to access Zillah's logic and thinking – seeing this as a means to understanding her understanding and misunderstanding. Having understood Zillah's mindset, she is now well placed to intervene, not by simply telling her the answer but by guiding her to construct the problem differently. If Kate had not probed Zillah's false logic here, she would not have understood why she got the wrong answer. In the event Zillah was helped to learn a crucial lesson – that you don't always bring in your own experiences to solve mathematical problems (Cooper and Dunne 1999).

Is this an example of assessment even if the teacher doesn't record it in some way? Not everything that is significant in classroom life needs to be written down. Recording, though important, is not assessing. Cameo 2 is an example of assessment that is beautifully integrated into teaching. It is worth noting that some assessment is planned in advance but some assessment occurs spontaneously in the light of classroom opportunities and events, like this one.

The importance of formative assessment and feedback

It may be helpful for the beginner teacher to think about formative assessment as being of two types: planned and interactive (Cowie and Bell 1999). Being formative, both are geared to supporting learning. Planned formative assessment, according to Cowie and Bell, is used to elicit permanent evidence of the thinking and achievement of pupils and such occasions are semi-formal and may occur at the beginning and end of a topic. A specific activity is set for the purpose of furnishing evidence that will be used to improve learning. Interactive formative assessment, on the other hand, takes place during teacher–pupil interaction – this is the kind of incidental, ongoing formative assessment that arises out of a learning activity. It cannot be anticipated and it has the potential to occur at any time. It involves 'noticing', 'recognizing' (what is significant) and 'responding' to pupil thinking (Cowie and Bell 1999: 107). To capitalize on such opportunities, the beginner teacher needs to talk with pupils and encourage pupils to ask questions about their work.

Over the past two decades we have learned a great deal about the kind of assessment that best promotes learning (Black and Wiliam 1998). Formative assessment is essential for all learners but seems to be especially important for so called 'low achievers'. Why is this the case?

First of all, formative assessment is designed to improve learning, not just measure it. In this sense it looks forward to the next step rather than merely looking back on what has been accomplished, without reference to future learning. Second, and more significantly, it provides vital information that the learner can use to bridge the gap between what s/he knows and needs to know or between what s/he can do and needs to be able to do. This information can be deemed 'feedback' if the learner uses it to bridge that gap (Black and Wiliam 1998).

Getting children to think about their learning and the processes of learning, e.g. how they learned something, is key to linking assessment and learning in practice (see Chapter 6). In Cameo 1, the two children had the opportunity to look back over work they had done, to articulate what was interesting, memorable and good about it, to note what the teacher said about it, and, through interaction with each other and the teacher, to define themselves as particular kinds of writers. Such attributions are important for learners' sense of identity and their feelings about what they might be capable of achieving next. Moreover, one can speculate that they had the opportunity to reflect on and talk about what constitutes successful writing. They had a chance to learn 'the rules of the game'. Making the rules of the game explicit to learners takes away the mystery – a mystery that remains if they merely get a score, a grade, a smiley face or even a comment like 'good try'. Contrast such responses with the following: 'What wonderful use of short sentences to build the suspense here', 'I would really like to know more about why Ted was afraid in your story', 'Excellent effort but watch the use of commas', 'A good try but let's discuss this'.

In the second cameo, the learner got feedback that she could apply there and then to move forward. And what was crucial here, in terms of a 'teachable moment', was the teacher's conversation with the learner. She didn't merely observe and assume Zillah's error was due to 'rounding down'. Only by probing her thinking could she determine the nature of her error and provide just the right feedback at just the right time.

It is likely that formative assessment is especially important for low achievers because it makes learning visible – they are not struggling to work out what the purpose of the task is or what the criteria for success are. The teacher makes this clear by her directions and guidance, by examples she gives, by demonstrating and modelling performances, and by providing the opportunity to talk, not only about what has been learned, but also about how it has been learned.

Classroom-based research in Medway and Oxfordshire (Black *et al.* 2003) identified several helpful strategies that teachers can use to support formative assessment, i.e. the kind of assessment that will yield feedback or information that learners can use to improve:

- sharing learning objectives or intentions with learners at the beginning of a lesson;
- revising these intentions at the end of a lesson and allowing learners to report back on what they have learned;
- encouraging children to think before responding to questions, i.e. giving them 'wait time';
- not making it a requirement that learners raise their hands for permission to speak;
- offering comments that are relevant to the particular qualities of the work (rather than marks or grades) when responding to children's written work.

One of the strategies discouraged by research (Black and Wiliam 1998) is making comparisons with other pupils. This is demotivating for pupils because it takes attention away from the specifics of the work itself.

Understanding the standard or getting a sense of what counts as good work is not a luxury but essential for a learner to make progress. However, simply knowing what is the standard is not straightforward. As Wiliam (2002) observes, telling the comedian whose audience is not laughing that he needs to be funnier is probably of little assistance! In order to improve, learners need more specific guidance; they need to have the success criteria 'unpacked' for them. In addition to the above, good (formative) assessment practice might include the following:

- making examples of work available to learners (as well as teachers!) with annotations identifying the way that the work meets the standards or success criteria;
- encouraging pupils to discuss samples of strong and weak performance;
- having learners say how a piece of work might be improved;
- facilitating and helping learners do peer assessment, e.g. in pairs, pupils mark one another's work and discuss their conclusions;
- having pupils devise questions appropriate for the assessment of their own work (rather than answering other people's questions).

The kinds of self- and peer-assessment noted above involve thinking about one's experiences and performances, reflecting on learning goals or destinations and articulating how to get there. These learning-oriented approaches to assessment recognize that the learner's active participation is pivotal.

A note about formative and summative assessment

Textbooks on assessment tend to distinguish between these two types. Formative assessment looks forward to the next steps of learning and summative assessment looks back and sums up achievement. However, summative assessment can also be used to inform future learning. For example, a prose summary of a child's writing samples, in the portfolios in Cameo 1, would constitute an example of summative assessment. However, this summary of attainment could also be used by the learners and the teacher to inform the next steps in writing. What is vital is the use to which assessment information is put – how it functions – and both formative and summative assessment can be used to inform teaching and learning.

Summative assessment and SATs

Sometimes people make the mistake of assuming summative assessment is the same as the external tasks and tests known as SATs. While these are indeed summative, they are not the only kind of summative assessment that goes on in schools, as the previous note clarifies.

Most of this chapter refers to assessment designed to support learning and is the kind of assessment the beginner teacher needs to understand really well. The external testing of pupils, which is designed to evaluate the extent to which standards are in line with expectations, is also important but is more straightforward in practice. The assessment tests and tasks are externally set and detailed guidance is given on when and how to administer and interpret the results.

However, given the references to assessment and standards in the media and sometimes in schools as well, the beginner teacher might be forgiven for thinking that the national testing of pupils – assessment *of* learning – at the end of a Key Stage is more demanding, more important and more time-consuming than assessment *for* learning. These false assumptions are made because SATs are 'high stakes' – they are used to construct league tables which are then published. League tables are seen by government as a way of pushing up standards and informing parents about school performance. Teachers often feel under considerable pressure to ensure their pupils do well in these assessments, sometimes 'teaching to the test', i.e. concentrating heavily in their teaching on those aspects that are assessed through the SATs. This marginalizes important aspects of the curriculum, such as PE, art, and music, narrows the range of assessment approaches adopted (for instance, over dependence on pencil and paper tests) and limits some pupils' opportunities to participate fully in their learning (Hall *et al.* 2004). While not denying the relevance of the national assessments, the challenge for teachers is to ensure that the main focus is on learning-oriented assessment.

Conclusion

The challenge for the beginner teacher, having recognized the significance of the learner's role in assessment and the integral nature of assessment and learning, is to assess children in a variety of ways, taking account of a range of evidence and a range of learning contexts. The best way to meet this challenge is to use good learning tasks as sources of evidence of learner's success and difficulty, to see the learner's thinking as central to the assessment process, and to involve learners in the assessment process.

Questions to set you thinking

The following are perspectives on assessment from two researchers, one from the United States, the other from the United Kingdom. On the basis of your own school experience as a pupil, as a student teacher and new teacher, and given your reading and study of the subject, what is your judgement of these perspectives? Consider the issue of whose interests are being served by the assessment systems we have in place in classrooms and in the nation generally.

1   Robert Reinecke (1998: 7) says:

    Assessments, formal or informal, considered or casual, intentional or not, powerfully affect people, particularly students. The assessment climate that students experience is a crucial component of instruction and learning. Students' assessment experiences remain with them for a lifetime and substantially affect their capacity for future learning ... emotional charge is part of the character of assessment information.

2   Dylan Wiliam (2002: 61), critical of the nature of national testing in England, poses the following questions:

    • Why are students tested as individuals, when the world of work requires people who can work well in a team?
    • Why do we test memory, when in the real world engineers and scientists never rely on memory: if they're stuck, they look things up.
    • Why do we use timed tests, when it is usually far more important to get things done right than to get things done quickly?

References

Black, P. and Wiliam, D. (1998) *Inside the Black Box: Raising Standards through Classroom Assessment*. London: Kings College School of Education.

Black, P., Harrison, C., Lee, C., Marshall, B. and Wiliam, D. (2003) *Assessment for Learning: Putting it into Practice*. Maidenhead: Open University Press.

Cooper, B. and Dunne, M. (1999) Anyone for tennis? Social class differences in children's responses to National Curriculum Mathematics testing, in P. Murphy (ed.) *Learners, Learning and Assessment.* London: Paul Chapman in association with the Open University.

Cowie, B. and Bell, B. (1999) A model of formative assessment in science education, *Assessment in Education,* 6(1): 101–16.

Hall, K. and Burke, W. (2004) *Making Formative Assessment Work: Effective Practice in the Primary Classroom.* Maidenhead: Open University Press.

Hall, K., Collins, J., Benjamin, S., Sheehy, K. and Nind, M. (2004) SATurated models of pupildom: assessment and inclusion/exclusion, *British Educational Research Journal,* 30(6): 801–17.

Nuttall, D. (1987) The validity of assessments, *European Journal of the Psychology of Education,* 11(2): 109–18.

Reinecke, R.A. (1998) *Challenging the Mind, Touching the Heart: Best Assessment Practice.* Thousand Oaks, CA: Corwin Press.

Wiliam, D. (2002) What is wrong with our educational assessment and what can be done about it? *Education Review,* 15(1): 57–62.

Suggested further reading

Carr, M. (2001) *Assessment in Early Childhood Settings: Learning Stories.* London: Paul Chapman. This is an excellent guide for the beginner teacher in assessing the learning and development of very young children. Carr develops the idea of 'learning stories' – a powerful means of staying close to children's real experiences and an imaginative way of avoiding mechanistic approaches.

Hall, K. and Burke, W. (2004) *Making Formative Assessment Work: Effective Practice in the Primary Classroom* Buckingham: Open University Press. This book explains and exemplifies formative assessment in practice, drawing on incidents and case studies from primary practice.

18 Observing closely to see more clearly: observation in the primary classroom

Linda Hargreaves and Sylvia Wolfe

Cameo 1

Somehow Dan always seems to be mobile or 'messing about' on the far side of the room, especially during group work sessions. His teacher decides to take a closer look at Dan's behaviour and devises a simple code: I = In base, O = Out of base and M = Moving about. Every 10 minutes or so, during the next practical session, she looks over to Dan and jots down I, M or O accordingly, noting his activities (see Figure 18.1). By doing this, she sees what Dan is doing at times when he is *not* attracting her attention. The results surprise her, for while there are many Ms and Os, she realises that:

1 his journeys are usually task-oriented rather than task-avoiding, e.g. finding a book, getting materials for the investigation;
2 the 'messing about' seems to be initiated by other children as Dan passes them, but the disturbances result from Dan obviously trying to get back to his investigation.

She realizes that she has assumed that Dan *causes* the disturbances because he is out of base. To check her initial observation she uses a similar observation technique with Dan in the next couple of practical sessions. Strangely enough, the number of Os and Ms decreases. If this is an 'observer effect', she is quite pleased about it.

Cameo 2

Vicki and Rachael are trainee teachers sharing a professional placement. They have a mutually supportive relationship and trust each other's feedback. Their PGCE course requires them to carry out a small-scale research study, using peer observations, if necessary. Vicki's research question is 'Is there any difference between boys' and girls' levels of participation in whole class numeracy and literacy sessions?' Her hunch is that boys tend to answer more questions in numeracy, while girls answer more literacy questions. Rachael carries out the observations in two literacy and two numeracy sessions using a simple 'blob' plan (see Figure 18.2).

Child: Dan **Curriculum area** science Weds 5th, Oct.
Task: Comparing supermarket washing-up liquids for suddiness: work out how to do fair test and then carry it out.

Time	I = In O = Out M = Mobile	Activity	Interactin g with …
1105	I	**Talking about soap suds task**	-own group
11.12	M	Collecting yogurt pot from sink. Sam goes to sink - picks up 2 pots - holds one to each eye - 'binoculars' Dan laughs/ back to place	Sam
11.20	I	Timing how long suds are lasting	No i/a
1130	M - O	Returning pots to sink. Sam is filling pots with hot water creating more suds. Dan turns away - S. grabs his sleeve and pulls him back - D. tugs himself free → back to table	Sam
1136	I	Writing /doing diagram	No i/a
11.45	M	Tidying up at Sam's group's table - gets cloth	Can't tell ??
11.55	I	(whole class - reporting back) listening intently	none

Figure 18.1 Tracking Dan

Rachel labels the blobs 'b' for boy and 'g' for girl. She records not only which children answer Vicki's questions (A) but also notes which children volunteer answers (V). Her observations confirm Vicki's hunch, but also show that the apparent gender bias lies in Vicki's selection of children to answer her questions, rather than in the children's own preferences. Similar numbers of girls and boys volunteer answers in all sessions, but Vicki tends to ask boys more often in the numeracy sessions and girls more often in literacy sessions: Vicki's expectations appear to be influencing the way she distributes questions. Accordingly, she

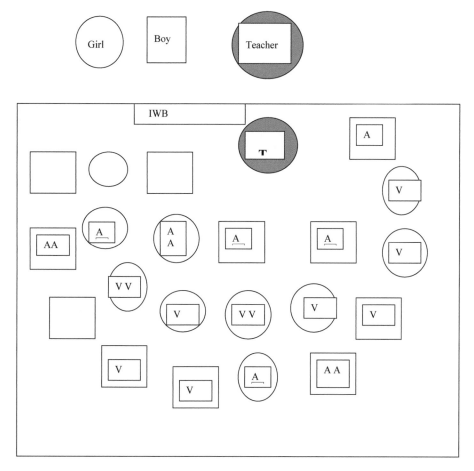

Key: V = volunteers   A = answers

Figure 18.2 Using a 'blob' chart to record who volunteers (V) and who answers (A) questions

makes a point of asking girls more often in numeracy and boys in literacy for a couple of sessions, and then asked Rachael to do another observation. This time a better balance is achieved.

Cameo 3
Twenty-two 4–5-year-old children share a big book with the teacher at the end of a long afternoon. The illustration is of a mouse standing on a ladder propped against a large strawberry that he intends to pick. Bihal and Salman are second language learners and the exchange is characterized by the teacher's emphasis on basic conceptual and language development, particularly regarding the introduction of correct mathematical vocabulary.

Participant	Linguistic and non-verbal behaviours
Bihal	He's got, that man's got a big tail (*points to illustration*)
Teacher	He has got a very big tail, hasn't he? A very long:: tail (.) (T holds the toy mouse up for the children to compare with the picture. She runs her finger along the tail in the picture) And can you see – does it look? Can you think of another word to say what his tail looks like? It's very (.) (*Extends tail*) A? (Anna has her hand up)
Anna	Straight
Teacher	Good girl. A very <u>straight</u> tail, isn't it? A very long, straight tail (.) (A child to the right of the Teacher is talking but his interruptions are ignored) What else is <u>straight</u> in this picture?
Salman	Umm [is a
Laura	[The leafs
Teacher	The leaves? (.)
Laura	Yeah
Teacher	Do you think they're straight? (.)
Laura	Mmm
James	No they're round (*draws circle in the air with a finger*)
Teacher	Can you see something else that's <u>straight</u>?
Anna	Yeah, the ladder sides (*points, moving finger up and down*)
Teacher	The ladder, that's right. I was thinking of the ladder, the sides of the ladder [they're very straight
James	[And [the bit that goes across (*gestures from side-to-side with hand as he speaks*)
Teacher	[and these parts (*points to rungs*) D'you know what these parts are called?
Sam	No
Teacher	The <u>rungs</u>. The <u>rungs</u> of the ladder.
James	No they're <u>steps</u>.
Teacher	Oh yeah they are like steps. That's another word for them.

Bihal's initiation alerts observers to gaps in his use of English – he refers to 'man' rather than 'mouse' and describes the tail as 'big' rather than 'long' or 'straight'. Anna and James add content and their own ideas to the exchange while Laura suggests that leaves are 'straight', a conceptual ambiguity that might usefully have been probed by the teacher. Although it might appear from the transcribed words that the teacher has a particular answer in mind, her almost leisurely tone of voice indicates a willingness to listen to and accept alternative ideas. The teacher's turns are supportive (the less insistent tone marked by gaps (.) in her utterances), and responsive to the children's words.

Introduction

'Observation' has been a fundamental part of training for early years' practitioners for many years (Oates 1991), but has recently become part of primary and secondary professional practice, as recognized in the *Standards for Qualified Teacher Status* (www.tda.gov.uk). It is central to the process of assessment, evaluation, reflection on practice and action research (see Chapters 13, 17 and 21).

Despite this belated recognition of its value, teachers still sometimes feel that the demands of observation can outweigh its benefits. In today's crowded curriculum, some teachers may feel it squanders teaching time, while others find it difficult to *hold back* their 'teacher's urge' to intervene when children are struggling with a problem. Discovering the strategies children use when left to work independently can reveal a great deal about their knowledge, skills and ingenuity, however (see Chapter 14), and children appreciate the teacher's *holding back*, as an 11-year-old pointed out recently, 'Like today, if she sees us getting into a pickle, she thinks she can sort it out, but usually we can do it ourselves. If we can't, then we can ask her for help. It's better if we do it ourselves.' He explained how he and another boy could sort out their 'pickles' and accommodate each other's needs: 'Like today, Carl's really tired so I'm writing it.' The tendency to intervene too soon can deny children the powerful learning gains to be achieved through socio-cognitive conflict with peers, as Piaget and others have pointed out (Wood 1998). The teacher could, instead, move close to the group and observe, i.e. *listen* to, their arguments as they 'unpickle' themselves. Inclusion of some observation time in a lesson plan, as the children work in groups (Cameo 3), or perhaps doing discreet 'spot checks' on individuals or groups (Cameo 1) can be extremely illuminating.

Unfortunately, for some teachers, observation of pedagogical practice has negative associations with the judgemental processes of school inspection. That kind of observation simply rates activities as good, bad or indifferent. Here, we are using observation to provide descriptive information about what teachers and/or children are actually doing without making value judgements. Evaluation might, or might not, come later in the process of interpretation.

Several initiatives, including the GTC(E)'s *Professional Learning Framework* (TPLF) (www.gtce.org), the criteria for *Chartered London Status* (www.teachernet.gov.uk), and the *Assessment for Learning* (AfL) group's research-based principles for the assessment of children's learning includes observation as a key professional skill (Black *et al.* 2002) (www.qca.org), all encourage the use of observation for professional development and as a research 'tool'. Observation of individual children is critical to *Foundation Stage* profiling. The principles for early years' education (perfectly applicable in primary and secondary classrooms with relevant objectives inserted), require that 'practitioners observe children and respond appropriately to help them make progress', by 'Mak[ing] systematic observations and assessments of each child's achievement, interests and learning styles; using these observations in planning learning experiences for the child, and matching their observations to the early learning goals' (DfEE/QCA 2000: 16).

New policies notwithstanding, observation will remain a key part of the professional practitioner's repertoire. In the rest of this chapter, we further justify the use of observation, suggest some simple pencil and paper recording techniques, before considering the use of more technologically advanced but easily accessible tools, such as video, MP3 and computerized systems, for observation purposes. We conclude with examples from observation-based research projects to inspire beginning teachers to examine similar themes in their own practice.

Looking and observing: What is the difference?

Cameo 1 reveals how Dan's teacher's impressions of his behaviour and perception that Dan was disturbing others were unjustified. Impressions may be quickly formed by looking at a child or a situation, but teachers must reassess their first impressions which could lead to expectations that could have a significant impact on a child's progress. Observation can help confirm, modify or reject our first impressions, systematically.

An important aspect of 'being systematic' is to write down/record observations so that they can be interpreted, analysed and reflected on away from the classroom. Writing them down as they happen forces us to focus our attention on specific behaviours. To achieve this, however, lesson plans need to include time (even just two minutes!) for observation. The teacher must decide:

- *why* the observation is taking place: the research question;
- *who* to observe: one child, a group, and/or a teacher;
- *where* to look: classroom, IT suite, playground;
- *what* behaviours to look for ('behaviour' is used generically throughout to include speaking, listening, non-verbal communication and physical activity);
- *when, how long* or *how often* to observe: whether to observe continuously, or use a 'time sampling' system, as in Cameo 1, or observe for a 30-second interval every 10 minutes;
- *how* to record the observations: notes, checklist, diagram, photographs, audio/video record.

Records of observations take many forms. Sharman *et al.* (2000) suggest numerous ways in which to conduct, record and present child observations. Wragg's (1999) guide to observation is especially useful, as are research methods textbooks, such as Bell (2005), Hopkins (1993) and, for 'first-time researchers', Roberts-Holmes (2005).

What kinds of observations – open-ended or more structured?

The answer to this question depends on:

- the purpose of the observation;
- the kinds of information sought;
- what is feasible in the time and space available.

If the aim is to find out what the children actually *say* or *do* in certain situations, long-hand notes, or an audio/video recording to be analysed later, will be most useful. If teachers already know what types of behaviour they are looking for, then structured observations, such as the use of a checklist or grid will be the most efficient method.

Child's Name: Simon (S)

Activity: Science : circuit with batteries and buzzers

Sitting/working with: Katie (K)

Each row is for 30 or 60 seconds' observation. This could be organized as a five minute block, 1 minute every 5 minutes, 2 x 5-minute periods or 10 observations spread over a session, day or half-day.

Time	What is target child actually doing?	Child interacts with:	Resources/ equipment being USED
9.30	Simon attaches wires by holding & place. Presses buzzer. "mine's working!"	Katie	battery wires buzzer unit
9.31	continues to press buzzer demonstrates to 3 children	3 children and Katie	"
9.32	watches other children doing theirs. Tries buzzer again no buzz. Partner tries &	Katie	"
	attach wires —says 'We have to 'tach them'. S. 'Do we?' Try & manipulate croc, clips	"	and crocodile clips
9.34	Katie tries & attach clips but they come off the terminals K: It's not going to work"	"	"
	Simon works buzzer again by holding wire on. Katie says 'Clip the black one on'	Katie	
9.35	Tries & clip π to battery. It falls off Ho!ho!ha! both Boy (R) comes over & watch.	Katie R.	"
9.36	S. 'ugh it's hard'. K. 'Should we ask Mrs. P.'? (S. ignores) Boy (R) watches. "Is it hot?" — S is holding wire on battery.	R	"
	S 'No it's cold' & rises on buzzing. Puts buzzer & face (to test for hot?) K. 'we've got to clip them on' How do we clip them on?		"

NOTES: Simon seems to see getting buzz as aim — he is not interested in making a circuit.
N.B. clips difficult for children to use. Too stiff?.

Figure 18.3 Individual child record

Observing children

Long-hand notes and open-ended observations are ideal for individual child studies. A simple 'semi-structured' format (e.g. Figure 18.3) means that observations over a similar period of time can be made of other children, or of the same child in a variety of situations.

Keeping in mind the influence of first impressions, it is important to practise making a factual account free from value-laden terms. For example:

> S. wanders lazily to get book from drawers and strolls back to seat
> flicks idly through pages to new page and gazes at blank page

presents a particularly negative view of what child S. did through the choice of words, such as *lazily*, *strolls*, *idly* and *gazes*. What S. *actually* did was:

- walk slowly to drawers and get book out;
- walk back, looking around;
- turn pages to find place and look at blank page.

A separate, more graphic 'commentary' might be added, thus helping the teacher become aware of his/her impressions.

Using more structured observation

A more structured observation system, based on a checklist or grid, and the use of 'time-sampling' can be particularly useful when observing a small number of children at the same time. Figure 18.4 shows a simple grid record used in the assessment of some basic science skills. It is based on just 2 minutes' observation. The column headings can be replaced by whatever skill or concept the teacher is assessing.

If several teachers want to observe the same aspects of children's behaviour, a checklist with shared definitions and examples of the behaviours to be observed will be most valuable. Initially, they should all observe the same few children (or video extract) to see how well their observations agree, that is, to check their 'inter-observer reliability'. Checklists are efficient to use. They can be accompanied by notes, but also obviate the need to write notes. A time pattern for observing events can be agreed in advance. Observations could be made instantaneously every 30 seconds, 2 minutes or even every 20 minutes for behaviours that are relatively easy to identify (see Cameo 1). For more complex behaviours, the observation might be divided into 30-second periods so that the observer can listen to the words being said, before coding. Figure 18.5 illustrates this method as the teacher has noted each time Louise showed any of the actions on the checklist during the time that she was being observed. This 'category' system shows each time a behaviour was observed during the 30 seconds, or 2 minutes, etc. that the observation lasted.

In Figure 18.6, the teacher has observed four children's social skills and simply noted

Date .20.9.......... Curriculum area(s) .Sci/tech......
Topic. fibres ....Task.. bridge task..............

Group 3	planning	measuring mass	measuring length	evaluation/ reflection
Dawn	✓✓✓		✓(talks)	
Julie	✓✓✓	✓?	✓✓✓	✓
Yvette	✓	*?check		

Examples/notes:

D: — now it'll need loads of these
   little ones

J: count them into 10s so it'll be
   100g in each pile

Y: Lets put the blue ones on first so
   it'll be more weights

D: Yeah. good idea (laughs)

Figure 18.4 Simple grid record for science

```
GESTURES                        Louise
smiles                          ///
nods                            /
faces/looks at speaker          ////
frowns
turns away

VERBAL BEHAVIOUR
asks a question
listens to other(s)             ////
offers own opinion
praises another child           /
interrupts speaker
asserts self
```

Figure 18.5 Time-sampled observation – individual child

	Clare	Jack	Mark	Louise
GESTURES				
smiles	/	/		/
nods in agreement	/			/
faces speaker	/	/		
frowns			/	
turns away			/	
VERBAL BEHAVIOUR				
asks a question	/			
listens to other(s)	/	/		
offers own opinion		/	/	
praises another child	/			
interrupts speaker		/		
asserts self		/		

Figure 18.6   Observing four children's social skills

each action once. This is called a *sign* system. It reveals which children did or did not use these actions in a situation designed to evoke them, but also allows the observer to listen for rarer skills, such as 'hypothesizing' in a science task or other evidence of higher-order thinking.

The patterns of ticks in Figure 18.6 reveal children's different social styles. It suggests, for example, that Louise participated positively with non-verbal gestures but did not speak, that Jack was more self-assertive than the others and that Clare was supportive of others.

Using diagrammatic records

A 'map-type' observation record is ideal when children are likely to be moving about, as in physical education, drama or the playground. It is also invaluable in the evaluation of classroom layout, and could even be useful for the teacher herself to ask another adult to track her movements, and note which groups or individuals get most or least attention. It might be used, for example:

- to identify 'bottlenecks';
- to track the movements of an individual child over a period of time (Figure 18.7);
- to evaluate the effects of a new room layout (Hastings and Chantry-Wood 2002);
- to record the distribution of teacher–pupil interactions, for example a small number of easily identifiably events when observing a large group (Cameo 2, Figure 18.2) (Hopkins 1993).

Observing teachers

Experienced teachers make it look easy to gain and hold the children's attention and because it looks so easy, the beginner might overlook *exactly* what the teacher is saying and doing. Sometimes teachers themselves do not recognize their own *skilled performances*, since communicative behaviours are often routinized at an unconscious level of practice. Observation can help the beginner identify the verbal and non-verbal signals that teachers use. Wragg (1999) suggests that a good way to start is by simply writing down *verbatim* two

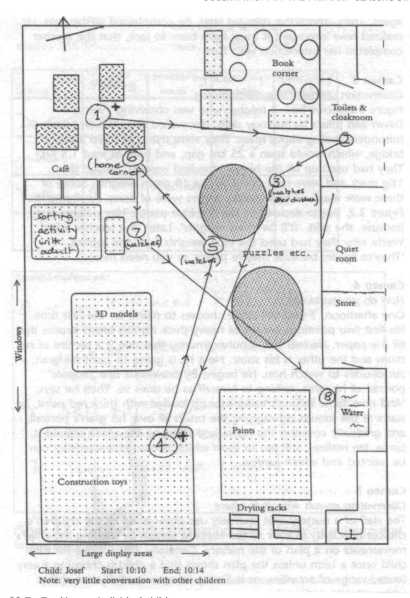

Figure 18.7 Tracking an individual child

or three of the teacher's questions and children's responses. Five minutes' observation using a page made out like Figure 18.8 and focusing on a specific aspect of the teacher's talk, will be more useful than attempting to observe the whole lesson, especially if it is possible to get the teacher to reflect on the observations after the session.

The column headings in Figure 18.8 serve as reminders to note down, in addition to the actual words, and the time, the teacher's *location*, *audience* and *non-verbal* behaviours. Teachers often use non-verbal communication to great effect and it can be worthwhile to observe this separately, recording, for example, position and posture, arms (open, folded,

ACTIVITY/TOPIC AREA....................................

Phase of session (underline): beginning   middle   end

Time	Locat-ion	Teacher's words	Non-verbal behaviour	Aud-ience

Notes about session: (any special features?)

Figure 18.8   Teacher Observation Sheet

pointing or gesturing?), eyes (making eye contact with children, scanning?) and facial expression (smiling, dead-pan, frowning?).

Beginning teachers often find that a certain phase of lessons does not go smoothly. Focused observation of how an experienced teacher tackles this phase, *recording* it in a simple format like Figure 18.8 and reflecting on it afterwards with the teacher, can help. Again, the act of recording forces the novice to focus on the strategies and tactics that the expert uses to gain or sustain the children's attention, calm them down or end the session.

When confident in identifying different types of talk, a checklist of, say, questions of different kinds, as shown in Figure 18.9, could be used to observe for a 2-minute period of teaching. Note the *'don't know'* category for anything that cannot be coded quickly.

The best-known method for the observation of teacher talk is *Flanders' Interaction Analysis Categories* (FIAC: Flanders 1970). FIAC is especially useful for observation of whole class teaching. It distinguishes between 'direct' teaching (lecturing, giving information or telling) and 'indirect' teaching (asking questions, listening to pupils' answers) as illustrated in Cameo 3. It is a semi-continuous system, consisting of ten codes, recorded every 3 seconds which is the typical rate of classroom interaction. Wragg (1999) gives more details. A simplified version would be to record 'T' (Teacher), 'P' (Pupil) or 'S' (Silence/no spoken interaction) every 3 seconds in a list (T T P T T S T . . .) according

Type of teacher talk date ...... topic .... times: start .... ends	1 number of uses in 3 min	2 number of uses in 3 min
QUESTIONS asking for a recap. of previous work asking closed questions (facts, recall) asking open questions (ideas, suggestions), other question (make note)	/ /// /	
TEACHER RESPONSES listening to a pupil (for 10 seconds minimum) positive feedback (more than just 'good') negative feedback other response (make note)	/ / (+++) // /	
STATEMENTS giving information (telling facts) giving instructions (how to do something), other statement (make note)	///	
ROUTINE TALK keeping control small talk, jokes, chat other	/ //	
Help! don't know what type of teacher talk	//	

Figure 18.9 Observing a specific aspect of teacher talk

to who is speaking. As Flanders found, the predominance of teacher talk over pupil talk soon becomes evident. FIAC is one of the earliest observational research methods, and leads into our final section.

Using observation and video for research and reflection

This final section refers to some large-scale research projects that have been based on systematic observation and/or video recording and analysis. They show how video can be used to support reflective practice and support pedagogical change. Although such projects are probably beyond the scope of most beginning teachers, observational skills can enable any teachers to pursue the same issues. ICT gadgets, such as notebooks, palm-held computers, interactive whiteboards, and the ease of use of video and digital cameras and MP3 recorders have transformed the possibilities for recording and analysing pedagogical behaviour.

The ORACLE studies (*Observational Research and Classroom Learning Evaluation*) were the first to use systematic observation extensively in England to investigate interaction in the 'enquiry-based' primary classrooms of the mid-1970s (Galton *et al.* 1980). Like Flanders, they found that 'direct' teacher talk still dominated the 'conversation'. Twenty years later, using the same structured observation system, Galton *et al.* (1999) found that teacher talk was even more dominant than in the 1970s. The strength of a structured observation system is that it can be applied to different contexts, or times, for comparative purposes. Thus, Blatchford (2003) used a similar structured system to examine the relationships between class size, classroom interaction and pupil achievement. Smith and Hardman (2003) developed a hand-held computerized system (the Noldus 'Observer') for coding and capturing classroom interactions, and investigated whether children with special educational needs experienced the same kinds of interaction as other children during the literacy hour (Hardman *et al.* 2005).

Video records provide an excellent basis for evaluation of, and reflection on, practice. In the SPRINT project (*Study of PRimary INteractive Teaching*), Moyles *et al.* (2003) videoed teachers engaged in interactive teaching, and used the videos as the basis for 'video-stimulated reflective dialogue' (VSRD) with the teachers, and subsequently coded the video using the ORACLE method. Early years practitioners in the Cambridgeshire Independent Learning (CIndLe) project used their videos for discussions of ways to foster independent learning within their settings (see Chapter 14). Myhill *et al.* (2006) provide a detailed guide on teachers' use of video for reflection, based on their 'TALK' project.

Video allows the actual *words spoken* (discourse) and the *meanings* constructed and exchanged between teachers and children to be studied even more closely when parts, even quite short sections, are transcribed (see Cameo 3). Hardman's researchers, for example, analysed the videoed discourse as well as coding the types of interaction (Mroz *et al.* 2000). They found that a very interactive pattern of 'initiation – response – feedback' (IRF) prevailed. This IRF pattern can restrict pupils' responses and inhibit expression of their ideas and arguments. Alexander (2006) refers to this kind of teaching talk, as 'recitation'. He has been working with teachers to reduce 'recitation', in favour of 'discussion' and 'dialogue' in their teaching talk, to enable pupils to articulate and share their ideas with teachers, and thus achieve 'common understanding through structured and cumulative questioning and discussion' (Alexander 2006: 38; North Yorkshire County Council 2006). The teachers involved videotaped themselves teaching, identified the teaching behaviours they wanted to change (e.g. the use of questions or pausing in speech) and evaluated their progress by comparing baseline videotapes with subsequent recordings. Some teachers shared tape extracts with the children and, thus, invoked children's meta-linguistic and meta-cognitive processes.

Video is not a panacea for the improvement of classroom discourse, however. Table 18.1 notes some of the advantages and problems associated with using video in classrooms. The ethical implications are of particular importance.

Hints and stumbling blocks

Cameo 1 shows that it is possible to teach and observe children at the same time but this takes advance planning and practice helps. When first starting to use classroom observation, remember that all observation is selective. Systematic or making timed observations seem rushed at first but becomes easier quickly when codes and layout are familiar. Children need time to get used to being observed and have to learn how to be self-sufficient when their teacher is observing. Teachers who observe regularly usually tell

Table 18.1 Advantages and problems of video observation

Some advantages Video	Some problems Video
allows reconstruction of aspects of the social situation or activity observed	may not capture all the information necessary to categorize behaviours accurately
can be reviewed and considered many times, from alternative perspectives and different disciplinary backgrounds (e.g. psychological, sociological, linguistic)	can affect or inhibit the people being observed (the observer effect). Although they may appear to acclimatize quickly, the camera's (or observer's) presence may then change the interaction observed
enriches the record of speech. It allows observers to track body language, note mediating artefacts – books and whiteboards	raises *ethical issues* in relation to ownership, anonymity, confidentiality, and future use of the video. Permission must be sought in advance to deter possible abuse or misuse of video data
with reflective dialogue can raise awareness, enhance reflection, and promote professional dialogue between teachers	requires a high level of trust and mutual support for shared reflection
offers a tool for assessment, monitoring language development and making cognitive and metacognitive processes 'visible'	can suffer from technical problems, such as shortage of power supplies, poor quality sound and space restrictions

the children that they are observing, and the children soon adapt and appreciate some feedback from the observations. Just a few minutes of focused observation of a child or another teacher is worthwhile. It will almost certainly reveal an alternative or surprising view of that person in the setting selected. We all have everything to gain by giving observation a try!

Questions to set you thinking

1 How would you use observation to investigate whether friendship pairs engage in more higher level talk (e.g. reasoning, debating) than teacher-allocated pairs?
2 What strategies could you use to free up short periods of time in which to observe the children?
3 What are the pros and cons of using video recordings for observational purposes in your current teaching context?

References

Alexander, R.J. (2006) *Towards Dialogic Teaching. Rethinking Classroom Talk* (3rd edn). Dialogos. (www.robinalexander.org.uk/dialogos.htm)

Bell, J. (2005) *Doing Your Research Project: A Guide for First-Time Researchers in Education, Health and Social Science.* Maidenhead: Open University Press.

Black, P., Harrison, C., Lee, C., Marshall, B. and Wiliam, D. (2002) *Working Inside the Black Box: Assessment for Learning in the Classroom.* London: King's College School of Education.

Blatchford, P. (2003) *The Class Size Debate: Is Small Better?* Maidenhead: Open University Press.

Department for Education and Employment/Qualifications and Curriculum Authority (2000) *Curriculum Guidance for the Foundation Stage.* London: DfEE.

Flanders, N. (1970) *Analysing Teacher Behaviour.* New York, NY: Addison-Wesley.

Galton, M., Hargreaves, L., Comber, C. and Wall, D. with Pell, T. (1999) *Inside the Primary Classroom – 20 Years On.* London: Routledge.

Galton, M., Simon, B. and Croll, P. (1980) *Inside the Primary Classroom.* London: Routledge.

Hardman, F., Smith, F. and Wall, K. (2005) Teacher-pupil dialogue with pupils with special needs in the National Literacy Strategy, *Educational Review*, 57(3): 299–316.

Hastings, N. and Chantry-Wood, K. (2002) *Reorganizing Primary Classroom Learning.* Maidenhead: Open University Press.

Hopkins, D. (1993) *A Teacher's Guide to Classroom Research* (2nd edn). Milton Keynes: Open University.

Moyles, J., Hargreaves, L., Merry, R., Paterson, A. and Esarte-Sarries, V. (2003) *Interactive Teaching in the Primary School: Digging Deeper into Meanings.* Maidenhead: Open University Press/McGraw-Hill.

Mroz, M., Smith, F. and Hardman, F. (2000) The discourse of the Literacy Hour, *Cambridge Journal of Education*, 30(3): 379–90.

Myhill, D., Jones, S. and Hopper, R. (2006) *Talking, Listening, Learning: Effective Talk in the Primary Classroom.* Maidenhead: Open University Press.

North Yorkshire County Council (NYCC) (2006) *Talk for Learning: Teaching and Learning through Dialogue.* (DVD pack containing text and 24 teaching extracts). NYCC/Dialogos (see Alexander, R.J.)

Oates, J. (1991) The competent adult, in Open University, *Working with Under Fives* (Resource Pack). Milton Keynes: Open University Press.

Roberts-Holmes, G. (2005) *Doing Your Early Years Research Project: A Step-by-Step Guide.* London: Sage Publications.

Sharman, C., Cross, W. and Vennis, D. (2000) *Observing Children: A Practical Guide* (2nd edn). London: Continuum.

Smith, F. and Hardman, F. (2003) Using computerized observation as a tool for capturing classroom interaction, *Educational Studies*, 29(1): 39–47.

Wood, D. (1998) *How Children Think and Learn* (2nd edn). Oxford: Blackwell.

Wragg, E.C. (1999) *An Introduction to Classroom Observation* (2nd edn). London: Routledge.

Suggested further reading

Alexander, R.J. (2006) *Towards Dialogic Teaching. Rethinking Classroom Talk* (3rd edn). Dialogos. (www.robinalexander.org.uk/dialogos.htm)

Dawes, L., Mercer, N. and Wegerif, R. (2002) *Thinking Together: A Programme of Activities for Developing Speaking Listening and Thinking Skills for Children aged 8–11.* Birmingham: Imaginative Minds.

Myhill, D., Jones, S. and Hopper, R. (2006) *Talking, Listening, Learning: Effective Talk in the Primary Classroom.* Maidenhead: Open University Press.

Wragg, E.C. (1999) *An Introduction to Classroom Observation* (2nd edn). London: Routledge.

19 Understanding challenging behaviour

Theodora Papatheodorou

Cameo 1

Maurice is 5-years-old, the middle child in a family of three. He is very bright with an excellent reading ability but continually seeks attention, positive or negative. He enjoys working one-to-one with an adult when the attention is focused on him; appears to think he is the only one in the class and that rules apply to everyone else but him. When tidying up, he always has to be the last one to come to the carpet; at the end of playtime he is always the last to join the line to go into class. He constantly tries to bend the rules and test the boundaries; calls out at inappropriate times, for example, if a visitor comes into class or during assembly he has to call out 'I'm Maurice and I'm 7-years-old'.

Cameo 2

Alice is 7-years-old and the youngest of five children. She has poor speech and very low self-esteem. She has self-injured by thumping herself on the forehead repeating 'I'm stupid'. She once knocked into a boy while in the playground and responded in a panicked manner telling him to hit her for the totally accidental incident. She will arrive in school and squeeze herself away between the wall and the book trolley. She is unable to accept any praise. For example, when told she had done something well, she would shake her head and, on one occasion, when a piece of her artwork was held up to show the rest of the class, she removed it, clearly feeling very uncomfortable.

Cameo 3

John is 5-years-old with two older siblings and one younger sister. Mother withdrew him from his first school 'because they could not cope with him'. A TA was employed to work one-to-one with John each afternoon. He shows aggressive behaviour towards adults but never towards the other children; he punches, kicks and spits at adults if they request him to do anything outside his own agenda. He will only speak in single words.

Mum said she could not cope with him. When the TA went to greet her at the end of one day, when he had been particularly well behaved, she expected negative feedback. When it was explained that she would receive a report about how good he had been, she did not know how to respond, saying she had hated school herself.

John's behaviour began to improve over time as he built a trusting relationship with the TA. The educational psychologist and speech and language therapist noticed progress during visits. After Easter a dramatic change was noticed – without any apparent reason, he regressed rapidly. Strategies that had been effective before the Easter break were ineffectual. John became increasingly aggressive towards adults and his behaviour continued to deteriorate. He began to upset other children in the class. Regular discussions were held between John's mother, the headteacher and SENCO.

Introduction

The first question raised from these cameos is, what constitutes challenging behaviour in an educational setting? Although the behaviours described were all perceived as being challenging for the teachers, they all differ in terms of symptoms, severity, duration and the impact they had on the children themselves and those working and playing with them.

The second question raised is, what contributes to such behaviour? Why do children behave the way they do? How do we understand their behaviour? For example, why is Maurice constantly seeking attention? Why does Alice show self-directed hostility and self-injuring behaviour? What has contributed to John's behaviour deterioration after a promising improvement?

The third question raised is how we deal with such behaviours. What can the teacher do to discourage Maurice's attention-seeking behaviour and other related disruptive behaviours or to raise Alice's self-esteem? What could have been done when changes in John's behaviour were first observed, to avoid such a setback. These questions will be the focus of the following discussion.

What is challenging behaviour?

In each of the three cameos the teachers used a number of statements to describe children's behaviour and arrived at some judgements as to the type of behaviour exhibited, that is, 'attention seeking' for Maurice, 'low self-esteem' for Alice and 'aggressive behaviour' for John. As a beginner teacher you may, or may not, agree with these judgements, but if the latter is the case, this should not be a surprise. Behaviour seen or perceived as being challenging or problematic by one teacher may be seen as being acceptable by another, depending on his/her temperament, time of the day or the context and circumstances under which the behaviour is happening (Galloway *et al.* 1982; Lawrence *et al.* 1984). However, there are certain parameters and criteria which determine whether a behaviour becomes challenging in the classroom. These include severity and persistence of the behaviour over a period of time, interference with the child's and other children's social and academic functioning, disruption of the learning and teaching process and behaviours which are considered as age- and gender-inappropriate and/or deviate from the expectations of a particular socio-cultural group (Mortimore *et al.* 1983; Gelfald *et al.* 1997).

Maurice's attention-seeking behaviour may not be of concern in terms of severity, but its persistence and interference with the teaching process (and indirectly with his and other pupils learning) becomes a challenge for the teacher. Alice's behaviour, on the other hand, may not interfere with the learning of other children and the teaching process, but its persistence, intensity, self-distracting and harming nature are equally challenging for the teacher who considers the child holistically. Finally, the severity of John's behaviour raises concerns as it is aggressive towards others, has an impact on his and others' safety and well-being and interferes with the teaching and learning process.

Behaviour classification and labelling

Depending on whether behaviours are directed towards others or the self, they are usually classified under two broad opposing categories variously labelled as:

Conduct problems	Personality problems
Externalizing problems	Internalizing problems
Anti-social behaviours	Neurotic behaviour
Acting out behaviours	Under-acting/withdrawn behaviour

In general, conduct problems include aggressive, non-compliant, disruptive, hyperactive and attention seeking behaviours. Personality problems include anxiety, inferiority, withdrawal, low self-esteem, passivity, depression and self-harming. For young children, there is a third category that of developmentally related problems that arise mainly from children's lack of awareness of, or inability to produce, acceptable behaviour. Developmentally related problems may include symptomatic behaviours of either conduct or personality problems (Papatheodorou 2005).

Maurice's and John's behaviours may be seen as falling under the category of conduct problems, whereas Alice's behaviour comes under personality problems. Considering his age, Maurice's behaviour may also be understood in terms of developmentally related problems. However, independently of how we may label and categorize behaviours, it is important to remember that this is an arbitrary and artificial division: there is much overlap between behaviours which are usually seen in a continuum rather than in terms of 'eithers or ors' (Papatheodorou 2005).

Labels, classification and categorization systems are useful devices for making sense of behaviours and can be used as mental frameworks and points of reference to plan and organize actions and/or decide about entitlement of support required. Labels, however, often have detrimental effects, such as stigmatization and exclusion, and unintended outcomes, such as self-fulfilling prophecies. Self-fulfilling prophecy is understood as an expectation or prediction (correct or false) which initiates a series of events (for example, teachers' responses and, in turn, pupils' reactions to such responses) that cause the original expectation or prediction to become true (Brophy and Good 1974).

There are clear warnings for beginner teachers to avoid making use of labels and classifications and, if they do so, to refer to behaviours, *not* to specific children: they should describe symptomatic behaviour on the basis of facts rather than assumptions and/or abstract concepts, deriving from categorization systems, and consider contextual factors. Indeed, in the three cameos, the teachers focused mainly on symptomatic behaviour, labelled the overall behaviour considering these symptoms, acknowledged the context within which the behaviours were exhibited and made some attempts to address the behaviour. Yet, exhibited behaviour remained largely unexplained and, where some kind of support was offered, this did not seem to alter behaviour (in Alice's case) or it was short-lived (in John's case).

Understanding challenging behaviour: a contextual framework

The teachers' responses to Alice's and John's challenging behaviours show that teachers see themselves as important factors in ameliorating challenging behaviours. Their first step in addressing the children's difficulties was to establish relationships that sent out messages of understanding, empathy and respect. In terms of interactional theories, the manner in which teachers and pupils relate to one another is of crucial significance in eliminating or accentuating challenging behaviours and pupil disaffection. We also now know that emotions, cognition and behaviour are dynamically interlinked. This means that the way we feel, affects the way we think and the way we think affects the way we behave (Carpenter and Apter 1988; Rolls 1999; Harden et al. 2003). Yet, the failure to change behaviour (in Alice's case) and/or sustaining initial changes (in John's case) shows that an emotionally safe environment created by one person in one context cannot compensate for possible multiple and long-lasting adverse influences.

Curricular demands and academic achievement have also been associated with children's challenging behaviour. Poor academic performance, in particular, has frequently been associated with challenging behaviour, but there is little consistency as to whether it is the cause or/and result. In general, it is now accepted that once initial causation (either challenging behaviour or poor academic performance) gets underway, gradually a more complex causal chain starts to operate (DfES, cited in Wicks-Nelson and Israel 1991; Clark 2003; McNamara 2003). For example, taking Alice's case, if the teacher continues to respond according to Alice's wishes, in time this response may have an adverse effect with her engagement with learning which in turn may further reinforce her low self-esteem. Similarly, if the teacher will not address Maurice's attention-seeking behaviour, over time this behaviour may interfere with his learning, which in the long term may have an adverse impact on his behaviour.

The physical environment of the classroom/school is another factor affecting pupils' behaviour (see Chapter 15). For example, uncomfortable and unmanageable learning environments leave pupils feeling neglected and alienated, whereas safe, predictable, encouraging and stimulating environments facilitate pupils' engagement with learning and positive behaviour. Large classrooms increase the level of motor activity and crowded conditions lead to aggressive behaviours; limited availability of learning resources may lead to instrumental aggressive behaviour, while high quality and appropriate learning resources offer children opportunities to interact with each other, learn problem-solving, stimulate their senses and stretch their bodies and emotions to new limits. It is now accepted that the ways in which space is organized implies certain order and determines how individuals behave (Jamieson *et al.* 2000; NPPS 2000).

The family context

When behaviour is not easily understood, teachers start seeking explanations that are outside of their sphere of influence and control, and consider factors that relate to the child her/himself and family circumstances (and failings). For example, in Cameo 3, John's LSA has already hinted potential parental/home influences on his behaviour. Indeed, age, gender, health and family circumstances, such as social class, family structure, rearing practices, quality of parenting and single parenthood, separation from parents or lack of stable environments, different expectations and experiences and cultural mismatch between family and school have all been the focus of research which has repeatedly shown that the kind of experiences which children have do affect their behaviour (Gelfand *et al.* 1997; Schaffer 1998; Weare 2000, and Chapter 5).

Beginner teachers need to acknowledge that no single event or factor can explain behaviour completely. Instead 'it is the totality of a child's experiences that matters' (Schaffer 1998: 109). Bronfenbrenner's (1995) idea of chrono-ecological theory suggests that behaviour is shaped, reinforced and maintained by complex and dynamic inter-relationships between multiple factors within and between different systems of influence that operate at micro (e.g. classroom/school, family unit) and macro level (policy-making agencies, societal values and attitudes) and over the life span of individuals (Bronfenbrenner 1995). It is acknowledged that a strong relationship with parents encourages good communication, parental participation and continuity for the child across the two systems – family and school.

A blueprint for assessment

During the past 30 years, symptomatic challenging behaviour has been, and, to a large extent, remains the focus of interventions. This is mainly due to the influences of behaviourism and behavioural theories which claim that behaviour is determined by the environment. So, changes in the environment (e.g. modifying teachers' responses to challenging behaviour; organizing appropriately the learning environment) would result to changes in behaviour. Yet, as Cameos 2 and 3 have shown, addressing symptomatic behaviour in one context and by one person (e.g. in the classroom by the teacher/learning support assistant) does not always bring about desired outcomes.

When challenging behaviours occur over a period of time, are frequent and severe, and/or do not respond to strategies employed by teachers in everyday teaching and learning practices, it is imperative that systematic assessment takes place to determine the nature of such challenging behaviours, contextual contributory factors and the intervention required (Ballard 1991; Campell 2002). Assessment is a team approach led by the SENCO and/or the Specialist Leader for Behaviour and Attendance, if the school has one, and actively involves the teacher. It seeks information from the child and his/her parents and, where and when necessary, other professionals with particular expertise (DfES 2001; Watson and Steege 2003).

Gathering information

Informal observations are usually the starting point for initiating formal and systematic observations conducted over a sustained and concentrated period of time and across different settings (see Chapter 18). Observations should take place in naturalistic environments, where challenging behaviours occur, and focus on the description of overt behaviour and situational events. At this stage, any interpretations of, and/or judgements on, the child's behaviour should be suspended or separately recorded to be used in discussions aiming to make sense of the information gathered (Quinn *et al.* 1998; Watson and Steege 2003, and Chapter 17).

Additional information may be gathered by reviewing, for example, records maintained by the school. These records provide general facts about the child (e.g. health problems, allergies, hearing, vision, etc.) and maybe information about her/his behaviour across different settings, background information about her/his family, the wider community and neighbourhood. Parents also provide important information and insights about the child's behaviour across different contexts and environments, her/his strengths and capabilities, contextual factors and how these may influence behaviour (see Chapter 5). Finally, the children themselves are an important source of information to allow them to give their version of events, express their feelings and provide an insight into the functions which their behaviour serves. However, receiving information from parents and listening to the child's voice is not an easy and straightforward affair; it requires sensitivity and empathy, time to build rapport and intuitiveness and tactfulness to reach to the core of the matter.

When collecting information, there is a danger of focusing primarily on challenging behaviours and ignoring the child's strengths and positive manifestations of behaviour (e.g. personal characteristics, predispositions and skills), emerging competencies and/or positive features. These will be used for planning an intervention programme that utilizes the child's strengths (Meisels and Atkins-Burnett 2000).

What to do with the information

Information collected must be carefully analysed and interrogated by the assessment team (see Chapter 17) by asking questions such as: where and when is the behaviour more likely to occur? Does the behaviour raise concerns across different contexts and situations? What has preceded (antecedents) and followed (consequences) the behaviour? Who else has been involved? How is the daily programme organized and structured? Is the daily programme too unpredictable? How is the physical environment organized? Is it possible for challenging behaviour to be secondary to other primary problems or difficulties? Is it more likely that 'bad' behaviour is noticed rather than 'good' behaviour?

The careful analysis of information must enable the assessment team to do the following:

1 Determine the symptomatic behaviours; whether the behaviour is happening in isolation or in conjunction with other behaviours and identify any recurring

patterns. For example, in Cameos 2 and 3, speech and language difficulties have been mentioned for both Alice and John.

2   Determine the frequency, duration and severity of challenging behaviours.
3   Identify the timing and location of the behaviour as well as others involved in challenging behaviour incidents.
4   Identify the functions which behaviour may serve (e.g. gaining attention in Maurice's case; avoiding attention in Alice's case).
5   Make hypotheses and attempt to establish possible factors that are not directly observable (e.g. the child's feelings and thoughts).
6   Establish what has been tried so far, when, where, by whom and for how long and whether it has worked or not (Papatheodorou 2005).

Responding to challenging behaviour

You can use the information gained to prepare a behaviour intervention plan that is individually tailored. It is accepted that universal and rigidly applied intervention programmes are of little value and their use is considered unwise; not all programmes are appropriate for all children. Evidence-based planning for intervention is beyond dispute and assessment provides the evidence required to plan for individualized intervention (Barrett 2000; Wolery 2000; Fox *et al.* 2002; Pretti-Frontczak *et al.* 2002; Visser 2002; McNamara and Hollinger 2003; Watson and Steege 2003).

Behaviour intervention plans aim to address the needs of an individual child through the existing curriculum and throughout everyday learning experiences in different settings (e.g. school, home). The behaviour intervention plan is expected to do the following:

* set out long-term goals and short-term objectives;
* identify intervention strategies and include a description of them – especially for new ones that have not been implemented before – explaining how and why they are used, environmental and curricula changes/modifications, and support and supplementary resources required (within school or other agencies);
* state the duration of the intervention plan, provide information about the monitoring process and identify the criteria to be used for its evaluation (Curtiss *et al.* 2002).

Long-term goals are usually set out on an annual basis and specify the time limit for achievement. Short-term objectives are the observable and measurable behaviours which are set out to be accomplished at regular intervals (e.g. mid- or end-term). In cases where short-term objectives are too many or the underlying factors are complex, these should be prioritized to address first of all behaviours that are most likely to have a knock-on effect on the overall behaviour. Short-term objectives should always remain manageable.

Behaviour management strategies

Depending on the complexity and severity of challenging behaviours and their function, the behaviour intervention plan may include a single, or range of, behaviour management strategies. A combination of strategies that are consistently applied at school and home by teachers and family members are more effective than a single strategy implemented in one context. As a general rule, behaviour management strategies should build upon the children's strengths and competencies and be embedded into their experiences. If management strategies are used to reduce or eliminate challenging behaviours, these should gradually be phased out as the child develops positive behaviours (Curtiss *et al.* 2002).

Behaviour management strategies implemented within the school context, should be interlinked and incorporated into daily planning, as this minimizes disruption and enables the child to receive support that is meaningfully embedded in the curriculum. Adhering to an inclusive ethos, provision made for an individual child may be different or additional to that offered to all children, but this should not exclude that child from the daily programme. However, it must be noted that some behaviours are so severe and intense that they require specialist intervention going beyond the input offered in the school.

As with assessment, parents should be consulted in all cases, participating in discussions and being part of any intervention programme (Wilson 2001; Fox and Dunlop 2002). Active parental involvement offers continuity and consistent application of behaviour management strategies across school and home and provides opportunities for parents and the family members to develop new skills and ways of interacting with the child. In terms of interactional theories, change in parental behaviour itself often alters the dynamics and patterns of interactions within the family that, in turn, influences the child's behaviour which again impacts on the family relationships.

Monitoring and evaluation

The introduced behaviour intervention plan must be monitored and evaluated regularly to determine its successful implementation and effectiveness. This involves the systematic collection of information, either informally or formally, throughout the implementation of the behaviour intervention plan and/or during specified periods of time (e.g. mid- or end-term). The information collected will be used to determine the extent to which short-term objectives and the overall goals of the programme have been met (Barrett 2000; Horner *et al.* 2001; Curtiss *et al.* 2002).

How do you decide what information to collect, when, how often and by whom? The short-term objectives of the intervention plan, broken down into small observable and measurable elements of behaviour, form the criteria for on-going (mid- or end-term) evaluation. Whether the overall goals have been achieved or not, is decided on the basis of information collected at the end of the intervention plan by using the same methods and sources as those used for the initial assessment of challenging behaviours. Such information will allow for direct comparability of behaviours at the beginning and end of the behaviour intervention plan period.

The fusion between assessment and intervention

If on-going evaluation demonstrates that the intended short-term objectives and long-term goals have been achieved, the intervention strategies may cease. If progress has been made, but not all objectives have been achieved the intervention strategies may continue and/or be modified. If no progress has been made, then the child's behaviour should be reassessed and, on the basis of the new information, a modified or new intervention plan may be devised. It is evident that assessment and intervention are on-going interactive processes that continuously inform each other rather than distinctly different processes conducted at different stages. Evidently, the fusion between assessment and intervention is necessary for addressing challenging behaviour (Kelly and Barnard 2000; Meisels and Atkins-Burnett 2000).

Conclusion

This chapter has attempted to provide a brief account of a complex and challenging issue that many beginner teachers face in their early professional lives: challenging behaviour in the classroom/school context. Four issues have been addressed: (1) what constitutes challenging behaviour; (2) how we understand challenging behaviour; (3) how we assess challenging behaviour; and (4) how we intervene to manage challenging behaviours. All four issues are clearly interlinked and impact on how challenging behaviour is addressed and managed to support children's well-being and their participation in the learning process.

Questions to set you thinking

1   Recall a case of challenging behaviour in your class and summarize briefly in writing what you did to address such behaviour. Now think what you might have done differently, considering the information in this chapter.
2   Get a copy of the school's behaviour policy. Can you summarize its underlying principles and procedures for dealing with challenging behaviour? Now read the behaviour policy again and think whether there are any issues that you may like to discuss with the SENCO in your school.
3   You may have already read the *Code of Practice for Special Educational Needs*. Revisit the document and think how your own practice and the school's behaviour policy fit in with the recommendations made.

References

Ballard, K.D. (1991) Assessment for early intervention; evaluating child development and learning in context, in D. Mitchell and R.I. Brown (eds) *Early Intervention Studies for Young Children with Special Needs*. London: Chapman and Hall.

Barrett, H. (2000) The politics and chemistry of early intervention, *Emotional and Behavioural Difficulties*, 5(2): 3–9.

Bronfenbrenner, U. (1995) Development ecology through space and time: a future perspective, in P. Moen, G.H. Elder and K. Luescher (eds) *Examining Lives in Context: Perspectives on Ecology of Human Development*. Washington, DC: American Psychological Publication.

Brophy, J.E. and Good, T.L. (1974) *Teacher-Student Relationships: Causes and Consequences*. New York, NY: Holt, Rinehart and Winston.

Campell, S.B. (2002) *Behavior Problems in Preschool Children*. New York, NY: The Academic Press.

Carpenter, R.L. and Apter, S.J. (1988) Research integration of cognitive-emotional interventions for behaviourally disordered children and youth, in M.C. Wang, M.C. Reynolds and H.J. Walberg (eds) *Handbook of Special Education Research and Practice*, vol. 2. Oxford: Pergamon Press.

Clark, T. (2003) Why behaviour training for schools (2nd edn). Paper presented at Teacher Training Agency's conference on behaviour management in teaching, Birmingham, March.

Curtiss, V.S., Mathur, S.R. and Rutherford, R.B. (2002) Developing behavioural intervention plans: a step-by-step approach. *Beyond Behavior*, (Winter Issue), 28–31. Available online. www.ccbd.net/documents/bb/developing_a_BIP_winter_02.pdf (accessed 12 April 2004).

Department for Education and Skills (2001) *Special Educational Needs Code of Practice*. London: DfES.

Fox, L. and Dunlop, G. (2002) Family-centered practices in positive behaviour support, *Beyond Behavior*, (Winter Issue), 24–6. Available online www.ccbd.net/documents/bb/family_positive_support_winter_02.pdf (accessed 12 April 2004).

Fox, L., Vaughn, B.J., Wyatte, M. L. and Dunlap, G. (2002) We can't expect other people to understand: family perspectives on problem behaviour, *Exceptional Children*, 68(4): 437–50.

Galloway, D., Ball, T., Blomfield, D. and Seyd, R. (1982) *Schools and Disruptive Pupils*. London: Longman.

Gelfand, D.M., Jenson, W.R. and Drew, C.J. (1997) *Understanding Child Behavior Disorders*. Fort Worth, TX: Harcourt Brace.

Harden, A., Thomas, J., Evans, J., Scanlon, M. and Sinclair, J. (2003) *Supporting Pupils with Emotional and Behavioural Difficulties (EBD) in Mainstream Primary Schools: A Systemic Review of Recent Research on Strategy Effectiveness (1999–2002). Research Evidence in Education Library*. London: EPPI-Centre, Institute of Education: Social Science Research Unit.

Horner, R.H., Sugai, G.A. and Todd, A.W. (2001) 'Data' need not be a four-letter word: using data to improve school wide discipline, *Beyond Behavior*, (Fall Issue), 20–2. Available online ccbd.net/documents/bb/ datanotbe4letterword.pdf (accessed 12 April 2004).

Jamieson, P., Fisher, K., Gilding, T., Taylor, P.G. and Trevitt, A.D.F. (2000) Place and space in the design of new environments, *Higher Education Research and Development*, 19(2): 221–37.

Kelly, J.F. and Bernard, K.E. (2000) Assessment of parent-child interaction: implications for early intervention, in J.P. Shonkoff and S.J. Meisels (eds) *Handbook of Early Childhood Intervention*. Cambridge: Cambridge University Press.

Lawrence, J., Steed, D. and Young, P. (1984) *Disruptive Children – Disruptive Schools?* London: Routledge.

McNamara, K. and Hollinger, C. (2003) Intervention-based assessment: evaluation rates and eligibility findings, *Exceptional Children*, 69(2): 181–93.

McNamara, S. (2003) Managing behaviour creatively, keynote speech at the *International Conference on Communication, Emotion and Behaviour* organized by SEBDA in Leicester, UK, 12–14 September.

Meisels, S.J. and Atkins-Burnett, S. (2000) The elements of early childhood assessment, in J.P. Shonkoff and S.J. Meisels (eds) *Handbook of Early Childhood Intervention*. Cambridge: Cambridge University Press.

Mortimore, P., Davies, J., Varlaam, A. and West, A. with Devine, P. and Mazza, J. (1983) *Behaviour Problems in Schools: An Evaluation of Support Centres*. London: Croom Helm.

NPPS (2000) *Age-Appropriate Design Guidelines for Playgrounds*. Available online: http://www.uni.edu/playground/tips/SAFE/ageappr_guidelines.html (accessed 6 April 2002).

Papatheodorou, T. (2005) *Behaviour Problems in the Early Years, A Guide for Understanding and Support*. London: Routledge.

Pretti-Frontczak, K., Kowalsi, K. and Douglas Brown, R. (2002) Pre-school teachers' use of assessment and curricula: a state wide examination, *Exceptional Children*, 69(1): 109–23.

Quinn, M.M., Gable, R.A., Rutherford, R.B., Nelson, C.M. and Howell, K.W. (1998) *Addressing Student Problem Behavior: An IEP's Team Introduction to Functional Behavioral Assessment and Behavior Intervention Plans*. Washington, DC: The Center for Effective Collaboration and Practice. Available online http://cecp.air.org/fba/problembehavior/funcanal.pdf (accessed 26 February 2004).

Rolls, E.T. (1999) *The Brain and Emotion*. Oxford: Oxford University Press.

Schaffer, R.H. (1998) *Making Decisions about Children* (2nd edn). Oxford: Blackwell.

Visser, J. (2002) The David Willis lecture 2001. Eternal verities: the strongest links, *Emotional and Behavioural Difficulties*, 7(2): 68–96.

Watson, S. and Steege, M. (2003) *Conducting School-Based Functional Behavioral Assessments: A Practitioner's Guide*. New York, NY: The Guilford Press.

Weare, K. (2000) *Promoting Mental, Emotional and Social Health: A Whole School Approach*, London: Routledge.

Wicks-Nelson, R. and Israel, A.C. (1991) *Behavior Disorders of Childhood*, (2nd edn). Englewood Cliffs, NJ: Prentice-Hall.

Wilson, W. (2001) The child care worker as a facilitator of family treatment, *The International Child and Youth Care Network*. Available online http://www.cyc-net.org/cyc-online/cycol-0501–family.html (accessed 25 March 2004).

Wolery, M. (2000) Behavioural and educational approaches to early intervention, in J.P. Shonkoff and S.J. Meisels (eds) *Handbook of Early Childhood Intervention*. Cambridge: Cambridge University Press.

Suggested further reading

Derrington, C. and Groom, B. (2004) *A Team Approach to Behaviour Management*. London: Paul Chapman. A practical book written primarily for SENCOs but equally useful for anyone who deals with the management of children's behaviour.

Papatheodorou, T. (2005) *Behaviour Problems in the Early Years: A Guide for Understanding and Support*. London: Routledge. Focusing on behaviour problems exhibited by young children, it discusses issues of terminology and definitions, factors associated with behaviour problems, screening, assessment and intervention procedures.

Porter, L. (2000) *Behaviour in Schools: Theory and Practice for Teachers*. Buckingham: Open University Press. A book that successfully integrates theory and practice for teacher use.

Watson, T.S. and Steege, M.W. (2003) *Conducting School-Based Functional Behavioural Assessments*. New York and London: Guilford Press. Focuses specifically on the assessment of the functions which behaviour serves.

20 Dialogue with difference: understanding race equality

Alison Shilela and Alan Bradwell

Cameo 1

Two Year 3 boys are in the playground at lunchtime. They have grown up together and are close friends. One boy is white and one is from a Pakistani background. They are playing 'Superman'. Both want to be Superman and neither wants to be the villain. They both lose their tempers and the white boy shouts, 'You can't play Superman because you are a Paki and all Pakis blow people up.' Both children burst into tears and the lunchtime supervisor comes over to calm them down.

Cameo 2

A black student teacher begins her qualifying school experience. She has had good reports from her previous school placements and feels well prepared for teaching. She has been advised by a (white) student that the mentor is extremely supportive and positive. However, as the first week progresses she finds her (white) mentor seems reluctant to support her, constantly picking up on insignificant aspects of classroom organization, using these as prompts to ask the question 'Are you sure teaching is the right thing for you?'

Cameo 3

A child who speaks little English joins a Year 6 class during the Autumn Term. The teacher decides that because she has so little English she will not be able to achieve at the projected levels of most of the children in her class for the SATs. The child is placed with the lowest achievers' group. The teacher plans to review her progress in English after a term and reconsider the grouping arrangements.

Introduction

This chapter explores the relationship between understandings of race equality manifested in the learning context and the lived experience of learners and practitioners. It emphasizes the need for collective commitment to engage with the dynamics of difference by taking into account the rapidly changing nature of the primary school workforce, the increasingly diverse ethnic profile of our primary children and the reality of under-achievement. This chapter aims to do the following:

- engage the reader with issues of race equality;
- enable beginning practitioners to address challenging situations in school with a degree of informed confidence;
- contribute to the development of a positive teaching philosophy.

It is divided into three parts:

- a framework for equality suggests a principled framework with which to analyse your classroom practice;
- understanding equality explores the political, theoretical and statistical background to race equality;
- analysis for equality in which the cameos are interrogated.

A framework for equality

Principles for good teaching

We begin with five *musts* for good teaching. The teacher *must* engage with:

- *the potential* for the future;
- *him/herself* as a teacher and with his/her background;
- *the learners* and their backgrounds;
- *the curriculum* and its background;
- *the learning* and its background.

Interaction with and between these aspects enables a discourse of dynamism resulting in a learning environment in which teachers and learners engage with, lead, manage and initiate change.

Change is the key thread running through these principles: all teaching is about change. We teach children to read, write, calculate and think at increasingly advanced levels. We change their social and economic skills so that they are better able to prosper as responsible members of society. But, we change children in a third way: we either prepare them to accept that some ethnic groups are more valued than others; or we prepare them to challenge this notion. This chapter is primarily about enabling you, as a beginner teacher, to see yourself and your school environment as powerful influencers, catalysts for change which challenge the practice of ethnic privilege.

Principles for equality

The Runnymede Trust has published guiding principles which enable us to gain a concrete understanding of this multifaceted concept, while offering practical approaches to planning (Runnymede Trust 2003). These principles, derived from the National

Curriculum (DfEE 1999) and the Race Relations (Amendment) Act (HMSO 2000) can be used as a framework for all curriculum planning. The principles are as follows:

1　Prioritize equality of opportunity and access.
2　Ensure excellence for all.
3　Support the development of cultural and personal identities.
4　Prepare pupils for citizenship.

These principles are also reflected as integral strands of the *Standards for Qualified Teacher Status* (TDA 2006). The relationship between the principles for good teaching and teaching for equality can be understood as *the dialogue with difference*. It is not enough, however, simply to believe in the principles. Dialogue with difference must be a considered, deliberate act.

Understanding equality

Our understandings of equality are formed in terms of our personal, professional and academic experiences. Classroom practitioners engage with understandings derived from a range of sources, including national, local authority and school policies; theories; colleagues; local communities; the children and their families. The interaction of different understandings influences the manifestation of equality in the classroom. Teachers lead the learning of a class. This leadership role includes taking responsibility for and to other adults who contribute to the learning context. A shared understanding of equality is a key component of the learning climate.

Political understandings: government education policy

The most recent changes in educational policy have included a strong move towards closer professional liaison between agencies concerned with the welfare of children. This is expressed in *Every Child Matters*, and the *Workforce Reform Agenda* (DfES 2003; TTA 2003; OfSTED 2005a). These policies have redefined the operational structure and remit of schools ensuring that everyone involved in child development is appropriately qualified and has a reasonable workload so that children may benefit from the best possible education.

　　This redefinition means an evolving experience for primary pupils, who traditionally might only have seen one teacher throughout the day. Pupils may now be taught by various people. Teaching assistants now have the opportunity to acquire professional qualifications which enable them to support classroom learning more effectively (see Chapter 16). Other professionals from outside the school, such as educational psychologists, may also support children in the classroom context. The need for close liaison is paramount. The onus is on the class teacher to orchestrate this liaison in order to create a coherent learning environment.

Theoretical understandings

Four different theories of equality in education inform this chapter:

- *multicultural education* which views all sets of cultural values equally;
- *anti-racist education* which challenges privilege, based on (the majority) ethnic, cultural or racial values;
- *common education* which privileges one set (majority) of ethnic, cultural or racial values;
- *intercultural education* which sees shared values evolving from engagement and negotiation.

Multicultural education

Multicultural education, developed in the 1970s and 1980s, was based on the notion that cultural diversity is to be celebrated as a source of enrichment. Multicultural education sought to challenge a 'Euro-centred' curriculum which preserved the idea of Western superiority. Schools following a multicultural curriculum would integrate a range of cultural manifestations in their provision, for example, see Gardner (2004).

Anti-racist education

This approach was adopted by the Inner London Education Authority in the late 1980s. It started from the premise that white people in Britain enjoy a position of power and privilege, based on their imperialist colonial heritage. Teachers were encouraged to confront their own prejudices and effect a shift in their own mindsets before attempting to challenge inequality in a learning context, for example, see Gaine (2001).

A common education

Education should be open to all sections of society who would be assimilated and integrated to the dominant culture as patriotic citizens. The roles of the school and the home, while complementary, would be separate. The school helps children learn the knowledge, skills, language and habits for successful social and economic participation in national society. Part of this approach was to learn a single national history and culture. Differences of custom and 'folkways' should belong to the home/church [*sic*]/local community (Ravitch 1991).

Intercultural education

Intercultural education recognizes that the identity of a nation is to be seen within international and global perspectives. The world has become increasingly interdependent. Britain can be seen as a microcosm of this interaction in that the British people are heterogeneous, representing a range of cultures, religions, languages and ethnic origins. This multifaceted 'Britishness' is a dynamic concept which is evolving as the result of interactions between the many differences (CRE 2005, 2006).

A way of looking at these interactions is suggested by Giroux's theory of border pedagogies (Giroux 1991). He argues that proponents of a common education see those from 'other' cultures as needing to be helped by members of the dominant culture to cross the borders to integrate within the dominant culture. Multicultural educators say that it is for the dominant culture to cross the border to understand the 'other' ethnicities, but the borders remain in place. Border pedagogy says that the new imagined culture of the community, be it national, local or international, will arise from dialogues taking place on the 'borders' between cultures. Such dialogues will take place wherever diversity meets – and the quality of the emerging discourse will depend on the commitment of each participating group to create new understandings.

The reality of inequality

The current UK government statistics acknowledge that pupils from different ethnic groups attain at different rates. At the Foundation Stage, Bangladeshi, African Caribbean, Black African and those who were classified as White Other and Black Other are underperforming (DfES 2005). The children who underachieve throughout their entire primary school education belong in the main to Black Caribbean, Black Other, Pakistani, Gypsy, Roma and Traveller children of Irish heritage.

Schools are required to report on the 'value-added' provision of their school. This means measuring pupil progress (e.g. the distance travelled) from individual starting points rather than simply measuring results through SATs. The statistics derived from these reports show that children from all minority ethnic groups make more progress than their white British peers when contextual factors, such as social and economic deprivation, are taken into account. Research shows that deprivation plays a larger role in underachievement than ethnicity (DfES 2005: 46).

The statistics also show that there is a changing profile of attainment with, for example, Bangladeshi and Pakistani pupils showing a rising profile of achievement while the attainment gap between White and Black African pupils has widened in every subject and in every Key Stage from 2003 to 2005. It has been shown that children from some minority ethnic groups consistently out-perform their white British peers at all Key Stages. These are Chinese, Indian and Mixed White and Asian pupils. However, although boys from Black Caribbean and Black Other are the lowest performers at GCSE level, these pupils are making faster progress than their White British peers (DfES 2005).

Although such patterns of attainment are longstanding, it does not mean that lower attainment among pupils from minority ethnic groups is inevitable. OfSTED (2005b) research suggests that no single ethnic group is innately less capable of success than any other. Additionally research shows that the attainment of children for whom English is an Additional Language (EAL) rises significantly with the improvement of their English language skills (Gillborn and Mirza 2000; OfSTED 2005b: 7). Changing rates of progress are noted in some minority ethnic groups, a key indicator of potential. The challenge for educators is to develop teaching and learning practices which are more likely to enable all children to achieve.

Analysing the cameos

In analysing the cameos, the differences are identified and engagement with the differences is deconstructed from an intercultural perspective. The situations are interrogated in terms of power relations and potential for change. An exemplar mapping framework is included for Cameo 1, to prompt reflection on the dialogue with difference using the framework described in Part 1, applying the framework for equality to show the different discourses and the role of the teacher in managing these cross-border dialogues. There is no single way of dealing with such difficult situations. However, using the framework will provide a guide as to how to engage with each situation from a theoretically informed position.

Cameo 1

- *Differences*: race, ethnicity, religion.
- *Issues* (musts for teaching and principles for equality): identity, equality of access, citizenship, curriculum, potential.
- *Power*: Children will fall out. What is worrying here is that the grounds for one being the hero and the other the villain is based on ethnicity. The white child is echoing information he has absorbed from sources which portray Islam and Pakistan as predominantly sources of terrorism (Adams and Moyles 2005).

   Name calling and references to religion using racial and ethnic stereotypes attack not only the individual addressee, but also his/her nationality, ethnic heritage, family background, religion and, in this case through the reference to bombing, his/her development as a responsible citizen. What might it mean for the Pakistani boy to be so rejected by a lifelong friend? How would it make him feel about himself, his family and his sense of belonging, to the school, the town, the country? How the school deals with the name calling will say much about the school's position on Islamaphobia, identified by the Runnymede Trust, as the fastest growing cause of racist attacks in Britain (Runnymede Trust 1997).

   We are all influenced by collective social values that are often insidiously expressed on television. Explicit news coverage is not the only way we receive information on ethnicity: advertisements are particularly influential. Monitoring a television channel over an evening can reveal much. How often are Muslims featured and how often is Islam portrayed positively and negatively? Subtle messages are also conveyed about people who are *not* represented: omission is a powerful form of exclusion. By omitting certain groups of people the received message is that the omitted groups do not feature in our 'normal' daily lives.

- *Change*: The first step in planning for equality is to start with the pupil's life experiences. How will we support the development of their personal and social identity? Identity is a dynamic and multifaceted concept. We normally belong to several different groups (e.g. British Pakistani, Muslim, vegetarian) with varying degrees of allegiance to each identifying characteristic. Allegiances may also change. The Commission for Racial Equality's research on Britishness revealed that when people are made to feel different or unusual in a community, an increased sense of allegiance to that 'difference' is expressed (CRE 2005: 8). This was shown to be true for Bangladeshi and Pakistani Muslims, who made it clear that since the events of 11 September 2001, religion has become an experienced difference with which they strongly identify.

   For classroom practitioners it is important to allow children the space to develop their own identities. Typically, children who feel valued and secure about their identity have the self-awareness that engenders empathy, enabling them to respect the needs of others. This sense of self within a larger community is an essential precursor to preparing pupils and young people for participation in society.

Negotiating, taking turns and reaching consensus are vital learning and social skills which can be integrated into learning activities. The children in this cameo have the power to ensure equality of access to the role of superheroes (see Table 20.1).

Cameo 2

- *Differences*: race, ethnicity.
- *Issues* (musts for teaching, principles for equality): engaging with self, expectations, identity, citizenship, potential, learning, collective commitment.
- *Power*: The mentor should be key in helping this student teacher realize her classroom potential. Yet here, the mentor seems to act in the opposite way. This scenario demonstrates a context in which institutionalized racism is manifested (Macpherson 1999). The underlying assumption is that the teaching profession is for white people, an unspoken and probably unconscious desire to maintain the status quo. The profession is dominated by white teachers. Teachers from minority ethnic backgrounds currently constitute only 10.5 per cent of the teaching population with the largest number of these teachers belonging to the 'White Other' category (DfES 2005). These figures reflect disproportionately to the primary pupil population, which currently constitutes 21 per cent pupils from minority ethnic groups (DfES 2005: 104). If there are white students in the school who are not being asked the same question and if the student had been told how supportive the mentor was from previous (white) students, then this is potentially a manifestation of racism.

  Insidious manifestations of racism such as this can result in reinforced low expectations and could adversely affect the performance of a potentially effective beginner teacher. The collective commitment to equality is under scrutiny here. School communities do not only consist of children. The mentor is in a powerful position as a 'gate keeper' to the profession. If we go back to the principles of good teaching and consider how the mentor is engaging with the potential of the future, we see that she challenges the student's decision to go into teaching. The mentor's role is not to question the student's career choice, but to support her in achieving it.

- *Change*: It may be that the attitudes expressed by other members of staff conflict with the messages you are trying to convey with regard to equality. However, we cannot expect to change others' attitudes overnight – as Klein (1993) suggests, 'Attitudes are extremely difficult to change ... children only pass through the school once, and can't be put on ice to await the slow process of teachers' attitude to change' (Klein 1993: 129). The implication here is that practice should exemplify whole school commitment to equality through engaging with difference on the daily basis at all levels.

Table 20.1 Mapping to show dialogue with difference

Dialogue with Difference	Equality of access	Identity	Excellence	Citizenship/participation
Engage with future potential	How does this situation reflect on classroom rules of behaviour?	How does this situation relate to your vision for the future? What practical steps can be taken to help restore confidence and trust?	How could you create the perfect playground conditions? What are the children's views?	How do pupils express their belief in their own potential? How are pupils enabled to work together, in teams, etc.? How are pupils helped to trust each other? How does this situation relate to the school's mission statement?
Engage with self	How can I ensure classroom principles for fairness apply at lunchtime?	How do I feel about the status of Islam, how does this affect my practice?	How do I present a balanced view? Do I understand Islamaphobia? How confident am I in dealing with controversial issues? Where would I go for support? What indicators can we use to show that practice is achieving equality?	Do my views and practice reflect those of the school? Can I take an active role in influencing policy or practice? Am I prepared to challenge negative viewpoints? Who is the named governor for Equality of Opportunity in the school? How close are links with the Muslim community?
Engage with learner	How can I enable children to become autonomous, responsible and caring in the playground?	How does the child identify with Islam? How do peers respond to Islam? Am I familiar with religions represented in class?	Are pupils receiving balanced and accurate information from different sources?	How do I enable pupils to manage conflict and work together?
Engage with curriculum	How much training have the lunchtime supervisors had? How much of the informal curriculum is influencing children's social development? How can I integrate issues into formal curriculum?	How is Islam portrayed in the curriculum?	Are materials balanced, up-to-date?	How do I manage the curriculum to enable children to engage with controversial issues?
Engage with learning	How often do children practise turntaking, negotiation, collaboration?	How do I integrate opportunities for cross-border dialogue about religion, in the classroom, staff room, etc.?	How do I enable pupils to detect bias, challenge stereotypes, take risks and pose questions?	How do learning activities reflect interactive and interdependent contexts?

Becoming a teacher does not give us immunity from our own socialization. Although it is essential to recognize the bias and stereotypes manifested by others, it is even more important to be able to recognize and decode our own attitudes and behaviours in terms of our upbringing as these influences can significantly affect our expectations of pupils, parents and other professionals and the ways in which we learn and teach.

Cameo 3

- *Differences*: language, possibly ethnicity.
- *Issues* (musts for teaching, principles for equality): expectations, identity, engagement with the learner, curriculum and learning, equality of access, excellence.
- *Power*: English is, if not the most, one of the most powerful global languages. Anyone watching a football match during the 2006 World Cup in Germany will have heard the announcement for all national anthems first of all in English. All referees were expected to have a required standard of English. Fluency in English is a vital tool in an individual's potential to prosper.

    Here, the teacher has confused the learning tool with the learning potential. This is a clear example of a teacher's low expectations of a child-based on language difference. The teacher expects the new child to perform poorly and puts her in the lowest achieving group. This model of deficit (expecting the lowest performance) reinforces low expectations. What effect might this have on the child's progress through the term and how will it affect the other children in the lowest achieving group? What message is given about the new child to the rest of the class through this grouping and how might it affect their future views whenever they meet anyone else whose English is limited?

- *Change*: Useful strategies for new arrivals can be found in Gibbons (2002) and DfES guidance on supporting pupils using EAL (DfES 2002; TTA 2000). Developing bilingual learners benefit from being placed with articulate children during activities that involve discussion. When learning a second language, children normally understand more than they are able to express and therefore may remain silent for up to a year, but this does not mean that they are not absorbing English language patterns and new concepts (Hall *et al.* 2001). The teacher should find out as much as possible about the child's first language. Is it written from right to left or left to right? How advanced is the child in her first language development? How is she continuing the development of her first language? How does she achieve in tasks set in her first language? Valuing other languages can be shown in many ways, for example, taking the register in different languages, using bilingual displays and dual language textbooks. Using other languages in our teaching gives formal recognition to the value of bilingualism (see Chapter 8).

    The link between language and culture can be misconstrued, for example, some languages have no word for 'please' or 'thank you', as respect is conveyed through tone or inflection. Direct translations can, therefore, appear rude to English-speaking people, who may then make assumptions about children with regard to behaviour.

Preparing pupils for participation in society means fostering a sense of interdependence. Children need to be able to engage with each other by valuing and exploring difference. An effective teacher enables this to happen by engaging with a vision for the future, the learners, the curriculum and the learning.

Conclusion

The chapter suggests that engagement with difference can equip all teachers, including the beginner teacher, to be a catalyst for change. Consciously or unconsciously, we are always engaging with the potential of the future while being cognisant of the past. Teaching for equality means ensuring that this engagement and cognisance are consciously used to lead the transformation from past structures and practices to new understandings based on dialogue with difference. Such cross-border pedagogy considers the learning environment to be the natural context for change. The primary teacher's role is key in establishing conditions in which all children can participate in change for a fairer future.

Questions to set you thinking

1 How much of the legislation in relation to racial equality, anti-discriminatory practices and equal opportunities do you know and understand?
2 What experiences have you had in working with children from different cultural backgrounds? Be honest with yourself: what has been your reaction to children and adults different from yourself?
3 What is your experience of working with children using English as an additional language? How far did you make efforts to use vocabulary in the child's home language? How far do you think this is important?

References

Adams, S. and Moyles, J. (2005) *Images of Violence: Responding to Children's Representations of Violence as They See It*. Lutterworth: Featherstone Publications.

Commission for Racial Equality (CRE) (2005) *Citizenship and Belonging: What is Britishness?* Available online: http://www.cre.gov.uk/research/britishness.html (accessed 14 August 2006).

Commission for Racial Equality (CRE) (2006) *How the CRE is Working towards a Fairer, More Integrated Britain*. Available online http://www.cre.gov.uk/policy/index.html.

Department for Education and Employment (1999) *The National Curriculum for England*. London: HMSO.

Department for Education and Skills (2002) *The National Literacy Strategy: Supporting Pupils Learning English as an Additional Language*. London: DfES.

Department for Education and Skills (2003) *Every Child Matters*. London: HMSO.

Department for Education and Skills (2005) *Ethnicity and Education: The Evidence on Minority Ethnic Pupils Aged 5–16* RTPG01–05. Available online http://www.dfes.gov.uk/rsgateway/DB/RRP/u014488/index.shtml (accessed 14 August 2006).

Gaine, C. (2001) If it's not hurting it's not working: teaching teachers about race, *Research Papers in Education,* 16(1): 93–113.

Gardner, P. (2004) *Teaching and Learning in Multicultural Classrooms.* London: David Fulton.

Gibbons, P. (2002) *Scaffolding Language: Scaffolding Learning.* Portsmouth: Heinemann.

Gillborn, D. and Mirza, S. (2000) *Educational Inequality: Mapping Race, Class and Gender.* London: OfSTED.

Giroux, H.A. (1991) Democracy and the discourse of cultural difference: towards a politics of border pedagogy, *British Journal of Sociology of Education,* 12(4): 501–19.

Hall, D., Griffiths, D., Haslam, L. and Wilkin, Y. (2001) *Assessing the Needs of Bilingual Pupils* (2nd edn). London: David Fulton.

Her Majesty's Stationery Office (2000) *Race Relations (Amendment) Act.* London: The Stationery Office.

Klein, G. (1993) *Education Towards Race Equality.* London: Cassell.

Macpherson, W. (1999) *The Stephen Lawrence Inquiry: Report of an Inquiry by Sir William Macpherson of Cluny.* London: The Stationery Office.

OfSTED (2005a) *Remodelling the School Workforce: A Report from OfSTED.* HMI 2596. Available online http://www.ofsted.gov.uk/publications/index.cfm?fuseaction=pubs.summaryand id=4115 (accessed 14 August 2006).

OfSTED (2005b) *Race Equality in Education.* London: Her Majesty's Inspectorate 589. Available online http://www.ofsted.gov.uk/publications/index (accessed 11 August 2006).

Ravitch, D. (1991) A culture in common, *Educational Leadership,* (December 1991/January 1992): 8–11.

Runnymede Trust (1997) *Islamaphobia: A Challenge for Us All.* London: Runnymede Trust.

Runnymede Trust (2003) *Complementing Teachers: A Practical Guide to Promoting Race Equality in Schools.* London: Granada Learning.

Teacher Development Agency (2006) *Professional Standards for NQTs.* Available online http://www.tda.gov.uk (accessed 26 June 2006).

Teacher Training Agency (2000) *Raising the Achievement of Minority Ethnic Pupils.* London: HMSO.

Teacher Training Agency (2003) *Raising Standards and Tackling Workload: A National Agreement.* Available online http://www.tda.gov.uk/remodelling/nationalagreement.aspx (accessed 14 August 2006).

Suggested further reading

Commission for Racial Equality (2005) *Citizenship and Belonging: What is Britishness?* Available online http://www.cre.gov.uk/research/britishness.html (accessed 14 August 2006).

DfES (2005) *Ethnicity and Education: The Evidence on Minority Ethnic Pupils aged 5–16* RTPG01-05. Available online http://www.dfes.gov.uk/rsgateway/DB/RRP/u014488/index.shtml (accessed 14 August 2006).

Gardner, P. (2004) *Teaching and Learning in Multicultural Classrooms.* London: David Fulton.

Runnymede Trust (2003) *Complementing Teachers: A Practical Guide to Promoting Race Equality in Schools.* London: Granada Learning.

21 Putting the bananas to bed! Becoming a reflective teacher

Siân Adams

Cameo 1

The teacher has carefully transformed the home area into a grocer's shop. The day's topic has a mathematical focus: the children are to go to the shop and engage in role play with the intention of using mathematical language previously modelled by the teacher. During the session, a child selects a bunch of bananas, wraps them in a tablecloth, and gently puts them to bed. The child speaks quietly to the bananas, before choosing a story and reading to them. When the teacher notices what the 4-year-old is doing, the book and cloth are removed and the child is encouraged to 'go shopping'.

Cameo 2

Ian has a Year 4 class with 24 children and is in his second year of teaching in a very small village school. He has been told by a peer appraiser that his 'teaching is excellent, class management is very good and the children are always attentive and well behaved'. Ian now wonders how to promote his own professional development – his very busy colleagues are supportive and encouraging, yet Ian observes 'I can't be that good already!'

Introduction

This chapter explores the ways in which practitioners may develop a reflective approach to practice. Many questions are raised which can guide the beginning teacher to make considered responses to episodes that frequently occur in the classroom. The two cameos – the first from KS1 and the second from KS2 – provide opportunities for examining ways in which reflective practice can support the professional development of teachers. Literature suggests there are many different levels and stages that occur during the development of a reflective approach to practice (Goodman 1991; Bain *et al.* 1999). Some of these stages are explored during the discussion of the first cameo. The second cameo approaches reflective practice from a different perspective through identifying practical ways in which beginning teachers might promote their own professional development.

The processes of reflective practice

Reflective practice is defined in many ways, including 'a way of being as a teacher' (Dewey 1933: 27) which indicates an approach to practice – the general attitude or disposition adopted by practitioners, rather than identifying specific reflective exercises – reflecting backwards, 'looking back and making sense of your practice' then using newly acquired insights to inform forward-looking reflection, in order 'to affect your future action' (Ghaye 1996: 124). This 'backward reflection' suggests certain skills and understandings are required to make sense and inform future actions. Before practitioners can 'make sense', they have to face the reality of their practice, through questioning, taking apart and confronting aspects of teaching and learning.

So, how is it possible to ensure that the potentially destructive process of confrontation and facing up to the uncertainties and dissatisfaction of practice, can become a positive process? First, it is important to understand the skills within reflective practice. Second, as has been suggested (McIntyre 1993), reflective practice requires considerable time in order to do the following:

- consider specific aspects of practice;
- step back from the immediacy and rawness of practice;
- deliberate;
- question;
- challenge;
- be challenged.

It also demands a repertoire of experiences and knowledge that are accumulated as practice matures. These experiences provide a bank of knowledge that is required in order to consider the variety of responses that might occur in any one situation. For instance, part of Ian's dilemma was that he knew enough to 'feel' dissatisfied with his lesson, yet did not have the experience nor the knowledge (1) to interpret aspects of teaching and learning; or (2) to plan for change.

Third, practitioners require supported challenge. This might be provided by peer support, through colleagues or, for example, through developing curriculum knowledge or exploring more about theories of children's learning.

Fourth, teaching is highly complex, so reflective practice benefits from a clearly defined framework, which guides the practitioner through a process of facing specific aspects of practice. This might lead to confronting dilemmas or challenging and questioning actions and beliefs. Through time and with support, practitioners begin to reconstruct – to build on beliefs and to modify practice in a way that promotes confident, self-assured pedagogy.

The four processes listed above will contribute to developing an overall approach to practice. The result of promoting a spirit of enquiry will be to deepen pedagogical understanding, to comprehend the complexities and interrelationship of teaching and learning.

In Cameo 1, the teacher in the reception class faces a dilemma when a child makes an unexpected response to the request to 'Go shopping'. Earlier, the teacher had transformed the play area into a well-resourced shop in order to provide opportunities for the children to incorporate shopping into their play. Plastic fruit and vegetables had been priced, shopping baskets provided, a small cashtill containing a variety of coins, and finally, notepads and pencils were placed in the shopping area for children to create shopping lists and issue receipts. The play was planned to support children's developing understanding of numeracy, through creating situations in which children may use number language (*Curriculum Guidance for the Foundation Stage* DfEE/QCA 2000). However, instead of using the resources as the teacher had planned, one child carefully selected a bunch of bananas, cuddled it into a blanket, walked out of the 'shop' to the book corner, chose a story, then read her 'baby ' a story. As she finished the story, she gently put the bananas to bed. The adult's immediate response was to remove the bananas and suggest the child 'goes shopping' rather than take time to support the child's mathematical understanding through imaginative and spontaneous play (DFES 2006).

In the past few years, the banana cameo has been presented to many different groups of practitioners, during staff meetings, training days and in seminars. Discussions about the dilemma faced by the Reception teacher have revealed many interesting aspects of reflective inquiry, and the ways in which practice is both informed and challenged by understanding teaching and learning. Some groups have responded to the emotional aspects within the cameo – others have explored the implications to teaching and curriculum policy. The responses illustrate complex, multi-layered aspects of teaching and are discussed under the following headings:

- emotional/affective response;
- pragmatic response;
- philosophical response;
- policy, ideological, curriculum issues;
- political, ethical or moral issues.

Emotional/affective response

The initial and most frequent responses to Cameo 1 have been affective – practitioners saying 'aaahh, how sweet' or 'how awful' before elaborating or offering any deeper comments. They have responded:

- to the emotion within the cameo – seeing a young child displaying an awareness of caring for an infant, being sensitive to the needs and feelings of others, behaving with sensitivity to a baby wanting to sleep or be cuddled and then gently placing the baby to bed;
- affectively – acknowledging the pedagogical dilemma of a child behaving with maturity and sensitivity but not within the framework of the teacher's learning intentions;
- to the polarity of sensitivities – a child apparently being sympathetic to the needs of a baby in stark relief to the apparent insensitive actions of an adult.

Interpretations and questions have also been based on the emotional needs of the child:

- Did the child have a young or new baby at home?
- Was the child exploring the intimacy of a new adult–child relationship within the family?
- Might the child be trying to come to terms with a new sibling, trying to understand her parents' responses of tenderness and affection to someone new?

Practitioners base their responses to this banana incident on their own pedagogical knowledge. This knowledge will include their understanding of how children learn and the ways in which that pedagogical knowledge informs their actions as teachers. Yet it is well documented that knowledge of teaching and learning is often buried under the sheer number of decisions which are made throughout the day – decisions about what to say to children, how to intervene, what resources to provide, how to respond to one question from a child, while also noting a child perhaps who is looking puzzled or inattentive or, as in this case, a child making an unexpected response to a planned situation. Under such relentless pressure, decisions can become intuitive – teachers often say such things as 'Well, I just do it … I don't have time to think about it.' The sheer 'busyness' of practice appears to prevent more explicit reasoning – decisions are made 'on the hoof' and practice moves forward, driven by further occasions where dilemmas are faced, decisions are made, responses made to the unexpected and the spontaneous requests and behaviours of children. At the end of the day, many dilemmas are buried under the weight of hosts of other spontaneous judgements. Unless practitioners have a system for recalling these actions and their accompanying decisions, their related values, beliefs and understanding remain embedded.

The process of scrutinizing the banana cameo has helped many practitioners articulate their own practice as they empathize with the immediate, complex dilemmas encountered by the Reception teacher.

Pragmatic response

The second level or type of response has been made about the practical ways in which the curriculum was being provided. Questions have been asked such as why was the teacher trying to encourage children to use mathematical language in this way? Some practitioners have suggested that these days children have few opportunities to go shopping – parents frequently discourage children from going out on their own, credit cards are often used, so the exchange of cash for goods may be an inappropriate method of exchange for children's play. There are also other more meaningful and relevant ways of encouraging children to use mathematical language in their play, such as visits to child-centred locations such as farms, galleries, museums or other venues that reflect the local culture and community.

It is possible that a more domestic setting, in which the 'bedtime story' might have encouraged the use of number in everyday situations (such as Penny Dale's *Ten in a Bed*, 2001). If children are encouraged to talk about their own experiences and interests, these ideas can be used as a starting point for planning the learning environment (see Chapter 6).

Philosophical response

The third level of reflection explored the teachers' constructs of play that often emerged as they talked about the cameos. Consider the words – 'the teacher had organized' – and 'told the children' to go shopping. These two phrases prompt questions about the ownership of play, i.e. the teacher had organized, the teacher told the children, but there was little evidence about how the teacher may also have inspired, motivated, involved, engaged or supported the child. Through careful, informed observation, the practitioner may have gained a clear understanding of possible next steps in the child's development and learning (see Chapter 17).

Cameos are often successfully used in the development of reflective practice. In observing practice through stories or cameos, practitioners are distanced from the harshness of scrutinizing their own practice. Some practitioners began to explore the level and range of decisions made by the reception teaching during the course of the lesson. For example, her immediate response – to remind the child to 'go shopping' – was intuitive. But was the content of her planning informed by an understanding of how children learn or was it informed by a commitment to fulfil curriculum demands? Readers are invited to explore and critically reflect upon the banana cameo and then devise new cameos, relevant to their own situations.

Curriculum response

At a fourth level many practitioners explore curriculum issues and the appropriateness of the teacher's learning intentions. Were there lost opportunities here? Could the child have been applying some aspects of her developing literacy skills? Is it possible she has just begun to explore the wonders of engaging in a story and wished to enjoy the intimacy of sharing a story – maybe she has observed others reading, or maybe this is the first time she has experienced this for herself? Many have explored ways in which a mathematical lesson might also make provision for other aspects of a child's development (Moyles and Adams 2001).

Political, ethical and moral issues

In discussions about this cameo, ethical and moral issues have been raised and various questions initiated, such as: were there outside forces or pressures here on the teacher resulting in a distorted view of the child's needs? Was the practitioner acting as arbiter, desperately trying to balance the needs of the child with the demands of the curriculum (Moyles and Adams 2000)? In these discussions, some groups of practitioners have explored the political issues, for example, considering the tensions that exist when curriculum initiatives are at odds with personal philosophies (Wood 1999). Through developing a critical, reflective approach to practice, it has been found that during many discussions, practitioners become more articulate, secure and able to justify practice in the face of challenge.

Reflection on Cameo 2

In the second cameo, Ian has just started his second year of teaching. From his training he knows that reflective practice is considered to be an effective way of promoting professional development. He is conscious that during a maths lesson, although all went according to his plan, somehow the lesson 'lacked excitement'. He comments 'I am sure one reason the children are well behaved is because the school is very formal, the classes small. The lessons do meet the learning objective but somehow it feels boring, safe and predictable.' He adds, 'If I was teaching in a more difficult area, or with a much larger class, I think the children would run rings around me.' Instinctively he feels that the lessons do not encourage engagement or independent thinking (see Chapter 14). However, without more experience, he does not have the knowledge to be discerning, nor the skills to determine more clearly how to build on his strengths, to create exciting, meaningful lessons. Similarly, in focusing on what might be 'wrong' in his lessons, he is at risk of overlooking very real and potentials strengths in his role as a developing teacher. Consider the affective responses he has made.

Affective response

Ian's first response was positive and affective – 'I am feeling good about this because the children were well behaved.' He acknowledges that 'feeling good' is a positive way to begin, yet later adds that he had expected reflective practice to be relevant only in the context of things going wrong. Often in the busyness of practice, teachers turn to reflection in an urgent need to salvage professional respect from a potentially negative experience. In this instance, Ian records his awareness of a need, at this stage in his career, to nourish professional confidence and to build on strengths rather than focus on weaknesses. However, he finds he is unsure about how to respond to a lesson that lacked luster rather than one that was heading for disaster.

The earlier discussion on reflective practice suggested that the process involves questioning and challenging, which may lead to confrontation. Ian has acknowledged or confronted his affective response to this situation – ' I am feeling good' – yet also senses a feeling of discomfort. This is a positive way to begin, for reflective practice involves confrontation – being prepared to face alternative ways of practising. We turn to the second level of reflective practice to explore ways in which Ian might further develop practice.

Pragmatic response

At this pragmatic level of reflection, Ian begins to examine the curriculum and relates his knowledge to theories of learning. He recalls that children learn best when engaged in practical authentic problems and able to relate to the context of the lessons. He can see that although the children completed the tasks he had set in his lessons, the problem-solving was far removed from any practical relevance to the pupils' experiences. This level of reflection tends to be pragmatic, so Ian might consider the resources that were used – were there adequate materials? Did the children have any choice or opportunities to make decisions? There was no provision in his plans (to use fractional notation, such as 2/3, $^3/_4$ and 7/10) for children to engage in relevant problem-solving. Through discussion, Ian considered whether he could have used the introduction to his lesson to relate this task to 'real-life', authentic problem-solving? Could he have stopped the class during the main activity and shared ideas and strategies for discussing alternative ways of completing the task, encouraging more open-ended engagement in the lesson?

He decided to change the next lesson and begin with a class discussion on the ways in which fractions might be used in everyday situations. Changing the learning intention into a more open-ended task might also have permitted the children to be more inventive during their deliberations. It is difficult to adopt reflective practice without a range of relevant experiences on which to draw. Yet Ian was able to identify the issues that might be developed. He could initiate discussion with his mentor and consider ways in which the lesson might have, on the surface, appeared to have been acceptable, yet confront the underpinning concerns that his practice was at odds with his emerging philosophy. He felt it was important to establish his own values and understanding, while also allowing himself to adopt a realistic and developmental approach to practice.

Evidence suggest that practitioners need time to promote a reflective approach to practice to work in a context in which professional discourse is encouraged, valued and promoted. Through asking specific questions of colleagues, it became possible for Ian to explore ways in which the teacher might make future lessons more exciting, motivating and relate his emerging philosophy to practice. Colleagues too have a responsibility to new teachers – for they will need help in becoming familiar with the curriculum, children and the many other pedagogical issues (Fletcher and Barrett 2004).

Through encouraging a culture of pedagogical discussion it was possible for Ian to maximize the experience and understanding of colleagues. There is also evidence that practitioners do not have sufficient opportunities to talk about practice, with the result that values, beliefs and understanding often become embedded, resulting in teachers commenting that 'Well, you just do these things don't you?' Yet, it was a resistance to 'just doing things' that resulted in Ian stopping, questioning, challenging and confronting his own and the complacency of this colleagues. It was hoped that through discussion, he would deepen pedagogical knowledge, enriched by his recent experience together with the theoretical understanding gained from his studies.

Reflective practice enables teachers to make sense of daily occurrence, ensuring the surfacing of tacitly held beliefs. Early in this chapter Ian wondered if being attentive was automatically a sign that children were learning. There is evidence that children do learn how to be pupils and that reflective enquiry must take account of the children's construct of learning. Heaslip (1994) suggests that children are 'exceedingly good guests' which 'can so easily lead practitioners into believing that the programme on offer is suitable as children will most likely seem "happy enough"' (Heaslip 1994: 107).

However, Ian felt a degree of disquiet about the children's apparent attentiveness. His construct of learning expected more than being adequately happy – he wanted the children to be inspired and motivated through his teaching. The comments he made provide evidence of moving from a focus of planning what to teach to deeper consideration of the ways in which children learn. Through discussion with colleagues, he developed a clear consideration of learning theories and deepening pedagogical under-standing that continued to impact his teaching style.

Berliner (1992) suggests that practitioner knowledge is partly based on experience and indicates that practitioner expertise is developed after applying that knowledge in familiar contexts. Berliner (1992: 245) states that pedagogical content knowledge develops through these processes of teaching, often from 'reflected-upon classroom experiences'. These experiences provide a repertoire of personalized knowledge that forms the basis of evidence for reflective practice. Ian's personal familiarity with the ways in which children respond in different situations has prompted a concern that the maths lesson did not offer adequate opportunities for their engagement in the lesson.

Having confronted that perception, being prepared to critically examine the 'bumpy' moments of teaching, he is now in a position to consider, or reconstruct, alternative ways of planning for future learning (Romano 2004). Through adopting a reflective approach to practice he is gaining deeper pedagogical understanding, promoting pedagogical development and change.

Conclusion

Reflective practice is a highly complex process. It involves thinking – critical thinking – about practice at many different levels. It is possible that the practitioner's own values will determine how reflective enquiry is approached. The child-centred practitioner might begin with affective considerations of the child's responses. The manager might consider policy implications. However, these layers of critical enquiry are not intended to be hierarchical – one approach is not necessarily better than the other. The range of responses begins to address the dynamic nature of pedagogy and includes consideration of the child and adult as learners.

Through the process of becoming 'reflective practitioners' many teachers find they develop pedagogical awareness: an ability to understand many of the situations and dilemmas faced in the classroom. Engaging in reflective enquiry is a highly complex process. It may involve identifying positive aspects of teaching and using them to cel-ebrate good practice and nourish self-confidence. However, it also involves confronting areas that might benefit from development. This process of confrontation requires sup-port from colleagues and the school, time to reflect and opportunity to question practice, beliefs or understandings about teaching and learning. Through 'eavesdropping' on many responses to the banana cameo, a range of possible reflective responses to one situation have been discovered. Ian's reflective response to his teaching has identified ways in which he can provide appropriate conditions for his maturing practice.

There are no right or wrong answers or responses to the cameos. Engaging in dis-cussion about these and countless other scenarios that occur each day in schools, con-tributes to an emerging pedagogical awareness. Understanding more about our own actions, thoughts, values and beliefs, and learning how to articulate them and expose them to scrutiny in a culture of support and professionalism, will lead to enriched understanding and changes in classroom and professional practices.

Confident, reflective pedagogues will result from supported, collaborative approaches to practice.

Questions to set you thinking

1 What do you know of your own strengths and weaknesses? How honest are you with/about yourself?
2 Regarding your own teaching, how honest are you when talking with tutors and mentor teachers about how you have felt about individual lessons/overall performance?
3 What kind of feedback makes you feel most challenged/reflective?

References

Bain, J., Ballantyne, R., Packer, J. and Mills, C. (1999) Using journal writing to enhance student teachers' reflectivity during field experience placements, *Teachers and Teaching: Theory and Practice*, 5(1): 51–74.

Berliner, D. (1992) Nature of expertise in teaching, in F. Oser, A. Dick and J. Patry (eds) *Effective and Responsible Teaching: The New Synthesis*. San Francisco, CA: Jossey-Bass Publishers.

Dale, P. (2001) *Ten in the Bed*. London: Walker Books.

Department for Education and Skills (DfES) (2006) *The Early Years Foundation Stage: Consultation on a Single Quality Framework for Services to Children from Birth to Five*. London: DfES.

Dewey, J. (1933) *How We Think: A Restatement of the Relation of Reflective Thinking to the Educative Process*. Chicago, IL: Henry Regenery.

Fletcher, S. and Barrett, B. (2004) Developing effective beginning teachers through mentor-based induction, *Mentoring and Tutoring*, 12(3): 321–33.

Ghaye, T. (1996) *An Introduction to Learning Through Critical Reflective Practice*. Newcastle-upon-Tyne: Pentaxion Press.

Goodman, J. (1991) Using a methods course to promote reflection and inquiry among preservice teachers, in R. Tabachnich and K. Zeichner (eds), *Issues and Practices in Inquiry-Oriented Teacher Education*. London: Falmer.

Heaslip, P. (1994) Making play work in the classroom, in J. Moyles (ed.) *The Excellence of Play*. Buckingham: Open University Press.

McIntrye, D. (1993) Theory, theorizing and reflection in initial teacher education, in J. Calderhead and P. Gates (eds) *Conceptualising Reflection in Teacher Development*. London: Falmer Press.

Moyles, J. and Adams, S. (2000) A tale of the unexpected: practitioners' expectations and children's play, *Journal of In-Service Education*, 26(2): 349–69.

Moyles, J. and Adams, S. (2001) *StEPs: A Framework for Playful Teaching*. Buckingham: Open University Press.

Qualifications and Curriculum Authority/Department for Education and Employment (2000) *Curriculum Guidance for the Foundation Stage*. London: DfEE.

Romano, S. (2004) Teacher reflections on 'bumpy moments' in teaching: a self-study, *Teachers and Teaching: Theory and Practice*, 10(6): 663–81.

Wood, E. (1999) The impact of the National Curriculum on play in reception classes, *Educational Research*, 41(1): 11–22.

Suggested further reading

Adams, S. (2005) Practitioners and play: reflecting in a different way, in J. Moyles (ed.) *The Excellence of Play*. Maidenhead: Open University Press.

Barnes, R. (1999) *Positive Teaching: Positive Learning*. London: Routledge.

Ghaye, A. and Ghaye, K. (1998) *Teaching and Learning through Critical Reflective Practice*. London: David Fulton Publishers.

Moyles, J. and Adams, S. with others (2001) *StEPs: A Framework for Playful Teaching*. Buckingham: Open University Press.

Conclusion
Achieving success: learning from continuing experiences

Janet Moyles, beginner teachers and tutors

One group of PGCE students, when asked to pass on their own messages to readers of this book, chose to make their offering in a 'Recipe for the perfect teacher' which is faithfully reproduced in Figure 22.1. It is such a good model of what it represents – warmth, humour and beliefs about primary teaching which characterize the new teachers of today – that it has been used in all three editions!

There have been many moves to make training much more school- or settings-based and these have to be welcomed IF they mean that students spend more time with *children* – the latter the focus of many students' desires to be teachers or early years practitioners in the first place! But, as emphasized in several of these chapters, the key element for all beginner teachers (and experienced ones!) is to reflect on – really think in-depth about – their practice and teaching opportunities (Day 2005). To be really effective teachers, they MUST be passionate about the teaching role and the impact they have upon children. This means understanding both the practice of teaching and having significant knowledge about the theory and underpinning research which informs effective learning and teaching (Pollard 2005).

Having worked in schools with teachers and being really excited about practice, many students come back to their ITE/ITT course desperate to know more about the theory and research behind classroom strategies, behaviour techniques or dealing with parents and to reflect on their practice. Teachers often find difficulty in articulating their effective practice as it is often 'second-nature' (Moyles and Adams 2001; Adams *et al.* 2004) – education tutors frequently have this information to hand plus the experience of dealing with adult groups to link the theory and practice effectively and efficiently.

The final statements in the book are left to those teachers just entering their first posts in primary schools all over the country and to those who are part of the teacher education system. Students just leaving ITE courses, and some who had left in the previous year, were asked to reflect on what advice they would wish to pass on to others in a similar situation. Teacher education tutors were also asked for their comments, and reflections were gathered from experienced teachers. The sample from all four groups constitutes much food-for-thought for beginner teachers and, undoubtedly, teachers at every stage in their careers.

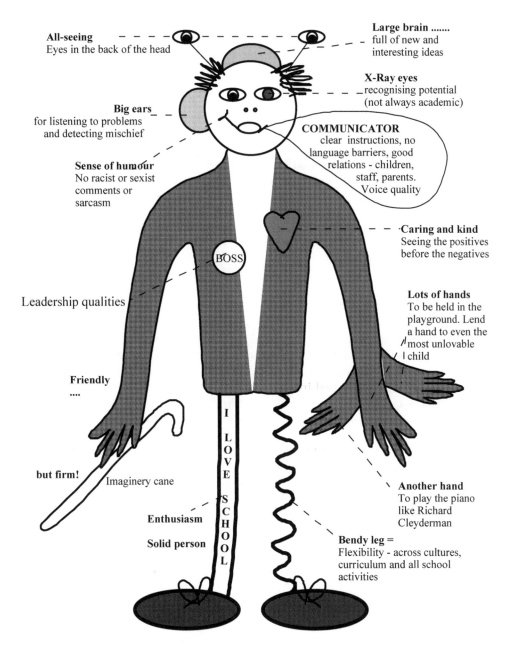

Figure 22.1 Recipe for the 'Perfect' Teacher

We hope that, having read this book, you will be able to adopt (and adapt) some of this advice as you set out on the complex but rewarding professional learning journey that is early years and primary teaching. Whereas some of the 'tips for teachers' might be familiar to you, there are others which, though unusual, are worth remembering. Many of these reiterate, albeit in a different way, the wealth of messages and insights which have comprised the chapters of this book.

Know your own self-worth: value the skills you have and enjoy the children with their skills and understanding. (tutor)

Be up-front about your weaknesses with mentor teachers and tutors: share with them your own ideas and priorities. They will be grateful to you for the knowledge of what they can help you with. (student teacher)

Avoid the perils of becoming a chocoholic – the pressure of the job leads to comfort eating on a massive scale. Save the choc for the day you've been on playground duty! (tutor)

I think everyone has a good cry during their first year of teaching – but it doesn't mean you're useless! (NQT)

Learn the children's names as quickly as you can and use them as much as possible. You must *act* like a teacher – look as if you expect children to listen to you and they probably will! (tutor)

Don't be too proud or too stubborn to learn from tutors and teachers: they have lots of experience and are there to help you to become a good teacher. (student teacher)

I've learned that all good teaching is based on relationships. Remember that children, like adults, tend to mirror the behaviour shown to them (especially if it's negative!) Always be patient, calm and courteous to the children whenever you can and don't 'lose your cool' (except as a deliberate strategy)! (teacher)

Treat children and others in school just as you would wish to be treated yourself. (tutor)

Try to ask yourself everyday – What did *I* learn in school/on the course today? (student teacher)

Make one weekend day your own and cultivate friends who are not teachers – you will find that they offer a hearty laugh at some of the antics which go on in schools and thus offer you a sense of proportion. (tutor)

On my final school experience, I found that using practical activities with the children was less stressful than endless paper exercises. I found out more about what and how children were learning. When children did produce paper work, I wrote comments on what they had shown they could do, or needed help to do, etc. and read this to the children. A lot of 5-year-olds appreciated this and it gave them motivation to try their best. (student teacher)

Good teachers have to be good learners. They have to learn *exactly* what it is the children (and they themselves) don't understand and then move heaven and earth to teach it so that they both *do* understand. (teacher)

Try out new things on a Friday afternoon: that way you (and the other staff) can forget any disasters by Monday! (tutor)

Do your evaluating and assessing straight away after a lesson, when things are fresh. It helps you to think and helps you to work out progression for the children. (student teacher)

Having done written assignments on your teacher education course, you must use them as a tool for your work in school – if you have found out the theory and reflected on how you or others put that into practice (or not!), stop and then think about *how* this will affect your practice. Don't just rush on regardless! (NQT)

Getting the class 'with you' so that the child misbehaving becomes embarrassed without you having to shout! First, give the child 'the withering look', then make them stand up (just for a little while), then ask them to settle down. It has usually worked for me. (student teacher)

Do remember that 'difficult' behaviour is usually the sign of an unhappy child – it is a challenge to you but it is not, at the end of the day, your *personal* problem. (tutor)

Don't forget to speak clearly and *listen* hard to what the children are telling you. (student teacher)

Don't make promises you can't keep. If you say 'The next child who talks I'll get your parents in' and someone talks, get the parents! (Worst still, you might be tempted to suggest you'll thrown them out of the window!) The corollary of this is *keep your promises*. (course tutor)

Especially with young children, don't be too shy to read stories in 'funny' voices. When I did, the children were 'knocked out' by my Oscar-winning performance and I think I commanded much more respect afterwards. (student teacher)

Yes – you'll be tired, worn out, all-in, kn———ed (and every other exhaustion word you can think of!). *But* it's worth it at the end of day when even one child shows you s/he has actually *learned* something new. (teacher)

These statements sum up nicely the comments by Butt (2003: 3):

> Underneath the surface ... lies a bedrock of teacher understanding about the principles of sound pedagogic practice. These principles are constructed from an appreciation of how children learn and from the self-knowledge that resulted from being a reflective teacher, skilled in understanding why things happen in the classroom.

Hear, hear!

References

Adams, S., Alexandra, E., Drummond, M.J. and Moyles, J. (2004) *Inside the Foundation Stage: Recreating the Reception Year*. London: Association of Teachers and Lecturers.

Butt, G. (2003) *Lesson Planning*. London: Continuum.

Day, C. (2004) *A Passion for Teaching*. London: RoutledgeFalmer.

Day, C. (2005) *A Passion for Teaching*. London: Routledge.

Moyles, J. and Adams (2001) *StEPs: A Framework for Playful Teaching*. Buckingham: Open University Press.

Pollard, A. (2005) *Reflective Teaching*. (2nd edn). London: Continuum.

Index